OXFORD READINGS IN PHILOSOPHY

Series Editor G. J. Warnock

REFERENCE AND MODALITY

REFERENCE
AND
MODALITY

EDITED BY
LEONARD LINSKY

OXFORD UNIVERSITY PRESS

Oxford University Press, Walton Street, Oxford OX2 6DP

OXFORD LONDON GLASGOW
NEW YORK TORONTO MELBOURNE WELLINGTON
KUALA LUMPUR SINGAPORE JAKARTA HONG KONG TOKYO
DELHI BOMBAY CALCUTTA MADRAS KARACHI
NAIROBI DAR ES SALAAM CAPE TOWN

ISBN 0 19 875017 X

© OXFORD UNIVERSITY PRESS 1971

First published 1971
Reprinted 1977 (with corrections), 1979

PRINTED IN GREAT BRITAIN
AT THE PITMAN PRESS, BATH

CONTENTS

INTRODUCTION

THE founders of modern logic dealt with the topics of these essays. Gottlob Frege wrote about them in 1892 in 'On Sense and Reference',[1] and in other works about the same time. Bertrand Russell first dealt with the problems in 1905 in 'On Denoting'.[2] But Frege's work was largely unstudied until nearly the middle of this century, and although Russell's Theory of Descriptions was anything but ignored, its applications to the problems of this volume were not given special attention until 1948 when Arthur Smullyan wrote the essay here reprinted.

The problems which concerned Frege and Russell were revived and placed in new perspectives by Willard Van Orman Quine beginning nearly thirty years ago. In the early 1940s Quine launched an attack on the concept of logical necessity and related notions which he has sustained and deepened up to the present day. The papers in this volume, except perhaps Saul Kripke's, are all direct responses to Quine's work and the bibliography lists but a part of a further extensive literature, the fallout of his writings.

In the introduction I shall say something about these views of Quine's and those of his critics and defenders. My aim is to acquaint the reader with the main issues of the collection and to indicate some respects in which these essays are related among themselves. Only some of the issues of these papers are touched upon and sometimes an author's conclusions are given without his supporting arguments. An introduction cannot be a substitute for the book. My goal is only to provide orientation.

I

A fundamental principle governing identity, says Quine in the first of his papers reprinted here, is that of *substitutivity*. *The terms of a true statement of identity are everywhere intersubstitutive, salva veritate.* Hardly is the principle stated than one finds cases contrary to it. The true identity 'Cicero = Tully' will not support the substitution of 'Cicero' for 'Tully' in ' "Tully" consists of five letters'. This is not a genuine paradox, for *substitutivity* is wrongly applied to terms in contexts in which they do not refer 'simply' to their objects. ' "Tully" consists of five letters' is not

---

[1] Translated in *Translations from the Philosophical Writings of Gottlob Frege*, edited by P. Geach and M. Black (Oxford: Basil Blackwell, 1952).
[2] *Mind*, 1905. Reprinted in *Logic and Knowledge*, edited by R. C. Marsh. London: Allen and Unwin, 1956).

about Cicero (= Tully) but about one of his names. Lapse of substitutivity merely reveals that the occurrence of the name supplanted is not 'purely referential' because 'the statement depends not only on the object, but on the form of the name'.[3] Quotation is only the most blatant of contexts in which terms can fail of purely referential occurrence. Consider, 'Philip believes that Tegucigalpa is in Nicaragua.' Misuse of *substitutivity* will take us from this and 'Tegucigalpa = the capital of Honduras' to the falsehood, 'Philip believes that the capital of Honduras is in Nicaragua.' Here again, for Quine, failure of substitutivity is only symptomatic of 'Tegucigalpa's' failure of purely referential occurrence at the place of substitution. '. . . the contexts "is unaware that . . ." and "believes that . . ." *resemble* the context of single quotes in this respect: a name may occur referentially in a statement S and not occur referentially in a longer statement which is formed by embedding S in the context "is unaware that . . ." or "believes that . . .".' Quine calls these contexts 'referentially opaque'. Logical modality provides another example.

(1) 9 is necessarily greater than 7,

and

(2) The number of planets = 9,

are true, but *substitutivity* would be misapplied to them to arrive at the falsehood

(3) The number of planets is necessarily greater than 7.

Affliction of modal contexts by referential opacity renders quantified modal logic a very obscure business, for we cannot *quantify into* referentially opaque contexts. We cannot go by existential generalization from (1) to

(4) $(\exists x)(x$ is necessarily greater than 7).

(4) lacks clear sense. 'What is this number which according to (4) is necessarily greater than 7. According to (1) from which (4) was inferred, it was 9, that is, the number of planets; but to suppose this would conflict with the fact that (3) is false.' The difficulty arises because necessary or contingent traits of objects are taken to belong to them not absolutely but according as one way of specifying them is used rather than another. Nine is taken to have necessary greaterness than seven according as it is specified in (1) but not as in (3). Hence the difference in truth value between

---

[3] All quotations in the introduction are from the author's contribution to this volume unless specifically indicated to the contrary.

(1) and (3) and the obscurity of (4). The modal logician, saddled as he is with (4), is thus committed to a metaphysical view, 'Aristotelian essentialism' to give it a name, according to which necessary and contingent properties *do* belong to objects irrespective of their modes of specification, if specified at all. 'Evidently', says Quine, 'this reversion to Aristotelian essentialism is required if quantification into modal contexts is to be insisted on'. He concludes, 'so much the worse for quantified modal logic'.

Arthur Smullyan responded to these arguments of Quine's by contending that they were fallacies turning on scope ambiguities of definite descriptions in modalized statements. Proper deployment of Russell's Theory of Descriptions reveals (3) to have two nonequivalent interpretations according as the scope of its contained definite description is taken as large or small. With the scope large (3) follows from (1) and (2) but that is all right, for so understood, says Smullyan, it is true. (3), with small scope accorded its contained description, is indeed false but no consequence of (1) and (2), so again, no paradox.

Ruth Barcan Marcus is one of the pioneering founders of quantified modal logic and she defends her work against Quine's attack. She does this from the vantage point of a general view about extensionality. For her, it comes in degrees. 'I will call a principle extensional if it either (a) directly or indirectly imposes restrictions on the possible values of the functional variables such that some intensional functions are prohibited or (b) it has the consequence of equating identity with a weaker form of equivalence.' If we identify equality with indiscernibility, it does come in degrees. 9 and the number of planets are indiscernible with respect to the stock of predicates available in classical predicate logic but they become discernible with the admission of modal predicates. Hence, for Mrs. Marcus, it is a fallacy to suppose that (2) supports substitution of '9' for 'the number of planets' in modal contexts such as (1). The identity sign of (2), she thinks, does not stand for 'true identity' but a weaker equivalence relation. If its singular terms were taken, however improbably, as genuine proper names, then (2) would indeed be, for her, a true identity; but then these terms would be everywhere intersubstitutive, so (3) would both be true and follow from its premises. 'The paradox', she says, 'evaporates.' Mrs. Marcus, like Smullyan, is invoking Russell's Theory of Descriptions, but another part of the theory. For Russell too (2) is not a true identity since it contains a definite description. In her appeal to genuine proper names, Mrs. Marcus again harks back to Russell. Like Smullyan she does not confront the issue of essentialism in her paper.

Quine has replied to these objections as follows: 'Notice to begin with that if we are to bring out Russell's distinction of scopes we must make two contrasting applications of Russell's contextual definition of description. But when the description is in a non-substitutive position, one of the two contrasting applications of the contextual definition is going to require quantifying into a non-substitutive position. So the appeal to scopes of descriptions does not justify such quantification, it just begs the question.'[4] Quine's second reason for rejecting the recourse to the Theory of Descriptions in defence of modality rests with his theory of the 'primacy of predicates'. According to Quine, all constant singular terms are eliminable in favour of general terms and bound variables. So if referential opacity is worth worrying about it must show its symptoms when the constant singular terms are gone. The argument against quantifying into opaque contexts can then still be made. Take the sentence

(5) $(\exists x)$ (necessarily x is odd).

'. . . let us ban singular terms other than variables. We can still specify things; instead of specifying them by designation we specify them by conditions that uniquely determine them. On this approach we can still challenge the coherence of (5), by asking that such an object x be specified. One answer is that

(6) $(\exists y) (y \neq x = yy = y + y + y)$.

But that same number x is uniquely determined also by this different condition: there are x planets. Yet (6) entails "x is odd" and thus evidently sustains "necessarily x is odd", while "there are x planets" does not.'[5] (6) and 'there are x planets' uniquely specify the same object. Does that object verify (5)? We might answer 'yes' if we start from (6) since it entails 'x is odd'. But if we start from 'there are x planets' we will answer 'no', since this latter specification does not entail 'x is odd'. Thus we are unable to specify an object which verifies (5). The idea of there being an object which is necessarily odd is incoherent. The only recourse for the modal logician is to essentialism according to which (6) is germane to (5) since it specifies its object essentially while 'there are x planets' specifies that same object accidentally and thus is irrelevant to (5).

Of the authors appearing here, Dagfinn Føllesdal is nearest to complete agreement with Quine. His paper deals with causal rather than logical modality, but is concerned only with features which the two modalities share. 'To make the parallelism between these arguments and those of Quine apparent', he says, 'Quine's wording will be used wherever possible.'

[4] *Words and Objections: Essays on the Work of W. V. Quine*, edited by D. Davidson and Jaakko Hintikka (Dordrecht—Holland: D. Reidel, 1969), p. 338.
[5] Ibid., p. 339.

The difficulties with causal necessity have their root in referential opacity. Suppose there is a well such that all who drink from it are poisoned. Let us suppose further that just one man has drunk from that well, a man born in place p at time t. Then presumably, it is true that,

(7) It is causally necessary that the man who drank from that well got poisoned.

It is also true that,

(8) The man who drank from that well = the man who was born in p at t.

But in spite of (7) and (8), it is false that,

(9) It is causally necessary that the man who was born in p at t got poisoned.

Attempted quantification into (7) yields

(10) $(\exists x)$ (it is causally necessary that x got poisoned).

'However, what is this object that got poisoned? The man who drank from the well, that is, the man who was born in p at t? But to suppose this would conflict with the fact that (9) is false.'

Føllesdal explores various ways of making an honest proposition of (10), thus legitimizing the quantified logic of causal necessity. One such way is suggested by Frege. When Frege came to deal with opaque contexts (he called them 'oblique'), he decided that names in them referred to their ordinary senses and not their ordinary references. Suppose that identity statements which are not merely true but necessarily true must contain terms whose ordinary senses are the same. (Frege, in fact, did not specify an identity condition for senses.) Then given Frege's principle identifying oblique reference with ordinary sense, necessary identity statements would sustain substitution in necessity contexts. If we now further suppose that all true identity statements are necessarily true, all our purported examples of the referential opacity of necessity will be swept aside and safely accounted fallacies.

At one time Quine thought that by intensionalizing the values of our variables we would render all true identities necessarily true and so clear the way to quantified modal logic. In a statement addressed to Rudolf Carnap and published in *Meaning and Necessity*, Quine says, 'I agree that such adherence to an intensional ontology, with extrusion of extensional entities altogether from the range of values of the variables, is indeed an effective way of reconciling quantification and modality. The cases of conflict between quantification and modality depend on extensions as values of variables. In your object language we may unhesitatingly quantify modalities because extensions have been dropped from among the values of the variables; even the individuals of the concrete world have disappeared, leaving only their concepts behind them.'[6] The purging of concrete individuals from the universe of discourse, Quine thought, would leave us with intensional objects no one of which could be uniquely specified by alternative conditions that fail of logical equivalence.

I am unable to construct a plausible argument that the purification suggested by Quine would have such beneficial consequences. At any rate, he was wrong about this and he says so. 'As a matter of fact, the worrisome charge that quantified modal logic can tolerate only intensions and not classes or individuals was a mistake to begin with. . . . I have been slow to see it, but the proof is simple.'[7] Suppose the condition 'φx' uniquely to determine the object x. Then, where 'p' is any truth not implied by 'φx', '$p \cdot \varphi x$' also uniquely determines x. But the two conditions 'φx' and '$p \cdot \varphi x$' are contingently and not logically coincident. This argument does not depend upon the extensionality of x, so intensionalizing the values of the variables will not evade it.

Suppose that we go at it the other way around and simply exclude those objects from our domain of discourse which admit of unique specifications by conditions which fail of necessary equivalence. 'There ceases to be any . . . objection to quantifying into modal position. Thus we can legitimize quantification into modal position by postulating that whenever each of two open sentences uniquely determines one and the same object x, the sentences are equivalent by necessity.'[8] We can put this opacity-annihilating postulate thus, where 'Fx' and 'Gx' are arbitrary open sentences and 'Fx and x only' is short for '(w) (Fw if and only if $w = x$)':

(11) If Fx and x only and Gx and x only then (necessarily (w) (Fw if and only if Gw)).

But this postulate annihilates modal distinctions along with the referential opacity of necessity. Let 'p' stand for any true sentence, it can be shown that 'Necessarily p'. Let y be any object and let $x = y$. Then

(12) (p and $x = y$) and x only

[6] *Meaning and Necessity* by Rudolf Carnap, 2nd edn. (Chicago, Illinois: The University of Chicago Press, 1956), p. 197.

[7] *Ways of Paradox* by W. Quine (New York: Random House, 1966), p. 182.

[8] *Word and Object* by W. Quine (Cambridge, Mass.: M.I.T. Press; New York and London: Wiley and Sons, 1960), p. 197.

and

(13) $x = y$ and x only.

Next, in our postulates take 'Fx' as '$p \cdot x = y$' and 'Gx' as '$x = y$', and it follows from (12) and (13) that,

(14) Necessarily (w) ((p and $w = y$) if and only if $w = y$).

(14) implies '(p and $y = y$) if and only if $y = y$' which implies 'p'. Hence, since what is implied by a necessary truth is a necessary truth, (14) implies that necessarily p. Q.E.D. Modal distinctions collapse.[9] Føllesdal tells the story in his paper, translating it to apply to causal rather than logical necessity.

Some, like Jaakko Hintikka,[10] have proposed abandoning substitutivity, in order to gain quantified modal logic. But Føllesdal argues that to restrict substitutivity in modal contexts is to abandon quantification as well. 'Quantification and substitutivity of identity go hand in hand.' The argument is as follows. Suppose we restrict substitutivity, denying it as a valid mode of inference in modal contexts. The justification for this is that an identity '$x = y$' may be true in this world and not true in some logically possible alternative to this world. (If '$x = y$' is also true in every logically possible alternative to this world, then its terms will also be unrestrictedly intersubstitutive in modal contexts.) This means that what corresponds to x, i.e. y, in this world are several objects (or none) in some logically possible alternative to this world. Now what will it mean under these conditions to say, e.g., '$(x)NFx$'. It means that everything is such that *it* has F in all possible worlds. Does x have F in all possible worlds? This question has no clear sense since 'it' has lost its unique reference in the possible world where '$x = y$' is false. Thus in order to make sense of quantification in modal contexts we must require that all true identity statements be necessarily true and this amounts to the requirement that identity be universally substitutive.

Restricting substitutivity in modal contexts or intensionalizing the values of the variables of modal logic are seen not to have the desired effects. Føllesdal proposes a third alternative, restrictions on the constant singular terms, or their complete elimination. He remarks, paradoxically, 'By insisting on the "primacy of predicates" and the eliminability of *all* singular terms in favour of general terms and variables, Quine . . . can be said to have levelled the road for modal logic.' Getting back to constant

[9] Ibid., p. 198.
[10] 'Quantifiers in Deontic Logic', by Jaakko Hintikka, *Societas Scientiarum Fennica, Commentationes Humanarum Litterarum* 23 (1957), No. 4.

singular terms, it is clear that they cause us difficulty only when they change their reference from possible world to possible world. Thus 'the number of planets' is nine in this world but not in other possible alternatives to it. And generally this will be true of definite descriptions. In order to avoid failures of substitutivity we are only required to exclude such terms and to require that all referring expressions have constant reference in all possible worlds. 'In order to avoid trouble, we should admit into our stock of singular terms only those descriptions which keep the same description in all . . . possible worlds.' The same restriction applies to all singular terms, constant and variable. None of this, of course, avoids essentialism. Rather, it implements it. Allowable names touch the essence of things and others do not. So Quine says, 'This plan of Føllesdal's is the formal implementation of the essentialism which, I have held, is the price of quantifying into opaque constructions.'[11] Føllesdal agrees.

II

Developments in modal logic took a new direction in the middle 1950s. Modal logic was provided with its semantics (model theory). In terms of this semantics various problems such as that of completeness could be formulated and solved. Saul Kripke's paper presents semantics for quantified modal logic and Jaakko Hintikka sketches the job for the propositional attitudes. I will not present the formal details since both papers are expository and the reader can find a compact presentation of Kripke's models in the first appendix of Terence Parsons' paper. Still, an informal heuristic account may be of help.

We begin with the idea of a *model structure* which is an ordered triple $\langle G, K, R \rangle$. K is a nonempty set of which G is an element and R is a reflexive relation defined on K: Intuitively K is the set of all possible worlds, G is the actual world and R is the relation of relative possibility. To say that one world is possible relative to another is to say that whatever is true in the former is possible in the latter. Thus intuitively R is required to be reflexive since what is true in a possible world H is possible in H. A *quantificational model structure* is a model structure together with a function ψ which assigns to each H ε K a set $\psi(H)$. Intuitively, $\psi(H)$ is the set of individuals existing in H (this may vary from possible world to possible world). For the semantics of quantified modal logic the relevant features about each possible world are (i) which things exist in that world and (ii) which things fall within the extensions of the predicates in that world. With regard to (ii), things are allowed to fall within the extension of a predicate in a possible world which do not according to (i) exist in that

---

[11] *Words and Objections*, p. 341.

world but do exist in another world possible relatively to it. A model (on a model structure) first fixes (ii) and then defines inductively a truth value for each formula A in each world H relatively to an assignment of objects (which need not exist in H) to the free variables of A. The quantifiers of A range only over objects existing in H. For a modalized closed sentence A the definition is,

> NA is true in the world H if and only if A is true in every world H' which is a possible world relatively to H.

A closed sentence is a valid sentence just in case it is true in G in every model on every model structure.

One might suppose that if quantified modal logic has its semantics in terms of which completeness can be proven, then surely there cannot be serious further questions of interpretation remaining, so that at last Quine's qualms can be set aside. But the creation of the new semantics has not terminated the philosophical controversy, though the issues have undergone reformulation. The question now arises as to the intelligibility of the semantics. There is no question, of course, as to the soundness of the mathematical results, or as to the semantics considered as a mathematical structure. There is no lack of clarity about the triple $\langle G, K, R \rangle$ consisting of a nonempty set K, a distinguished element of that set G, and a reflexive relation R defined on K. But this structure provides an account of *modality* only if K is regarded as the set of possible worlds and R as relative possibility and G as the actual world. So the structure must have an intuitive sense relating to *necessity*, and the philosophical controversy concerns the clarity of the relevant intuitions.

Terence Parsons bases his search for the essentialist commitments of modal logic on Kripke's semantics, and he comes up (happily) empty-handed. Parsons distinguishes several varieties of essentialism and several senses in which modal logic might be committed to it. He finds modal logic uncontaminated. 'I also argue', he says, 'that work in quantified modal logic need not even presuppose the *meaningfulness* of essentialist claims *in any objectionable sense*.' Parsons distinguishes individual essences which belong so intimately to their objects that not more than one thing *could* have them, and general essences which distinct individuals are not prohibited from sharing. His discussion is concerned solely with general essences. Parsons recognizes that it is individual essences which concern us in the problem of identifying individuals across possible worlds. 'Roughly, an object in one world is identified with an object in another world just in case they have the same individual essence.'

Parsons' investigation concerns a brand of essentialism about general essences. The doctrine holds (roughly) that there are general essences which some things have and which other things lack. A system of quantified modal logic (specifically, one of the systems of the class discussed by Kripke) is, according to Parsons, capable of commitment to essentialism in one or more of three senses. Let an *essential* sentence be one (roughly) which is general and which ascribes a necessary property to some things which it asserts that other things lack. Then a system of quantified modal logic is committed to essentialism in the first sense if '(i) It has some essential sentence as a theorem.' In this sense, Parsons proves that his systems fail of essentialist commitment. They fail of commitment to essentialism in the second sense as well. According to this, a system of quantified modal logic is committed to essentialism if '(ii) It has no essential sentence as a theorem, but nevertheless requires that some essential sentence be true—in the sense that the system, together with some obvious and uncontroversial non-modal facts, entails that some such sentence be true.' According to the third sense, a system is committed to essentialism if '(iii) The system allows the formulation (and thus presupposes the *meaningfulness* of) some essential sentence.'

The importance of this last sense of 'commitment' is this. Although modal logic has been shown not to be committed to the *truth* of essentialism, it must be committed to the *meaningfulness* of essentialism, 'for quantified modal logic simply *is* that symbolism within which essential sentences are formulable'. Thus quantified modal logic is committed to essentialism in sense (iii). But Parsons holds that there *need* be nothing objectionable in this. It is thought to be objectionable because it is thought that truth-conditions for essential sentences cannot be given in a determinate and clear way. But that is not true. The antiessentialist modal logician 'has a simple method of assigning determinate (and natural) truth-conditions to all essential sentences. That is to make them all false in all possible worlds'. Freedom of commitment in senses (i) and (ii) allows 'a freedom of any objectionable commitment in the third sense'.

My own essay takes up the doctrine of individual essences which Parsons put aside. Two individuals are the same across possible worlds if and only if they have the same individual essence. Consider the manner in which a model assigns a truth value to the sentence '$(\exists x)NFx$' in a world H. '$(\exists x)NFx$' is true in H if and only if there is some thing which exists in H such that *it* has F in all worlds possible relative to H. What does it mean to say of an object that it is identical with an object in another possible world? What is the criterion of identity across possible worlds? These questions are requests for explication of the doctrine of individual essence. So one can grant all that Parsons shows and still object to modal logic as involving us in an unintelligible metaphysics. And Quine agrees that here is where the essentialism involved in such systems as Kripke's surfaces. He says, in his response to the essay of David Kaplan in this volume, 'In any event Kaplan and I see eye to eye, negatively, on essentialism as applied to particulars. The result is that we can make little sense of identification of particulars across possible worlds. And the result of that is that we can make little sense of quantifying into necessity contexts when the values of the variables are particulars.'[12] So I see vindication for Quine in the semantics for modal logic, only I do not conclude 'so much the worse for modal logic' for I think I can see sense in essentialism. Whenever we talk about what might have happened to a thing but did not, we invoke the idea of that thing (the *same* thing) in another possible world in which what *might* have happened to it but did not (in the actual world) *did* happen. If we can understand this language about what might have been, we can identify individuals across possible worlds. And surely we do understand such talk, at least so I argue in my paper.

III

The essays discussed so far take necessity as centre of interest, but there are very close similarities between necessity and what Russell called 'propositional attitudes'. Propositional attitudes are for example, believing, supposing, denying; activities which, for Russell, take propositions as their objects. Belief may be taken as typical of the lot. Quine's second essay, and those following it in this book, deal with various aspects of the propositional attitudes. The most prominent feature which logical necessity shares with belief is referential opacity. This is shown in the example about Philip and Tegucigalpa cited above. There is an important asymmetry in Quine's attitude to these two classes of opaque contexts. He dismisses quantified modal logic as committed to an unacceptable metaphysics, and he can do this with a clear conscience because he believes that science and mathematics have no use for necessity. The concept of belief cannot thus be dismissed as unintelligible. He says, 'What makes me take the propositional attitudes more seriously than logical modality is a different reason: not that they are clearer, but that they are less clearly dispensable. We cannot easily forswear daily reference to belief, pending some substitute idiom as yet unforeseen. We can much more easily do without reference to necessity.'[13]

The principal considerations of Quine's second paper turn on an ambiguity in belief statements. Consider 'Ralph believes that someone is a

[12] Ibid., p. 343.   [13] Ibid., p. 344.

spy.' This may be paraphrased as 'There is someone whom Ralph believes to be a spy', and represented thus,

(15) $(\exists x)$ (Ralph believes that x is a spy).

Here 'belief' is said to have its 'relational' sense. Or 'belief' may have its likelier 'notional' sense, in which case our original statement may be paraphrased as, 'Ralph believes there are spies' and represented thus,

(16) Ralph believes that $(\exists x)$ (x is a spy).

'The difference', says Quine, 'is vast; indeed if Ralph is like most of us (16) is true and (15) is false'; (15) presages an arrest. In later work, Quine distinguishes two senses of belief, 'transparent' (as in (15)) and 'opaque' (which is here called 'notional'). He says, 'In my treatment of belief I distinguished an opaque and a transparent version, but in modal logic I got no further than the opaque.'[14] (15) does not involve quantification into an opaque context for here 'belief' has its transparent sense.

Yet, for Quine, that sense is odd, as is brought out by the following story.[15] Tom insists 'Tully did not denounce Catiline. Cicero did.' In the transparent sense, Tom believes that Cicero, i.e. Tully, denounced Catiline, and in that same sense he believes that Tully did not denounce Catiline. So in the transparent sense, Tom believes both that Tully did, and that Tully did not, denounce Catiline. Quine says, 'This is not yet a self-contradiction on our part or even on Tom's for a distinction can be reserved between (a) Tom's believing that Tully did and that Tully did not denounce Catiline, and (b) Tom's believing that Tully did and did not denounce Catiline.'[16] This oddity is the price we pay for

(17) $(\exists x)$ (Tom believes that x denounced Catiline).

(17) demands the transparent sense of belief. Quine prefers to avoid quantification into belief, even transparent belief. 'Thus in declaring belief invariably transparent for the sake of "Someone is such that Tom believes that he denounced Catiline" . . . we would let in too much. It can sometimes best suit us to affirm "Tom believes that Cicero denounced Catiline" and still deny "Tom believes that Tully denounced Catiline", at the cost— on *that* occasion—of "Someone is such that Tom believes that he denounced Catiline". In general what is wanted is not a doctrine of transparency or opacity of belief, but a way of indicating, selectively and

[14] Ibid., p. 343–44.
[15] *Word and Object*, p. 148.
[16] Ibid., p. 148.

changeably, just what positions in the contained sentence are to shine through as referential on any particular occasion.'[17]

In the second part of his paper, Quine suggests, provisionally, the following way of doing this. We settle on a single sense of belief, the opaque sense, and think of this as a relation between a believer and an *intension* named by a 'that'-clause. Intensions named by such clauses without free variables—intensions of degree 0—are propositions. There are also intensions of degree 1, or attributes named by prefixing a variable to a sentence in which it has a free occurrence; so $z(z$ is a spy) is the attribute spyhood. We name higher degree intensions by prefixing multiple variables in the same fashion. Now we can recognize a dyadic sense of belief between a believer and a proposition,

(18) Tom believes that Cicero denounced Catiline.

And we can also recognize a triadic sense of belief holding between a believer, an attribute, and an object,

(19) Tom believes $y(y$ denounced Catiline) of Cicero.

And tetradic belief,

(20) Tom believes $yz(y$ denounced $z)$ of Cicero and Catiline.

With this apparatus, we can steadfastly maintain a policy of not quantifying into propositional attitude expressions, but now it takes the form of not quantifying into names of intensions. We can still represent relational belief as, e.g., by (19) in which 'Cicero' occupies a quantifiable position. In place of the troublesome (17), we get the relatively unproblematic

(21) $(\exists x)$ (Tom believes $y(y$ denounced Catiline) of $x)$.

I call this 'relatively' unproblematic because it, along with (18), (19), and (20), contains a name of an intension. These, for Quine, are 'creatures of darkness'.

In the final section of his paper Quine suggests a way of retaining the merits of the above analysis while avoiding the intensions. 'Instead of speaking of intensions we can speak of sentences, naming these by quotation. Instead of:

w believes that . . .

we may say:

w believes-true ". . .".

[17] Ibid., p. 149.

Instead of:

> w believes $y(\ldots y \ldots)$ of x

we may say:

> w believes "$\ldots y \ldots$" satisfied by x.'

An argument against any analysis which takes linguistic expressions as objects of the propositional attitudes is put forth in the short paper by Alonzo Church in this volume. A statement of the form 'w believes-true "$\ldots$" in L' cannot convey the same meaning as one of the form 'w believes that $\ldots$' for neither follows from the other in the absence of some extraneous information about the language L. Church makes the point by appeal to a translation test. The statement

Meinong believes that there are objects such that there are no such objects, does not convey the same information as

Meinong believes the proposition meant by 'there are objects such that there are no such objects' in English.
These go into German respectively as

> *Meinong glaubt, dass es gibt Gegenstände, von denen gilt, dass es dergleichen Gegenstände nicht gibt.*
> *Meinong glaubt diejenige Aussage, die* „There are objects such that there are no such objects" *auf Englisch bedeutet.*

A German speaker innocent of English gets entirely different information from the German sentences, so the English sentences also convey different information. This argument does not disturb Quine, turning as it does on the notion of synonymy. The difficulty he sees in taking sentences as objects of the propositional attitudes is that these sentences must be referred to a language if the sentences containing them are to have their desired senses. But Quine finds the principle of individuation for languages as obscure as it is for intensions. Thus he finds his best efforts to legitimize the propositional attitudes defeated.

David Kaplan, with his quantifiers, goes where Quine fears to tread, into the propositional attitudes. Quine tends to treat terms in all opaque contexts in conformity with his treatment of them in the context of quotation. Quotation, for Quine, is the referentially opaque context *par excellence*. In quotation, terms occur as mere accidents of orthography, not in any logically or semantically relevant sense. Contrast this view with Frege's. Where Quine sees an accidental occurrence, Frege sees ambiguity. Instead of failure of reference, Frege sees shift of reference. The contexts which Frege calls 'oblique' and Quine 'opaque', Kaplan calls 'intermediate'.

The occurrence of 'nine' in 'Nine is greater than seven' is a *vulgar* occurrence, and its occurrence in 'Canine' is an *accidental* occurrence, while its occurrence in 'Necessarily nine is greater than seven' is *intermediate* between these.

Even terms in the context of quotation, according to Frege, perform their referential function. He does not hold that they are mere orthographic accidents there, parts of larger terms including the quotation marks. An expression in the context of quotation denotes itself. On this view it makes sense to quantify into the context of quotation and this is the foundation of Kaplan's approach to the problem of quantifying into necessity and propositional attitude contexts.

Kaplan takes sentences within the scope of 'necessarily' and 'believes' to denote themselves, so in his analysis they appear between quotes after these words. Using corners to represent Frege-quotes and Greek variables to range over expressions there is then nothing obscure about

(22) $(\exists \alpha)$ (α numbers the planets and $N^\ulcorner \alpha$ is greater than five$^\urcorner$),

which is simply false because expressions do not number planets. The difficulty is that '. . . the Fregean formulations appear to lack the kind of recurrence of a variable both within and without the necessity context that is characteristic of quantified modal logic. . . .' This difficulty can be overcome by taking advantage of the fact that numerals, although they do not number planets, denote the things that do. Kaplan uses Church's denotation predicate 'Δ' to attain the desired connection between expressions within and without modal contexts. The following corrects what is wrong with (22):

$(\exists y)$ (y numbers the planets and $\exists \alpha(\Delta(\alpha, y)$ and $N^\ulcorner \alpha$ is greater than five$^\urcorner$)). And there is no obscurity about

(23) $(\exists \alpha)$ ($\Delta(\alpha,$ nine) and $N^\ulcorner \alpha$ is greater than five$^\urcorner$),

which is true and avoids essentialism. (23) is a Fregean version of Quine's relational

(24) Nec('x is greater than five', nine),

with 'nine' in referential position. The trouble now is that the corresponding Fregean version of

(25) Nec('x = the number of planets', nine)

is also true understood as

(26) $\exists \alpha(\Delta(\alpha,$ nine) and $N^\ulcorner \alpha =$ the number of planets$^\urcorner$)

in view of the facts that

  N ⌜the number of planets = the number of planets⌝

and

  Δ('the number of planets', nine).

At this point Kaplan introduces an idea already hinted at by Mrs. Marcus and Føllesdal, standard names. These are names '. . . which are so intimately connected with what they name that they could not but name it. I shall say that such a name *necessarily denotes* its object, and I shall use "Δ_N" to symbolize this more discriminating form of denotation.' This leads to replacement of (23) with

  $\exists\alpha(\Delta_N(\alpha,$ nine) and N⌜α is greater than five⌝)

as the analysis of (24), and replacement of (26) by

  (27) $\exists\alpha(\Delta_N(\alpha,$ nine) and N⌜α = the number of planets⌝)

as the analysis of (25). (27) has the advantage of being false. Similar difficulties affect Kaplan's Fregean treatment of belief and similar 'solutions' are available, except that another notion is needed for the propositional attitudes, that of a *vivid* name. The analysis in terms of standard names and vivid names, of course, does not avoid essentialism. It embraces it.

I

REFERENCE AND MODALITY

W. V. O. QUINE

I

ONE of the fundamental principles governing identity is that of *substituti-vity*—or, as it might well be called, that of *indiscernibility of identicals*. It provides that, *given a true statement of identity, one of its two terms may be substituted for the other in any true statement and the result will be true*. It is easy to find cases contrary to this principle. For example, the statements:

(1) Giorgione = Barbarelli,

(2) Giorgione was so-called because of his size

are true; however, replacement of the name 'Giorgione' by the name 'Barbarelli' turns (2) into the falsehood:

Barbarelli was so-called because of his size.

Furthermore, the statements:

(3) Cicero = Tully,

(4) 'Cicero' contains six letters

are true, but replacement of the first name by the second turns (4) false. Yet the basis of the principle of substitutivity appears quite solid; whatever can be said about the person Cicero (or Giorgione) should be equally true of the person Tully (or Barbarelli), this being the same person.

In the case of (4), this paradox resolves itself immediately. The fact is that (4) is not a statement about the person Cicero, but simply about the word 'Cicero'. The principle of substitutivity should not be extended to contexts in which the name to be supplanted occurs without referring simply to the object. Failure of substitutivity reveals merely that the

From *From a Logical Point of View*, by W. Quine (New York: Harper and Row, 1961), pp. 139–57. Reprinted by permission of the publishers of the cloth edition, Cambridge, Mass.: Harvard University Press, Copyright, 1953, 1961, by the President and the Fellows of Harvard College.

occurrence to be supplanted is not *purely referential*,[1] that is, that the statement depends not only on the object but on the form of the name. For it is clear that whatever can be affirmed about the object remains true when we refer to the object by any other name.

An expression which consists of another expression between single quotes constitutes a name of that other expression; and it is clear that the occurrence of that other expression or a part of it, within the context of quotes, is not in general referential. In particular, the occurrence of the personal name within the context of quotes in (4) is not referential, not subject to the substitutivity principle. The personal name occurs there merely as a fragment of a longer name which contains, beside this fragment, the two quotation marks. To make a substitution upon a personal name, within such a context, would be no more justifiable than to make a substitution upon the term 'cat' within the context 'cattle'.

The example (2) is a little more subtle, for it is a statement about a man and not merely about his name. It was the man, not his name, that was called so and so because of his size. Nevertheless, the failure of substitutivity shows that the occurrence of the personal name in (2) is not *purely* referential. It is easy in fact to translate (2) into another statement which contains two occurrences of the name, one purely referential and the other not:

(5) Giorgione was called 'Giorgione' because of his size.

The first occurrence is purely referential. Substitution on the basis of (1) converts (5) into another statement equally true:

Barbarelli was called 'Giorgione' because of his size.

The second occurrence of the personal name is no more referential than any other occurrence within a context of quotes.

It would not be quite accurate to conclude that an occurrence of a name within single quotes is *never* referential. Consider the statements:

(6) 'Giorgione played chess' is true,

(7) 'Giorgione' named a chess player,

each of which is true or false according as the quotationless statement:

(8) Giorgione played chess

[1] Frege spoke of *direct* (*gerade*) and *oblique* (*ungerade*) occurrences, and used substitutivity of identity as a criterion just as here. See his 'On Sense and Reference', trans. Max Black, in *Philosophical Writings of Gottlob Frege* (Oxford: Blackwell, 1952).

is true or false. Our criterion of referential occurrence makes the occurrence of the name 'Giorgione' in (8) referential, and must make the occurrences of 'Giorgione' in (6) and (7) referential by the same token, despite the presence of single quotes in (6) and (7). The point about quotation is not that it must destroy referential occurrence, but that it can (and ordinarily does) destroy referential occurrence. The examples (6) and (7) are exceptional in that the special predicates 'is true' and 'named' have the effect of undoing the single quotes—as is evident on comparison of (6) and (7) with (8).

To get an example of another common type of statement in which names do not occur referentially, consider any person who is called Philip and satisfies the condition:

(9) Philip is unaware that Tully denounced Catiline,

or perhaps the condition:

(10) Philip believes that Tegucigalpa is in Nicaragua.

Substitution on the basis of (3) transforms (9) into the statement:

(11) Philip is unaware that Cicero denounced Catiline,

no doubt false. Substitution on the basis of the true identity:

Tegucigalpa = capital of Honduras

transforms the truth (10) likewise into the falsehood:

(12) Philip believes that the capital of Honduras is in Nicaragua.

We see therefore that the occurrences of the names 'Tully' and 'Tegucigalpa' in (9)–(10) are not purely referential.

In this there is a fundamental contrast between (9), or (10), and:

Crassus heard Tully denounce Catiline.

This statement affirms a relation between three persons, and the persons remain so related independently of the names applied to them. But (9) cannot be considered simply as affirming a relation between three persons, nor (10) a relation between person, city, and country—at least not so long as we interpret our words in such a way as to admit (9) and (10) as true and (11) and (12) as false.

Some readers may wish to construe unawareness and belief as relations between persons and statements, thus writing (9) and (10) in the manner:

(13) Philip is unaware of 'Tully denounced Catiline',

(14) Philip believes 'Tegucigalpa is in Nicaragua',

in order to put within a context of single quotes every not purely referential occurrence of a name. Church argues against this. In so doing he exploits the concept of analyticity, concerning which we have felt misgivings[1a]; still his argument cannot be set lightly aside, nor are we required here to take a stand on the matter. Suffice it to say that there is certainly no *need* to reconstrue (9)–(10) in the manner (13)–(14). What *is* imperative is to observe merely that the contexts 'is unaware that . . .' and 'believes that . . .' *resemble* the context of the single quotes in this respect: a name may occur referentially in a statement *S* and yet not occur referentially in a longer statement which is formed by embedding *S* in the context 'is unaware that . . .' or 'believes that . . .'. To sum up the situation in a word, we may speak of the contexts 'is unaware that . . .' and 'believes that . . .' as *referentially opaque*.[2] The same is true of the contexts 'knows that . . .', 'says that . . .', 'doubts that . . .', 'is surprised that . . .', etc. It would be tidy but unnecessary to force all referentially opaque contexts into the quotational mold; alternatively we can recognize quotation as one referentially opaque context among many.

It will next be shown that referential opacity afflicts also the so-called *modal* contexts 'Necessarily . . .' and 'Possibly . . .', at least when those are given the sense of *strict* necessity and possibility as in Lewis's modal logic.[3] According to the strict sense of 'necessarily' and 'possibly', these statements would be regarded as true:

(15) 9 is necessarily greater than 7,

(16) Necessarily if there is life on the Evening Star then there is life on the Evening Star,

(17) The number of planets is possibly less than 7,

and these as false:

(18) The number of planets is necessarily greater than 7,

(19) Necessarily if there is life on the Evening Star then there is life on the Morning Star,

(20) 9 is possibly less than 7.

[1a] See *From a Logical Point of View*, pp. 23–37.

[2] This term is roughly the opposite of Russell's 'transparent' as he uses it in his Appendix C to *Principia*, 2nd edn., Vol. 1.

[3] Lewis, C. I., *A Survey of Symbolic Logic* (New York: Dover, 1918) Ch. 5; Lewis and Langford, *Symbolic Logic* (New York, 1932; 2nd printing New York: Dover, 1951) pp. 78–89, 120–66.

The general idea of strict modalities is based on the putative notion of *analyticity* as follows: a statement of the form 'Necessarily . . .' is true if and only if the component statement which 'necessarily' governs is analytic, and a statement of the form 'Possibly . . .' is false if and only if the negation of the component statement which 'possibly' governs is analytic. Thus (15)–(17) could be paraphrased as follows:

(21) '9 > 7' is analytic,

(22) 'If there is life on the Evening Star then there is life on the Evening Star' is analytic,

(23) 'The number of planets is not less than 7' is not analytic,

and correspondingly for (18)–(20).

That the contexts 'Necessarily . . .' and 'Possibly . . .' are referentially opaque can now be quickly seen; for substitution on the basis of the true identities:

(24) The number of planets = 9,

(25) The Evening Star = the Morning Star

turns the truths (15)–(17) into the falsehoods (18)–(20).

Note that the fact that (15)–(17) are equivalent to (21)–(23), and the fact that '9' and 'Evening Star' and 'the number of planets' occur within quotations in (21)–(23), would not of themselves have justified us in concluding that '9' and 'Evening Star' and 'the number of planets' occur irreferentially in (15)–(17). To argue thus would be like citing the equivalence of (8) to (6) and (7) as evidence that 'Giorgione' occurs irreferentially in (8). What shows the occurrences of '9', 'Evening Star', and 'the number of planets' to be irreferential in (15)–(17) (and in (18)–(20)) is the fact that substitution by (24)–(25) turns the truths (15)–(17) into falsehoods (and the falsehoods (18)–(20) into truths).

Some, it was remarked, may like to think of (9) and (10) as receiving their more fundamental expression in (13) and (14). In the same spirit, many will like to think of (15)–(17) as receiving their more fundamental expression in (21)–(23).[4] But this again is unnecessary. We would certainly not think of (6) and (7) as somehow more basic than (8), and we need not view (21)–(23) as more basic than (15)–(17). What is important is to appreciate that the contexts 'Necessarily . . .' and 'Possibly . . .' are,

---

[4] Cf. Carnap, *The Logical Syntax of Language* (New York: Harcourt Brace; London: Routledge & Kegan Paul, 1937), pp. 245–59.

like quotation and 'is unaware that . . .' and 'believes that . . .', referentially opaque.

II

The phenomenon of referential opacity has just now been explained by appeal to the behaviour of singular terms. But singular terms are eliminable, we know, by paraphrase. Ultimately the objects referred to in a theory are to be accounted not as the things named by the singular terms, but as the values of the variables of quantification. So, if referential opacity is an infirmity worth worrying about, it must show symptoms in connection with quantification as well as in connection with singular terms.[5] Let us then turn our attention to quantification.

The connection between naming and quantification is implicit in the operation whereby, from 'Socrates is mortal', we infer '$(\exists x)$ (x is mortal)', that is, 'Something is mortal'. This is the operation which was spoken of earlier[5a] as *existential generalization*, except that we now have a singular term 'Socrates' where we then had a free variable. The idea behind such inference is that whatever is true of the object named by a given singular term is true of something; and clearly the inference loses its justification when the singular term in question does not happen to name. From:

There is no such thing as Pegasus,

for example, we do not infer:

$(\exists x)$ (there is no such thing as x),

that is, 'There is something which there is no such thing as', or 'There is something which there is not'.

Such inference is of course equally unwarranted in the case of an irreferential occurrence of any substantive. From (2), existential generalization would lead to:

$(\exists x)$ (x was so-called because of its size),

that is, 'Something was so-called because of its size'. This is clearly meaningless, there being no longer any suitable antecedent for 'so-called'. Note, in contrast, that existential generalization with respect to the purely referential occurrence in (5) yields the sound conclusion:

$(\exists x)$ (x was called 'Giorgione' because of its size),

that is, 'Something was called 'Giorgione' because of its size'.

---

[5] Substantially this point was made by Church, in *Journal of Symbolic Logic*, 7 (1942), 100 ff.

[5a] *From a Logical Point of View*, p. 120.

The logical operation of *universal instantiation* is that whereby we infer from 'Everything is itself', for example, or in symbols '$(x) (x = x)$', the conclusion that Socrates = Socrates. This and existential generalization are two aspects of a single principle; for instead of saying that '$(x) (x = x)$' implies 'Socrates = Socrates', we could as well say that the denial 'Socrates $\neq$ Socrates' implies '$(\exists x) (x \neq x)$'. The principle embodied in these two operations is the link between quantifications and the singular statements that are related to them as instances. Yet it is a principle only by courtesy. It holds only in the case where a term names and, furthermore, occurs referentially. It is simply the logical content of the idea that a given occurrence is referential. The principle is, for this reason, anomalous as an adjunct to the purely logical theory of quantification. Hence the logical importance of the fact that all singular terms, aside from the variables that serve as pronouns in connection with quantifiers, are dispensable and eliminable by paraphrase.[6]

We saw just now how the referentially opaque context (2) fared under existential generalization. Let us see what happens to our other referentially opaque contexts. Applied to the occurrence of the personal name in (4), existential generalization would lead us to:

(26) $(\exists x)$ ('x' contains six letters),

that is:

(27) There is something such that 'it' contains six letters,

or perhaps:

(28) 'Something' contains six letters.

Now the expression:

'x' contains six letters

means simply:

The 24th letter of the alphabet contains six letters.

In (26) the occurrence of the letter within the context of quotes is as irrelevant to the quantifier that precedes it as is the occurrence of the same letter in the context 'six'. (26) consists merely of a falsehood preceded by an irrelevant quantifier. (27) is similar; its part:

'it' contains six letters

[6] See *From a Logical Point of View*, pp. 7f, 13, and 166f. Note that existential generalization as of p. 120 does belong to pure quantification theory, for it has to do with free variables rather than singular terms. The same is true of a correlative use of universal instantiation, such as is embodied in R2 of Essay V, ibid.

is false, and the prefix 'there is something such that' is irrelevant. (28), again, is false—if by 'contains six' we mean 'contains exactly six'.

It is less obvious, and correspondingly more important to recognize, that existential generalization is unwarranted likewise in the case of (9) and (10). Applied to (9), it leads to:

$(\exists x)$ (Philip is unaware that x denounced Catiline),

that is:

(29) Something is such that Philip is unaware that it denounced Catiline.

What is this object, that denounced Catiline without Philip's having become aware of the fact? Tully, that is, Cicero? But to suppose this would conflict with the fact that (11) is false.

Note that (29) is not to be confused with:

Philip is unaware that $(\exists x)$ (x denounced Catiline),

which, though it happens to be false, is quite straightforward and in no danger of being inferred by existential generalization from (9).

Now the difficulty involved in the apparent consequence (29) of (9) recurs when we try to apply existential generalization to modal statements. The apparent consequences:

(30) $(\exists x)$ (x is necessarily greater than 7),

(31) $(\exists x)$ (necessarily if there is life on the Evening Star then there is life on x)

of (15) and (16) raise the same questions as did (29). What is this number which, according to (30), is necessarily greater than 7? According to (15), from which (30) was inferred, it was 9, that is, the number of planets; but to suppose this would conflict with the fact that (18) is false. In a word, to be necessarily greater than 7 is not a trait of a number, but depends on the manner of referring to the number. Again, what is the thing x whose existence is affirmed in (31)? According to (16), from which (31) was inferred, it was the Evening Star, that is, the Morning Star; but to suppose this would conflict with the fact that (19) is false. Being necessarily or possibly thus and so is in general not a trait of the object concerned, but depends on the manner of referring to the object.

Note that (30) and (31) are not to be confused with:

Necessarily $(\exists x)$ ($x > 7$),

Necessarily $(\exists x)$ (if there is life on the Evening Star then there is life on x), which present no problem of interpretation comparable to that presented by (30) and (31). The difference may be accentuated by a change of example: in a game of a type admitting of no tie it is necessary that some one of the players will win, but there is no one player of whom it may be said to be necessary that he win.

We had seen, in the preceding section, how referential opacity manifests itself in connection with singular terms; and the task which we then set ourselves at the beginning of this section was to see how referential opacity manifests itself in connection rather with variables of quantification. The answer is now apparent: if to a referentially opaque context of a variable we apply a quantifier, with the intention that it govern that variable from outside the referentially opaque context, then what we commonly end up with is unintended sense or nonsense of the type (26)–(31). In a word, we cannot in general properly *quantify into* referentially opaque contexts.

The context of quotation and the further contexts '. . . was so called', 'is unaware that . . .', 'believes that . . .', 'Necessarily . . .', and 'Possibly . . .' were found referentially opaque in the preceding section by consideration of the failure of substitutivity of identity as applied to singular terms. In the present section these contexts have been found referentially opaque by a criterion having to do no longer with singular terms, but with the miscarriage of quantification. The reader may feel, indeed, that in this second criterion we have not really got away from singular terms after all; for the discrediting of the quantifications (29)–(31) turned still on an expository interplay between the singular terms 'Tully' and 'Cicero', '9' and 'the number of planets', 'Evening Star' and 'Morning Star'. Actually, though, this expository reversion to our old singular terms is avoidable, as may now be illustrated by re-arguing the meaninglessness of (30) in another way. Whatever is greater than 7 is a number, and any given number x greater than 7 can be uniquely determined by any of various conditions, some of which have '$x > 7$' as a *necessary* consequence and some of which do not. One and the same number x is uniquely determined by the condition:

(32) $x = \sqrt{x} + \sqrt{x} + \sqrt{x} \neq \sqrt{x}$

and by the condition:

(33) There are exactly x planets,

but (32) has '$x > 7$' as a necessary consequence while (33) does not. *Necessary* greaterness than 7 makes no sense as applied to a *number* x; necessity attaches only to the connection between '$x > 7$' and the particular method (32), as opposed to (33), of specifying x.

Similarly, (31) was meaningless because the sort of thing x which fulfils the condition:

(34) If there is life on the Evening Star then there is life on x,

namely, a physical object, can be uniquely determined by any of various conditions, not all of which have (34) as a necessary consequence. *Necessary* fulfilment of (34) makes no sense as applied to a physical object x; necessity attaches, at best, only to the connection between (34) and one or another particular means of specifying x.

The importance of recognizing referential opacity is not easily overstressed. We saw in §1 that referential opacity can obstruct substitutivity of identity. We now see that it also can interrupt quantification: quantifiers outside a referentially opaque construction need have no bearing on variables inside it. This again is obvious in the case of quotation, as witness the grotesque example:

($\exists x$) ('*six*' contains 'x').

III

We see from (30)–(31) how a quantifier applied to a modal sentence may lead simply to nonsense. Nonsense is indeed mere absence of sense, and can always be remedied by arbitrarily assigning some sense. But the important point to observe is that granted an understanding of the modalities (through uncritical acceptance, for the sake of argument, of the underlying notion of analyticity), and given an understanding of quantification ordinarily so called, we do not come out automatically with any meaning for quantified modal sentences such as (30)–(31). This point must be taken into account by anyone who undertakes to work out laws for a quantified modal logic.

The root of the trouble was the referential opacity of modal contexts. But referential opacity depends in part on the ontology accepted, that is, on what objects are admitted as possible objects of reference. This may be seen most readily by reverting for a while to the point of view of §1, where referential opacity was explained in terms of failure of interchangeability of names which name the same object. Suppose now we were to repudiate all objects which, like 9 and the planet Venus, or Evening Star, are nameable by names which fail of interchangeability in modal contexts. To do so would be to sweep away all examples indicative of the opacity of modal contexts.

But what objects would remain in a thus purified universe? An object x must, to survive, meet this condition: if S is a statement containing a referential occurrence of a name of x, and S' is formed from S by sub-stituting any different name of x, then S and S' not only must be alike in truth value as they stand, but must stay alike in truth value even when 'necessarily' or 'possibly' is prefixed. Equivalently: putting one name of x for another in any analytic statement must yield an analytic statement. Equivalently: any two names of x must be synonymous.[7]

Thus the planet Venus as a material object is ruled out by the possession of heteronymous names 'Venus', 'Evening Star', 'Morning Star'. Corres-ponding to these three names we must, if modal contexts are not to be referentially opaque, recognize three objects rather than one—perhaps the Venus-concept, the Evening-Star-concept, and the Morning-Star-concept.

Similarly 9, as a unique whole number between 8 and 10, is ruled out by the possession of heteronymous names '9' and 'the number of the planets'. Corresponding to these two names we must, if modal contexts are not to be referentially opaque, recognize two objects rather than one; perhaps the 9-concept and the number-of-planets-concept. These concepts are not numbers, for the one is neither identical with nor less than nor greater than the other.

The requirement that any two names of x be synonymous might be seen as a restriction not on the admissible objects x, but on the admissible voca-bulary of singular terms. So much the worse, then, for this way of phrasing the requirement; we have here simply one more manifestation of the super-ficiality of treating ontological questions from the vantage point of singular terms. The real insight, in danger now of being obscured, was rather this: necessity does not properly apply to the fulfilment of conditions by *objects* (such as the ball of rock which is Venus, or the number which numbers the planets), apart from special ways of specifying them. This point was most conveniently brought out by consideration of singular terms, but it is not abrogated by their elimination. Let us now review the matter from the point of view of quantification rather than singular terms.

From the point of view of quantification, the referential opacity of modal contexts was reflected in the meaninglessness of such quantifica-tions as (30)–(31). The crux of the trouble with (30) is that a number x may be uniquely determined by each of two conditions, for example, (32) and (33), which are not necessarily, that is, analytically, equivalent to each other. But suppose now we were to repudiate all such objects and retain only objects x such that *any two conditions uniquely determining*

---

[7] See *From a Logical Point of View*, p. 32. Synonymy of names does not mean merely naming the same thing; it means that the statement of identity formed of the two names is analytic.

x are analytically equivalent. All examples such as (30)–(31), illustrative
of the referential opacity of modal contexts, would then be swept away.
It would come to make sense in general to say that there is an object
which, independently of any particular means of specifying it, is necessarily
thus and so. It would become legitimate, in short, to quantify into modal
contexts.

Our examples suggest no objection to quantifying into modal contexts
as long as the values of any variables thus quantified are limited to *intensional objects*. This limitation would mean allowing, for purposes of
such quantification anyway, not classes but only class-concepts or attributes, it being understood that two open sentences which determine the
same class still determine distinct attributes unless they are analytically
equivalent. It would mean allowing, for purposes of such quantification,
not numbers but only some sort of concepts which are related to the
numbers in a many-one way. Further it would mean allowing, for purposes
of such quantification, no concrete objects but only what Frege[7a] called
senses of names, and Carnap[7b] and Church have called individual concepts.
It is a drawback of such an ontology that the principle of individuation of
its entities rests invariably on the putative notion of synonymy, or analyticity.

Actually, even granted these dubious entities, we can quickly see that the
expedient of limiting the values of variables to them is after all a mistaken
one. It does not relieve the original difficulty over quantifying into modal
contexts; on the contrary, examples quite as disturbing as the old ones
can be adduced within the realm of intensional objects. For, where A
is any intensional object, say an attribute, and 'p' stands for an arbitrary
true sentence, clearly

(35) $A = (\imath x)[p \cdot (x = A)]$.

Yet, if the true sentence represented by 'p' is not analytic, then neither is
(35), and its sides are no more interchangeable in modal contexts than are
'Evening Star' and 'Morning Star', or '9' and 'the number of the planets'.

Or, to state the point without recourse to singular terms, it is that the
requirement lately italicized—'any two conditions uniquely determining
x are analytically equivalent'—is not assured merely by taking x as an
intensional object. For, think of 'Fx' as any condition uniquely determining x, and think of 'p' as any nonanalytic truth. Then '$p \cdot Fx$' uniquely
determines x but is not analytically equivalent to 'Fx', even though x
be an intensional object.

[7a] 'On Sense and Reference.'
[7b] *Meaning and Necessity*, 2nd edn. (Chicago, Ill.: Univ. of Chicago Press, 1956).

It was in my 1943 paper that I first objected to quantifying into modal contexts, and it was in his review of it that Church proposed the remedy of limiting the variables thus quantified to intensional values. This remedy, which I have just now represented as mistaken, seemed all right at the time. Carnap adopted it in an extreme form, limiting the range of his variables to intensional objects throughout his system. He did not indeed describe his procedure thus; he complicated the picture by propounding a curious double interpretation of variables. But I have argued[8] that this complicating device has no essential bearing and is better put aside.

By the time Church came to propound an intensional logic of his own,[8a] he perhaps appreciated that quantification into modal contexts could not after all be legitimized simply by limiting the thus quantified variables to intensional values. Anyway his departures are more radical. Instead of a necessity operator attachable to sentences, he has a necessity predicate attachable to complex names of certain intensional objects called propositions. What makes this departure more serious than it sounds is that the constants and variables occurring in a sentence do not recur in Church's name of the corresponding proposition. Thus the interplay, usual in modal logic, between occurrences of expressions outside modal contexts and recurrences of them inside modal contexts, is ill reflected in Church's system. Perhaps we should not call it a system of modal logic; Church generally did not. Anyway let my continuing discussion be understood as relating to modal logics only in the narrower sense, where the modal operator attaches to sentences.

Church and Carnap tried—unsuccessfully, I have just argued—to meet my criticism of quantified modal logic by restricting the values of their variables. Arthur Smullyan took the alternative course of challenging my criticism itself. His argument depends on positing a fundamental division of names into proper names and (overt or covert) descriptions, such that proper names which name the same object are always synonymous. (Cf. (38) below.) He observes quite rightly on these assumptions, that any examples which, like (15)–(20) and (24)–(25), show failure of substitutivity of identity in modal contexts, must exploit some descriptions rather than just proper names. Then he undertakes to adjust matters by propounding, in connection with modal contexts, and alteration of

---

[8] In a criticism which Carnap generously included in his *Meaning and Necessity*, pp. 196f.

[8a] Church, A., 'A Formulation of the Logic of Sense and Denotation', in Henle, P., Kallen, H. M., and Langen, S. K. (eds.), *Structure, Method and Meaning: Essays in Honour of Henry M. Sheffer* (New York: Liberal Arts Press, 1951), pp. 3–24.

Russell's familiar logic of descriptions.[9] As stressed in the preceding section, however, referential opacity remains to be reckoned with even when descriptions and other singular terms are eliminated altogether.

Nevertheless, the only hope of sustaining quantified modal logic lies in adopting a course that resembles Smullyan's, rather than Church and Carnap, in this way: it must overrule my objection. It must consist in arguing or deciding that quantification into modal contexts makes sense even though any value of the variable of such a quantification be determinable by conditions that are not analytically equivalent to each other. The only hope lies in accepting the situation illustrated by (32) and (33) and insisting, despite it, that the object x is question is necessarily greater than 7. This means adopting an invidious attitude toward certain ways of uniquely specifying x, for example (33), and favouring other ways, for example (32), as somehow better revealing the 'essence' of the object. Consequences of (32) can, from such a point of view, be looked upon as necessarily true of the object which is 9 (and is the number of the planets), while some consequences of (33) are rated still as only contingently true of that object.

Evidently this reversion to Aristotelian essentialism[10] is required if quantification into modal contexts is to be insisted on. An object, of itself and by whatever name or none, must be seen as having some of its traits necessarily and others contingently, despite the fact that the latter traits follow just as analytically from some ways of specifying the object as the former traits do from other ways of specifying it. In fact, we can see pretty directly that any quantified modal logic is bound to show such favouritism among the traits of an object; for surely it will be held, for each thing x, on the one hand that

(36) necessarily $(x = x)$

and on the other hand that

(37) $\sim$ necessarily $[p \cdot (x = x)]$,

where 'p' stands for an arbitrary contingent truth.

Essentialism is abruptly at variance with the idea, favoured by Carnap, Lewis, and others, of explaining necessity by analyticity[11]. For the appeal

[9] Russell's theory of descriptions, in its original formulation, involved distinctions of so-called 'scope'. Change in the scope of a description was indifferent to the truth value of any statement, however, unless the description failed to name. This indifference was important to the fulfilment, by Russell's theory, of its purpose as an analysis or surrogate of the practical idiom of singular description. On the other hand, Smullyan allows difference of scope to affect truth value even in cases where the description concerned succeeds in naming.

[10] *From a Logical Point of View*, p. 22.

[11] Ibid., p. 30.

to analyticity can pretend to distinguish essential and accidental traits of an object only relative to how the object is specified, not absolutely. Yet the champion of quantified modal logic must settle for essentialism.

Limiting the values of his variables is neither necessary nor sufficient to justify quantifying the variables into modal contexts. Limiting their values can, however, still have this purpose in conjunction with his essentialism: if he wants to limit his essentialism to special sorts of objects, he must correspondingly limit the values of the variables which he quantifies into modal contexts.

The system presented in Miss Barcan's pioneer papers on quantified modal logic differed from the system of Carnap and Church in imposing no special limitations on the values of variables. That she was prepared, moreover, to accept the essentialist presuppositions seems rather hinted in her theorem:

(38) $(x)(y)\{(x = y) \supset [\text{necessarily } (x = y)]\}$,

for this is as if to say that some at least (and in fact at most; cf. '$p \cdot Fx$') of the traits that determine an object do so necessarily. The modal logic in Fitch, follows Miss Barcan on both points. Note incidentally that (38) follows directly from (36) and a law of substitutivity of identity for variables:

$(x)(y)[(x = y \cdot Fx) \supset Fy]$.

The upshot of these reflections is meant to be that the way to do quantified modal logic, if at all, is to accept Aristotelian essentialism. To defend Aristotelian essentialism, however, is not part of my plan. Such a philosophy is as unreasonable by my lights as it is by Carnap's or Lewis's. And in conclusion I say, as Carnap and Lewis have not: so much the worse for quantified modal logic. By implication, so much the worse for unquantified modal logic as well; for, if we do not propose to quantify across the necessity operator, the use of that operator ceases to have any clear advantage over merely quoting a sentence and saying that it is analytic.

IV

The worries introduced by the logical modalities are introduced also by the admission of attributes (as opposed to classes). The idiom 'the attribute of being thus and so' is referentially opaque, as may be seen, for example, from the fact that the true statement:

(39) The attribute of exceeding 9 = the attribute of exceeding 9
    goes over into the falsehood:
The attribute of exceeding the number of the planets = the attribute of exceeding 9

under substitution according to the true identity (24). Moreover, existential generalization of (39) would lead to:

(40) $(\exists x)$ (the attribute of exceeding x = the attribute of exceeding 9)

which resists coherent interpretation just as did the existential generalizations (29)–(31) of (9), (15), and (16). Quantification of a sentence which contains the variable of quantification within a context of the form 'the attribute of . . .' is exactly on a par with quantification of a modal sentence.

Attributes, as remarked earlier, are individuated by this principle: two open sentences which determine the same class do not determine the same attribute unless they are analytically equivalent. Now another popular sort of intensional entity is the *proposition*. Propositions are conceived in relation to statements as attributes are conceived in relation to open sentences: two statements determine the same proposition just in case they are analytically equivalent. The foregoing strictures on attributes obviously apply to propositions. The truth:

(41)   The proposition that $9 > 7$ = the proposition that $9 > 7$ goes over into the falsehood:

The proposition that the number of the planets > 7 = the proposition that $9 > 7$.

under substitution according to (24). Existential generalization of (41) yields a result comparable to (29)–(31) and (40).

Most of the logicians, semanticists, and analytical philosophers who discourse freely of attributes, propositions, or logical modalities betray failure to appreciate that they thereby imply a metaphysical position which they themselves would scarcely condone. It is noteworthy that in *Principia Mathematica*, where attributes were nominally admitted as entities, all actual contexts occurring in the course of formal work are such as could be fulfilled as well by classes as by attributes. All actual contexts are *extensional* in the sense already explained.[12] The authors of *Principia Mathematica* thus adhered in practice to a principle of extensionality which they did not espouse in theory. If their practice had been otherwise, we might have been brought sooner to an appreciation of the urgency of the principle.

We have seen how modal sentences, attribute terms, and proposition terms conflict with the nonessentialist view of the universe. It must be

---

[12] *From a Logical Point of View*, p. 30.

kept in mind that those expressions create such conflict only when they are quantified into, that is, when they are put under a quantifier and themselves contain the variable of quantification. We are familiar with the fact (illustrated by (26) above) that a quotation cannot contain an effectively free variable, reachable by an outside quantifier. If we preserve a similar attitude toward modalities, attribute terms, and proposition terms, we may then make free use of them without any misgivings of the present urgent kind.

What has been said of modality in these pages relates only to strict modality. For other sorts, for example, physical necessity and possibility, the first problem would be to formulate the notions clearly and exactly. Afterwards we could investigate whether such modalities, like the strict ones, cannot be quantified into without precipitating an ontological crisis. The question concerns intimately the practical use of language. It concerns, for example, the use of the contrary-to-fact conditional within a quantification; for it is reasonable to suppose that the contrary-to-fact conditional reduces to the form 'Necessarily, if p then q' in some sense of necessity. Upon the contrary-to-fact conditional depends in turn, for example, this definition of solubility in water: To say that an object is soluble in water is to say that it would dissolve if it were in water. In discussions of physics, naturally, we need quantifications containing the clause 'x is soluble in water', or the equivalent in words; but, according to the definition suggested, we should then have to admit within quantifications the expression 'if x were in water then x would dissolve', that is, 'necessarily if x is in water then x dissolves'. Yet we do not know whether there is a suitable sense of 'necessarily' into which we can so quantify.[13]

Any way of imbedding statements within statements, whether based on some notion of 'necessity' or, for example, on a notion of 'probability' as in Reichenbach, must be carefully examined in relation to its susceptibility to quantification. Perhaps the only useful modes of statement composition susceptible to unrestricted quantification are the truth functions. Happily, no other mode of statement composition is needed, at any rate, in mathematics; and mathematics, significantly, is the branch of science whose needs are most clearly understood.

Let us return, for a final sweeping observation, to our first test of referential opacity, namely, failure of substitutivity of identity; and let us suppose that we are dealing with a theory in which (a) *logically* equivalent formulas are interchangeable in all contexts *salva veritate* and (b) the logic of classes

---

[13] For a theory of disposition terms, like 'soluble', see Carnap, 'Testability and Meaning', *Philosophy of Science*, 3 (1936), 419–71.

is at hand.[14] For such a theory it can be shown that *any* mode of statement composition, other than the truth functions, is referentially opaque. For, let ϕ and ψ be any statements alike in truth value, and let $\Phi(\phi)$ be any true statement containing ϕ as a part. What is to be shown is that $\Phi(\psi)$ will also be true, unless the context represented by 'Φ' is referentially opaque. Now the class named by $\hat{\alpha}\phi$ is either V or Λ, according as ϕ is true or false; for remember that ϕ is a statement, devoid of free α. (If the notation $\hat{\alpha}\phi$ without recurrence of α seems puzzling, read it as $\hat{\alpha}(\alpha = \alpha \,.\, \phi)$.) Moreover ϕ is logically equivalent to $\hat{\alpha}\phi = $ V. Hence, by (a), since $\Phi(\phi)$ is true, so is $\Phi(\hat{\alpha}\phi = $ V). But $\hat{\alpha}\phi$ and $\hat{\alpha}\psi$ name one and the same class, since ϕ and ψ are alike in truth value. Then, since $\Phi(\hat{\alpha}\phi = $ V) is true, so is $\Phi(\hat{\alpha}\psi = $ V) unless the context represented by 'Φ' is referentially opaque. But if $\Phi(\hat{\alpha}\psi = $ V) is true, then so in turn is $\Phi(\psi)$, by (a).

---

[14] See *From a Logical Point of View*, pp. 27, 87.

II

MODALITY AND DESCRIPTION

Arthur F. Smullyan

There are logicians who maintain that modal logic violates Leibniz's principle that if x and y are identical, then y has every property of x. The alleged difficulty is illustrated in the following example due to Quine.[1]

(a) It is logically necessary that 9 is less than 10.

(b) 9 = the number of the planets.

(c) Therefore, it is logically necessary that the number of the planets is less than 10.

The premises of this argument are true, the conclusion is false, and yet the conclusion appears to be derived by means of the logical precept that if x is y then any property of x is a property of y. Such is the paradox of modal logic. But the difficulty is obviated if we draw a distinction. We must distinguish between statements of the following forms:

(d) The so-and-so satisfies the condition that it is necessary that Fx.

and

(e) It is necessary that the so-and-so satisfies the condition that Fx.

The reader at this stage is bound to feel as though he were being asked to distinguish between Tweedledum and Tweedledee. Possibly, it will be of assistance to him to remark that statements of type (d) are sometimes synthetic, whereas those of type (e) are never synthetic. I will ask the reader to believe that James is now thinking of the number 3. If, now, some one were to remark, 'there is one and only one integer which James is now thinking of and that integer is necessarily odd', then he would be stating a contingent truth. For that there is just one integer which James now thinks of, is only an empirical fact. This statement could just as well be expressed in the form, (d), 'The integer, which James is now

[1] W. Quine, 'Notes on Existence and Necessity', *Journal of Philosophy*, XL (1943), 113–27.

We assume, at this stage of the discussion, that '9' and '10', as they occur in the illustration, are *names* of familiar logical *properties*. This is in order to simplify the introductory discussion. In due course we shall consider the problem in a more general way.

thinking of, satisfies the condition that it is necessarily odd.' In contrast, the statement, 'It is necessary that James's integer is odd', which is of the form, (e) is an impossible statement and not a contingent one. If not necessary, then necessarily not necessary: at least, so we assume.

The conclusion, (c) is of the form, (e), and it does not follow logically from (a) and (b). Leibniz's law does not require that (a) and (b) entail (c). What Leibniz's law does permit us to infer from the premisses (a) and (b) is the statement,

(f) As a matter of brute fact, the number of planets satisfies the condition that it is necessary that x is less than 10.

It is to be noted that this sentence (f) is true, synthetic and not paradoxical. On the other hand, the statement (c) is not only incorrectly inferred from the premisses, but is, moreover, logically impossible. For it is false, and, as we have already said, a false sentence which attributes necessity is *logically* false. We have just noted that (c) is of the form (e), whereas the valid conclusion is of the form (d).

In order to show that the difficulty is not essentially connected with Leibniz's principle, we shall consider another specious but equally instructive argument. We shall assume the truth of a synthetic sentence

(1) $E!(\imath x)(Fx)$

and we assume the principle

(2) $(x)[N(x = x)]$, where 'N' means what we express by the idiom, 'it is necessary that'.

The critics of modal logic might very well allege that we are by that logic committed to infer from (1) and (2) the statement,

(3) $N[(\imath x)(Fx) = (\imath x)(Fx)]$.

The absurdity of this derivation will soon be made apparent to the reader. What we are committed by modal logic to infer is the quite different statement,

(4) $(\exists x) (Fu \equiv_u u = x . N(x = x))$.

This statement is not at all equivalent to

(5) $N[(\exists x) (Fu \equiv_u u = x . x = x)]$, which is logically equivalent to (3).

The reader will note that if in place of (1) we had written '$N[E!(\imath x)(Fx)]$' we could then have deduced (5) which says that it is necessary that $(\imath x)(Fx)$ is self-identical or, in other words, that it is necessary that there exists just one instance of the property F. But from the premises (1) and (2) we may validly infer only (4) which asserts that *in fact* one and only one instance of F exists satisfying the condition that it is necessarily self-identical. The reader will already have observed that (4) is a statement of the sort (d), whereas (3) and (5) are statements of type (e).

The student of logic will at this stage remind us of theorem *14.18 of *Principia Mathematica* which is the sentence,

$$\vdash : . \; E!(\imath x)(\varphi x) . \; \supset \; : (x) . \; \psi x . \; \supset \; \psi(\imath x)(\varphi x).$$

Does not this formula enable us to deduce (5), which is equivalent to (3), from (1) and (2)? Surely, all we need to do is to perform these substitutions on *14.18, viz., substitute 'f' for 'φ', 'N($x = x$)' for 'ψx', and use *modus ponens* twice? But the student who so objects is committing the subtle fallacy of misreading the scope of the description, '$(\imath x)(\varphi x)$'. In *Principia Mathematica* it is assumed that the scope of a description is the smallest formula containing that description, unless it is to the contrary indicated. In the case of *14.18, the scope of the second occurrence of the descriptive phrase is '$\psi(\imath x)(\varphi x)$'. It is only by neglecting this consideration that one is led to deduce (3) from (1) and (2) in place of the correct deduction of (4).

But the tireless objector will try once more. 'Surely', we can hear him saying, 'in case "E!$(\imath x)(\varphi x)$" is true, the scope of the descriptive phrase can be ignored and "$(\imath x)(\varphi x)$" may be treated as a name.' But this is an error which impedes the development of modal logic. It cannot be demonstrated [because it is not so] that if f is *any* function of propositions, then

$$E!(\imath x)(\varphi x) : \; \supset \; : f\{[(\imath x)(\varphi x)] . \; \chi(\imath x)(\varphi x) . \} . \; \equiv \; . \; [(\imath x)(\varphi x)] . \; f\{\chi(\imath x)(\varphi x)\}.$$

What *can* be regarded as established is *14.3 in *Principia Mathematica* which asserts that when 'E!$(\imath x)(\varphi x)$' is true and when '$(\imath x)(\varphi x)$' occurs in a *truth-functional* context, then the scope of '$(\imath x)(\varphi x)$' does not affect the truth value of the sentence in which it occurs. *14.3 reads as follows:

$$\vdash : . \; p \equiv q \; \supset_{p,q} : . \; f(p) \equiv f(q) : E!(\imath x)(\varphi x) : \; \supset \; : f\{[(\imath x)(\varphi x)] . \; \chi(\imath x)(\varphi x) . \}.$$
$$\equiv \; . \; [(\imath x)(\varphi x)] . \; f\{\chi(\imath x)(\varphi x)\}.$$

However, in non-truth-functional contexts the scope of the description, even when E!$(\imath x)(\varphi x)$, does matter to the truth value of the context. From (4) we cannot deduce (5). From (f) we cannot deduce (c).

One of the possible sources of the confusion which we are trying to eliminate is to be found in *Principia Mathematica* itself where the authors inadvertently assert, on p. 186, vol. I,

> 'It should be observed that the proposition in which $(\imath x)(\varphi x)$ has the larger scope always implies the corresponding one in which it has the smaller scope, . . .'

It is evident that this pronouncement holds good only when truth functional contexts are in question. In non-truth-functional contexts, the contention fails to hold. We cannot, for example, derive from the sentence $[(\imath x)(\varphi x)] \cdot N(\psi(\imath x)(\varphi x))$., the sentence, $N(\psi(\imath x)(\varphi x))$, although the description in the latter proposition has the smaller scope. This is an important difference between intensional and extensional contexts.

Let us now return to the specious argument with which we began, in which (c) was derived from (a) and (b). This argument may be taken as illustrating the abstract form

$$N(Fy)$$
$$\underline{y = (\imath x)(\varphi x)}$$
$$\therefore N[F(\imath x)(\varphi x)]$$

The fallacy implicit in this mode of argument consists in taking the scope of the description in the conclusion to be '$F(\imath x)(\varphi x)$'. That is to say, the valid argument-form is rather

$$N(Fy)$$
$$\underline{y = (\imath x)(\varphi x)}$$
$$\therefore [(\imath x)(\varphi x)] \cdot N(F(\imath x)(\varphi x)).$$

For the second premiss of this argument is, by definition, equivalent to

$$(\exists x)(\varphi z \equiv_z z = x : y = x),$$

which, in conjunction with the first premise, yields

$$(\exists x)(\varphi z \equiv_z z = x : y = x \cdot N(Fy)).$$

This, by Leibniz's law gives

$$(\exists x)(\varphi z \equiv_z z = x \cdot N(Fx))$$

which is the same proposition as

$$[(\imath x)(\varphi x)] \cdot N(F(\imath x)(\varphi x)).$$

The reader should note that to obtain the conclusion, $N(F(\imath x)(\varphi x))$, it would be possible to strengthen the second of the premisses. I.e., the following argument-form is valid:

$$N(Fy)$$
$$\underline{N(y = (\imath x)(\varphi x))}$$
$$\therefore N(F(\imath x)(\varphi x))$$

Similarly,

$$(x)N(Fx)$$
$$\underline{N(E!(\imath x)(\varphi x))}$$
$$\therefore N(F(\imath x)(\varphi x))$$

and

$$(x)N(Fx)$$
$$\underline{E!(\imath x)(\varphi x)}$$
$$\therefore [(\imath x)(\varphi x)] \cdot N(F(\imath x)(\varphi x))$$

are valid argument-forms.

The intention of this paper is to show that the unrestricted use of modal operators in connection with statements *and* matrices embedded in the framework of a logical system such as *Principia Mathematica* does not involve a violation of Leibniz's principle. In order to show this, we have, of course, utilized Russell's method of contextual definition of descriptive phrases and we shall, in the sequel, and for the same reason, adopt contextual definitions of class abstracts.

In the light of our discussion so far, it may suggest itself to the reader that the modal paradoxes arise not out of any intrinsic absurdity in the use of the modal operators but rather out of the assumption that descriptive phrases are names. It may indeed be the case that the critics of modal logic object primarily not to the use of modal operators but to the method of contextual definition as employed, e.g., in Russell's theory of definite descriptions. In this case, however, it would be in the interest of clarity to indicate the prior grounds on which their objections to the theory of descriptions are based.

It is natural in this connection to refer to the reviews of Alonzo Church which antedate important parts of this discussion by about five years.[2] In his review of Quine's essay, to which we principally refer, Church argues that the modal paradoxes indicate that if modal operators are used in a system in which descriptions and class abstracts are construed as names, then these operators must be prefixed not to sentences in the

[2] A. Church, *Journal of Symbolic Logic*, 7 (1942), 100.

system but to the names of their *senses*. One may agree with this hypothetical proposition of Church and use it to defend the contention that *since* we *do* ordinarily prefix modal operators to sentences we are by this fact committed to a logical system in which descriptions *are* contextually defined. This is not to deny, of course, the legitimacy of other constructions. In particular, Church's preference is to prefix modal operators to the names of the senses of sentences rather than to the sentences themselves. But the theory of descriptions appears to have a peculiar relevance to our ordinary use of modal notions. Other sections of Church's review may be adduced as corroboration of our contention that the logical modalities need not involve paradox when they are referred to a system in which descriptions and class abstracts are contextually defined.

We have been discussing logical systems in which descriptions are treated in accordance with the theory of descriptions. But there are logicians who will say that the theory of descriptions is really a 'proposal to do without descriptions'. This is Church's view in the review cited. And it *is* a possible interpretation to make; but to many it will seem preferable to regard a logical system as containing not only formulae in primitive notation but also the abbreviations of those formulae which are effected by the use of descriptive phrases and other defined *idioms*. In semantical discussions this latter interpretation is particularly useful because although we may wish to deny that descriptions are names we may yet wish to insist that some of them *describe* objects. Being a meaningless noise is not the only alternative to being a name.

Our discussion of the argument (abc) may seem to have depended, at certain crucial points, upon our decision to interpret the expression, 'the number of the planets' as a definite description. What would have been the situation had the phrase in question been interpreted as a class abstract, as synonymous with '$\hat{x}(x$ is equinumerous with the set of planets)' for example?

The analysis which we have been expounding applies to this interpretation also provided that class abstracts are not treated as names but as incomplete symbols. We shall briefly indicate how this may be shown in the case of systems which use class variables in addition to property variables. Essentially the same analysis holds more generally for systems such as *Principia Mathematica* which have only property variables and which seek to dispense with the assumption of classes. But there are subtleties[3] connected with such reductive techniques which are not germane

---

[3] See R. Carnap, *Meaning and Necessity* (Chicago, Ill.: Univ. of Chicago Press, 1947), pp. 147–50, where certain inelegancies of the *Principia* approach to class theory are indicated.

to our thesis, and, accordingly, we shall restrict our discussion to logical systems in which class variables are used.

One procedure for treating class abstracts is that followed by Quine,[4] namely to use expressions of the form '$\hat{x}(A)$' as abbreviations of the correlative descriptions '$(\imath\alpha)(A \equiv_x x\epsilon\alpha)$'. If this procedure is followed our entire preceding analysis becomes directly relevant.

A second but essentially equivalent procedure is to provide a contextual definition, in a manner reminiscent of *Principia Mathematica*, defining all contexts of the form '$f\hat{x}(Gx)$'. In order to eliminate confusions of the sort with which this paper is concerned it is essential to employ scope prefixes in connection with class abstracts. This provision is automatically secured by the first method which explicitly interprets class abstracts as singular descriptions. But if the idiom of abstraction is to be introduced in the second way it should be done with explicit reference made to the scope of the abstraction. Thus:

$$[\hat{x}(Gx)] . F\hat{x}(Gx) =_{df} (\exists\alpha)(Gx \equiv_x x\epsilon\alpha . F\alpha)$$

Of course it is not customary to use scope prefixes in connection with class abstracts. In extensional systems they would be of little use particularly if it were assumed that every correctly formed matrix determines a class. However, in modal logic, their importance is readily seen from a study of the modal paradoxes.

Since we are here concerned to combine modalities with a logic which assumes the existence of classes, it appears natural to stipulate

(s1) $N(\exists\alpha)(\varphi x \equiv_x x\epsilon\alpha)$

(s2) $N[x\epsilon\alpha \equiv_x x\epsilon\beta \supset \alpha = \beta]$

We shall find it convenient for the present purpose informally to assume the theory of types. Also, the symbol for identity is to be so construed as to satisfy Leibniz's law.

It should be noted that if in place of (s1) we had stipulated

(s3) $(\exists\alpha)N[\varphi x \equiv_x x\epsilon\alpha]$

we would then be able to derive paradoxical results. This may be shown as follows:

Assume that '$Fx \equiv_x Gx$' is a contingent truth. By (s3) we have both

$(\exists\alpha)(N[Fx \equiv_x x\epsilon\alpha])$

---

[4] W. Quine, 'New Foundations for Mathematical Logic', *The American Mathematical Monthly*, 44 (1937), 70–80.

and

$$(\exists\beta)(N[Gx \equiv {}_x x\,\epsilon\,\beta])$$

which jointly imply

$$(\exists\alpha)(\exists\beta)[N(Fx \equiv {}_x x\,\epsilon\,\alpha)\,.\,N(Gx \equiv {}_x x\,\epsilon\,\beta)].$$

This statement implies

$$(\exists\alpha)(\exists\beta)[N(Fx \equiv {}_x x\,\epsilon\,\alpha)\,.\,N(Gx \equiv {}_x x\,\epsilon\,\beta) : Fx \equiv {}_x x\,\epsilon\,\alpha : Gx \equiv {}_x x\,\epsilon\,\beta].$$

We may now insert the empirical truth, '$Fx \equiv {}_x Gx$', inside the scope of the quantifiers to obtain

$$(\exists\alpha)(\exists\beta)[N(Fx \equiv {}_x x\,\epsilon\,\alpha)\,.\,N(Gx \equiv {}_x x\,\epsilon\,\beta) : Fx \equiv {}_x x\,\epsilon\,\alpha : Gx \equiv {}_x x\,\epsilon\,\beta :$$
$$Fx \equiv {}_x Gx].$$

Using (s2) we derive

$$(\exists\alpha)(\exists\beta)[N(Fx \equiv {}_x x\,\epsilon\,\alpha)\,.\,N(Gx \equiv {}_x x\,\epsilon\,\beta)\,.\,\alpha = \beta],$$

which is equivalent to

$$(\exists\alpha)(\exists\beta)[N(Fx \equiv {}_x x\,\epsilon\,\alpha : Gx \equiv {}_x x\,\epsilon\,\beta)\,.\,\alpha = \beta].$$

Using Leibniz's law, we have

$$(\exists\alpha)(\exists\beta)[N(Fx \equiv {}_x x\,\epsilon\,\alpha : Gx \equiv {}_x x\,\epsilon\,\alpha)],$$

which in turn implies $N(Fx \equiv {}_x Gx)$, which contradicts the hypothesis that '$Fx \equiv {}_x Gx$' is a contingent truth.

Thus it is that (s3) does give rise to the paradox that no true formal equivalences are contingent. It is for this reason that (s1) was preferred. It is presumed that (s1) gives rise to no such untoward consequences.

The modal paradox (abc) may now equally well be viewed as illustrating the following argument-form:

$$\hat{x}(Ax) = \hat{x}(Bx)$$
$$\underline{\quad N[f\hat{x}(Ax)] \quad}$$
$$\therefore N[f\hat{x}(Bx)]$$

The scope of the abstract is to be understood to be the shortest formula containing the abstract unless it is otherwise indicated.

It will be duly noted that the conclusion cannot be deduced from the premisses. However, if the operator, 'N', is prefixed to the first premiss then the conclusion can correctly be obtained. Again, if in the second premise and conclusion the class abstract is given maximum scope, the conclusion would be valid. This is simply to say again what was said before in reference to descriptions. It is not, essentially, the unrestricted use of modal operators which violates Leibniz's law. It is rather that the modal paradoxes arise out of neglect of the circumstance that in modal contexts the scopes of incomplete symbols, such as abstracts or descriptions, affect the truth value of those contexts.

It is of course possible to design languages in such wise that modal operators would be employed in a different way than that considered here. It is not the intention of this paper to discuss every use or meaning of the idiom 'it is necessary that—' but only to show that one usage, so far as we yet know, does not incur paradoxes nor, in particular, violation of Leibniz's law.

EXTENSIONALITY
Ruth B. Marcus

THE continued development of intensional logics, and concern with problems of their interpretation has had a rather curious effect. It has reinforced the notion, unjustifiable in my opinion, that extensionality is an unambiguous concept. This presumed clarity is usually singled out as the virtue of extensional systems, to say nothing of their metaphysical advantages. The assertion that in mathematics and empirical science one does not *need* to traffic in non-extensional notions which are fuzzy and troublesome, has become a virtual platitude. Yet a cursory examination of the literature does not reveal any well-defined theory of extensionality, although it is possible to find a core of agreement. Indeed, there are differences as to (a) what are the principles of extensionality, (b) which objects are or ought to be extensional, and (c) which formal systems are extensional.

My purpose in this paper is to arrive at a characterization of extensionality in terms of these differences which may be helpful in connection with some familiar problems of interpreting intensional systems.

Principles of extensionality. Consider first some unspecified system of material implication L with theory of types. On the propositional level, extensionality takes the form of a substitution principle:

(1) If p is equivalent$_1$ to q then A is equivalent$_2$ to B,

   where B is the result of replacing one or more occurrences of p in A by q.

As stated, (1) is of course ambiguous. The ambiguity concerns the meaning of 'equivalence$_1$' and 'equivalence$_2$'. A minimal requirement of an equivalence relation is that it be reflexive, transitive and symmetrical. These conditions are met by a variety of relations ranging from identity to having the same weight, and further interpretation is required. Our concern is with logically definable relations of equivalence.

Using the abbreviations 'eq$_1$' and 'eq$_2$', let us first consider principles

From *Mind*, n.s., 69 (1960), 55–62. Reprinted by permission of the author and the Editor of *Mind*.

in which eq_1 and eq_2 have the same meaning. If they are taken as identity, (1) becomes

(1.1) If pIq then AIB (where 'I' names the identity relation)

and is merely explicative of the notion of identity. Suppose what is intended is

(1.2) If '$p \equiv q$' is a tautology then '$A \equiv B$' is a tautology.

In what sense is (1.2) an extensionality principle? Only in that it eliminates as possible predicates of propositions, certain intensional predicates such as 'believed by John'. Not all intensional predicates are precluded by (1.2). In particular, modal predicates such as 'logically necessary' would not falsify (1.2). Ordinarily, variables which range over predicates of propositions are dispensable, and consequently (1.1) is often provable as a strong form of the substitution theorem.

Most commonly, eq_1 and eq_2 are interpreted as material equivalence without the modifying condition of (1.2):

(1.3) If $p \equiv q$ then $A \equiv B$.

Here (1) is taken to mean that if p and q have the same truth value, whether contingently or necessarily, then A and B have the same truth value. As contrasted with (1.2), (1.3) is a strongly extensional principle for it disallows all intensional predicates of propositions. Here again, where variables which range over propositional predicates are not introduced, (1.3) is provable as the substitution theorem.

Consider, again on the level of propositions, principles in which eq_1 and eq_2 are not the same. If eq_1 is taken as identity and eq_2 material equivalence, then (1) becomes

(1.4) If pIq then $A \equiv B$.

(1.4) like (1.1) is explicative of the identity relation. [The converse of (1.4) is of course another matter involving as it does the assumption of Leibniz's law, in addition to being strongly extensional.]

If we take eq_1 as material equivalence and eq_2 as identity, we have

(1.5) If $p \equiv q$ then AIB

which in the first instance, where A is p, becomes

(1.51) If $p \equiv q$ then pIq.

In contrast to (1.4), (1.5) is very strongly extensional since it not only eliminates intensional predicates of propositions but assimilates propositions to truth values.

What I am trying to make apparent by this necessarily crude and informal analysis, is that even on the level of propositions, we cannot talk of *the* thesis of extensionality but only of stronger and weaker extensionality principles. I will call a principle *extensional* if it either (a) *directly or indirectly imposes restrictions on the possible values of the functional variables such that some intensional functions are prohibited or* (b) *it has the consequence of equating identity with a weaker form of equivalence.* Obviously (a) and (b) are interdependent. On the basis of this characterization, (1.2), (1.3), and (1.5) are all principles of extensionality, in order of increasing strength. It should now be clear why there is often disagreement as to whether a given formal system is or is not extensional. There is, for example, a literature of tiresome arguments as to whether the formal system of *Principia* is extensional. It is all a matter of deciding how extensional a system must be to be properly so-called. There are by contrast, logicians such as Alonzo Church who does talk in terms of degrees of extensionality. A more reasonable approach would be to assert, in connection with *Principia*, that the formal system as interpreted in the first edition is less extensional than the interpretation proposed by the second edition, since the latter assumes an analogue of (1.5) which is stronger than (1.2).

Consider next another set of principles which are more frequently associated with the theory of extensionality. Principles which relate the equivalence of classes (or attributes) to the equivalence of their defining functions.

(2) If $(x)(F(x) \text{ eq}_1 G(x))$ then $F \text{ eq}_2 G$.

In addition to the interpretation of eq_1 and eq_2, one must specify whether F and G are predicate variables, class variables, or non-committal functional variables. I cannot give an exhaustive account of the many possible variations of (2). In a weakly extensional system, eq_1 might be taken as tautological equivalence, eq_2 as identity, F and G functional variables, as follows:

(2.1) If $(x)(F(x) \equiv G(x))$ is tautological, then FIG.

By the criterion of extensionality stated above, (2.1) is weakly extensional since it precludes some intensional contexts. On the other hand (2.1) permits us to state an identity between the terms '9' and '3^2' but not '9' and (on the assumption that it can be construed as an expression of proper type level) 'the number of planets'. A stronger alternative (referred to most often as *the* extensionality principle) asserts identity of functions as a consequence of formal equivalence.

(2.2) If $(x)(F(x) \equiv G(x))$ then *FIG*.

In languages which distinguish classes from attributes, the distinction is sometimes maintained by postulating (2.2) for classes and perhaps (2.1) for attributes. This has the effect of eliminating intensional contexts involving class names but allowing such contexts for attribute names. Such is the interpreted procedure of *Principia*. The concept of identity in *Principia* is systematically ambiguous not only as prescribed by the theory of types, but on the same type level. In the second order predicate calculus, 'identity' means something different for classes than for attributes, and has still another import for individuals. My preference is for the alternative procedure of giving uniform meaning to 'identity' and to talk of attributes and classes as being equal, but not identical. Functional *equality* would be defined as

(3) $(F = G) \rightarrow_{df} (x)(F(x) \equiv G(x))$

where $F = G$ is *not* equated to *FIG*. On the basis of known substitution theorems, the substitution of F for G in strongly extensional contexts is still permissible and in such contexts $F = G$ is *like FIG*. This permits us to say that the class of mermaids and the class of Greek gods are equal but not identical and that in strongly extensional contexts (arithmetic ones for example) we are concerned only with their equality, so that the name of one may be substituted for the other.

It seems to me that much of the discussion these past few years concerning apparent breakdowns of substitutivity principles in intensional contexts and its presumably devastating results for logic and mathematics are largely terminological. I am not (as Quine[1] insists in his review of two of my papers on quantified modal logic) proposing that there be more than one kind of identity, but only that the distinctions between stronger and weaker equivalences be made explicit before, for one avowed purpose or another, they are obliterated.

The usual reason given for reducing identity to equality [(3) (2.2)] is that it provides a simpler base for mathematics, mathematics being concerned with aggregates discussed in truth functional contexts, not with predicates in intensional contexts. Under such restrictive conditions, the substitution theorem can generally be proved for equal (formally equivalent) classes, with the result that equality functions *as* identity.

Establishing the foundations of mathematics is not the only purpose of logic, particularly if the assumptions deemed convenient for mathematics do violence to both ordinary and philosophical usage. I am not

---

[1] W. V. O. Quine, *Journal of Symbolic Logic*, 12 (1947), 95–6.

disturbed by the possibility of equal, non-identical classes or attributes, *e.g.* man and featherless biped. To me it seems reasonable that there are many empty classes of the same type, *e.g.* mermaids and Greek gods, equal but not identical. And why should the non-identity of the numbers n and $n+1$ depend on the enumeration of different things in the world? To subsume mathematics under logic is not to equate them. A much broader base is indicated in the direction of intensional systems such as the modal logics. I will try to show that the apparent difficulties of interpreting such systems are not genuine, but analogous to a rejection of a non-Euclidean geometry because it allows parallel lines to meet.

To complete this analysis, I must consider another set of modifications of identity involving Leibniz's law.

The identity of indiscernibles. Sometimes identity is introduced as

(4) If $(\phi)(\phi(x) \text{ eq } \phi(y))$ then xIy.

The usual interpretation of eq is as material equivalence:

(4.1) If $(\phi)(\phi(x) \equiv \phi(y))$ then xIy.

Another possibility is in terms of tautological equivalence.

(4.2) If $(\phi)(\phi(x) \equiv \phi(x))$ is a tautology, then xIy.

The converse of (4) is of course explicative of identity. The status of (4) itself is not quite so clear. It has also been accepted as a truism and merely explicative. However, I do not regard Ramsey's[2] reservations about (4) as entirely spurious. He objected to taking (4.1) as definitive of identity on the ground that it is logically possible for two things to have all their properties in common and still be two. Such a possibility is excluded by (4.1). To argue that if they are two then they are distinguishable as having two different names will not do for Ramsey, since they may be unknown, unnamed, and still two.

According to our characterization of extensionality, instances of (4) may therefore be interpreted as extensionality principles in that they equate identity with the slightly weaker relation of indiscernibility which requires that to be distinct means to be *discernibly* distinct.[3]

---

[2] F. P. Ramsey, *The Foundations of Mathematics* (London: Routledge & Kegan Paul; and New York: Harcourt Brace, 1931), pp. 30–2.

[3] I am aware that interpreting (4) in this way is somewhat paradoxical since (4) has the effect of establishing a logical priority of the concept of 'property' over that of 'class' whereas in an extensional system the emphasis is held to be on the class concept. If such usage is intolerable the characterization of extensionality can be appropriately modified.

Interpreting intensional systems. Quine[4] states: 'When modal logic is extended (as by Miss Barcan) to include quantification theory, . . . serious obstacles to interpretation are encountered.' These difficulties revolve about the substitution of equivalences in contexts involving 'knows that', 'is aware that', and in particular 'is necessary that', and 'is possible that'. Quine describes such contexts as being referentially opaque. It is the point of this paper to show that the opacity lies with Quine's use of such terms as 'identity', 'true identity', 'equality'. The above analysis leads to the dissolution of at least some of the problems of interpretation associated with intensional contexts.

Among the equivalence relations which can be introduced into L are identity, indiscernibility, tautological equivalence, material equivalence. On the functional level, these are listed in order of decreasing strength, for there is some model, some permissible range of values, which prevents our equating them except by explicit postulate. It should be noted that for variables of lowest type, there are only identity and indiscernibility. Indeed a recent paper of Bergmann[5] on *Individuals* may be understood as an attempt to explicate the notion of individuals as those entities for which only the strongest equivalence relation holds.

Consider now modal functional calculi such as my[6] extension of the Lewis systems. In such languages (2.1) can be stated directly as

(5) If $N((x)(F(x) \equiv G(x)))$ then FIG (where N is interpreted as logical necessity)

(4.2) becomes

(6) If $N((\phi)(\phi(x) \equiv \phi(y)))$ then xIy

and (1.1) is

(7) If $N(P \equiv Q)$ then PIQ.

[4] W. Quine, 'The Problem of Interpreting Modal Logic', *Journal of Symbolic Logic*, 12 (1947), 43–8.

[5] G. Bergmann, 'Individuals', *Philosophical Studies*, IX (1958), 78–85. (My interpretation of this paper rests on the assumption that the statement of (Ext) involves a typographical error.)

[6] R. C. Barcan (Marcus): 'A Functional Calculus of First Order Based on Strict Implication', *Journal of Symbolic Logic*, 11 (1946), 1–16; 'The Deduction Theorem in a Functional Calculus of First Order Based on Strict Implication', ibid. 115–18; 'The Identity of Individuals in a Strict Functional Calculus of Second Order', ibid. 12, 12–15.

Within these extended systems, I have been able to prove theorems which relate different kinds of equivalence. It is possible to show

> (8) Given $P \equiv Q$, P is not everywhere interchangeable with Q, but only in restricted non-modal contexts. Given $N(P \equiv Q)$, then the substitution theorem is unrestricted.

This theorem has the effect of prohibiting the substitution of 'Socrates is a featherless biped' for 'Socrates is a man' in 'It is necessary that if Socrates is a man then Socrates is a man'. That the substitution theorem for strict equivalence differs from the theorem for material equivalence, is not paradoxical, but a more adequate formalization of a known distinction.

It is when Quine[7] refers to

> (9) The number of planets equals nine

as a 'true identity', without hint of ambiguity that we become aware that his fundamental criticism is directed not toward presumed paradoxes but toward the intensional point of view. As indicated above (9) is *not* unambiguous except in a strongly extensional language.

Let us assume for the moment that '9' and 'the number of planets' are expressions of the same type level and can meaningfully be equated. Quite apart from interpretation in terms of the theory of descriptions, within the modal language the problem revolves about substituting 'the number of planets' for '9' in

> (10) $N(9 > 7)$.

But such a substitution is prohibited by (8), for (9) does not assert tautological equivalence, and the substitution would have to be made within the scope of a modal operator. The paradox evaporates. By the same token, since

> (11) $N(9 = (5+4))$, '5+4' can replace '9' in (10).

The problem of the Morning Star and the Evening Star is resolved in an analogous way.[8] For, like (9),

[7] W. Quine, *From a Logical Point of View* (Cambridge, Mass.: Harvard Univ. Press, 1953), p. 144. [See above, p. 21].

[8] The paragraph which follows restates a point made by F. B. Fitch in 'The Problem of the Morning Star and the Evening Star', *Philosophy of Science*, xvi (1949), 137–40.

(12) The Evening Star equals the Morning Star

is not unambiguous. If (12) involves proper names of individuals then 'the Evening Star' may replace 'the Morning Star' without paradox in

(13) It is necessary that the Evening Star is the Evening Star

for the only equivalence relation between individuals are identity and indiscernibility. Indeed, although it appears as if (4.1) and (4.2) express two kinds of indiscernibility, they can be *proved* strictly equivalent within a modal system. Quine's[9] failure to note the latter in his review of my paper had the unfortunate result of perpetuating a non-existent paradox.

If, on the other hand, (12) is about classes or properties, then it states a non-tautological equality, not an identity, and consequently, the conditions of the substitution theorem (8) prevent the substitution of 'the Morning Star' for one of the occurrences of 'the Evening Star' in (13). At the risk of too much repetition, we are not asserting that the substitution *ought* not to be made on the basis of some pre-formal analysis, but that they are prohibited by the theorems provable[10] in such extended systems.

I have tried in this brief paper, to characterize the theory of extensionality, and to show that logical systems are more or less extensional. Their extensionality depends on the kinds of contexts and predicates which are prohibited, and the degree to which the relation of identity is equated to weaker forms of equivalence. I also tried to show that a more broadly based logic in the direction of modalities need not do violence to the foundations of mathematics, and the supposed paradoxes involved in interpreting such intensional systems are not genuine.

---

[9] See n. 4 above. Quine's failure to notice that (4.1) and (4.2) are materially equivalent in s2^2 and strictly equivalent in s4^2 and s5^2 leads him to conclude that modal logic must deal with individual concepts rather than individuals. In a recent letter Quine forwarded copies of a note to the editor of *The Journal of Symbolic Logic*, and his publisher correcting the error.

[10] The substitution principle (8) is a rough restatement of substitution theorems for some of the extended modal calculi. The theorems are proved at the end of the first paper listed in n. 6 p. 49 above.

IV

QUANTIFICATION INTO CAUSAL CONTEXTS[1]

DAGFINN FØLLESDAL

IN this paper I will discuss some problems connected with contrary-to-fact conditionals, scientific laws, confirmation, and some types of probability statements and disposition terms. These problems are analogous to those that Professor Quine, in several articles and books,[2] has pointed out for the logical modalities.

In *From a Logical Point of View*, after having shown that quantification into contexts of logical modality encounters serious difficulties, Quine continues:

What has been said of modality in these pages relates only to strict modality. For other sorts, for example, physical necessity and possibility, the first problem would be to formulate the notions clearly and exactly. Afterward we could investigate whether such modalities, like the strict ones, cannot be quantified into without precipitating an ontological crisis. The question concerns intimately the practical use of language. It concerns, for example, the use of the contrary-to-fact conditional within a quantification; for it is reasonable to suppose that the contrary-to-fact conditional reduces to the form 'Necessarily, if *p* then *q*' in some sense of necessity. Upon the contrary-to-fact conditional depends in turn, for example, this definition of solubility in water: To say that an object is soluble in water is to say that it would dissolve if it were in water. In discussions of physics, naturally, we need quantifications containing the clause '*x* is soluble in water', or the equivalent in words; but, according to the definition suggested, we should then have to admit within quantifications the expression 'if *x* were in water then *x* would dissolve', that is, 'necessarily if *x* is in

From *Boston Studies in the Philosophy of Science*, Vol. II, ed. Cohen and Wartofsky (New York: Humanities Press, 1965), pp. 263–74. Reprinted by permission of the publishers.

[1] I am grateful to W. Quine for helpful remarks.
[2] W. Quine: 'Notes on Existence and Necessity', *Journal of Philosophy* XL (1943), 113–27. Reprinted in Leonard Linsky (ed.), *Semantics and the Philosophy of Language* (Urbana: Univ. of Ill. Press, 1952); 'The Problem of Interpreting Modal Logic', *Journal of Symbolic Logic*, 12 (1947), 43–8; *From a Logical Point of View* (Cambridge, Mass., 1953, 1961); 'Three Grades of Modal Involvement', *Proceedings of XIth International Congress of Philosophy* (Brussels, 1953), Vol. 14, pp. 65–81; 'Quantifiers and Propositional Attitudes', *Journal of Philosophy*, LIII (1956), 177–87; *Word and Object* (Cambridge, Mass.: M.I.T. Press; and New York and London: Wiley and Sons, 1960).

water then x dissolves'. Yet we do not know whether there is a suitable sense of 'necessarily' into which we can so quantify.[3]

Obviously, much is at stake here; the usefulness of the notions of physical necessity, contrary-to-fact conditionals, etc., depends largely on whether one can quantify into them, as illustrated e.g. in Quine's example that I just quoted, concerning solubility in water. If one cannot find a quantifying into these contexts, then these notions, together with a wealth of related notions, will probably have to be abandoned, to the extent that they cannot be made clear without appeal to physical necessity, e.g. in the case of dispositions by conceiving them as enduring structural traits of objects.[4]

However, it seems to me that arguments analogous to those of Quine against quantification into logical modalities apply to the contexts of physical necessity and related contexts as well. The first part of my paper will be an attempt to show this. To make the parallelism between these arguments and those of Quine apparent, Quine's wording will be used wherever possible.

Adapting an example from Chisholm's 'The contrary-to-fact conditional,'[5] let us suppose that there is a well which is such that anyone who drinks from it gets poisoned. Let us further suppose that just one man has drunk from that well (and of course got poisoned). Then, presumably, the following is true:

(1) it is causally necessary that the man who drank from that well got poisoned.

Let us now further suppose that this man was born in place p at time t, i.e. that the following is true:

(2) the man who drank from that well = the man who was born in p at t.

Now in spite of (1) and (2), presumably

(3) it is causally necessary that the man who was born in p at t got poisoned.

is false.

[3] Quine, *From a Logical Point of View*, pp. 158–9. [See above, p. 33].
[4] Cf. Quine, *Word and Object*, p. 46.
[5] Roderick M. Chisholm, 'The Contrary-to-fact Conditional', *Mind*, 55 (1946), 289–307. Reprinted in Feigl, and Sellars (eds.), *Readings in Philosophical Analysis* (New York: Appleton Century Crofts, 1949).

To see how causal contexts fare with respect to quantification, let us now try to apply existential generalization to (1). We get:

(4) $(\exists x)$ it is causally necessary that x got poisoned.

However, what is this object that got poisoned? The man who drank from the well, that is, the man who was born in p at t? But to suppose this would conflict with the fact that (3) is false.

This then is a straight causal parallel to one of Quine's arguments against quantification into contexts of logical necessity.[6]

Our problem relates to Nelson Goodman's problem in 'A query on confirmation'[7] that the degree of confirmation may vary widely with the way the given evidence is described.

The trouble in our example clearly springs from the fact that the objects over which we quantify can be uniquely described in ways that are not causally equivalent. Hoping to make sense of quantification into causal contexts, one might therefore try to weed out from one's universe of discourse all such 'stubborn' objects that can be uniquely specified in ways that fail of causal equivalence. That is, one may require that whenever each of two open sentences 'Fx' and 'Gx' uniquely determines one and the same object x, the sentences are causally equivalent. In symbols

(5) If $(w)(Fw \equiv . w = x)$
    and $(w)(Gw \equiv . w = x)$
    then (it is causally necessary that $(w)(Fw \equiv Gw)$)

But this postulate annihilates causal distinctions, for as pointed out by Quine in an exactly parallel argument concerning the logical modalities,[8] let 'p' stand for any true sentence, let y be any object in our purified universe of discourse, and let $x = y$. Then

(6) $(w)(p . w = y . \equiv . w = x)$

(7) $(w)(w = y . \equiv . w = x)$

By (5), next, with its 'Fw' taken as '$p . w = y$' and its 'Gw' as '$w = y$', we can conclude from (6) and (7) that

(8) it is causally necessary that $(w)(p . w = y . \equiv . w = y)$

---

[6] One might try to avoid this dilemma by arguing that (3) is perhaps true after all, if we understand it properly. However, this can easily be shown to lead to a collapse of causal distinctions. In fact, the weeding out of 'stubborn' objects, which will be discussed shortly, amounts to this.

[7] Nelson Goodman, 'A Query on Confirmation', *Journal of Philosophy*, XLIII (1946), 383–5.

[8] Quine, *Word and Object*, pp. 197–8.

But the quantification in (8) implies in particular '$p . y = y . \equiv . y = y$' which in turn implies 'p', so from (8) we conclude

it is causally necessary that p.

So, causal distinctions collapse.

But, one may object, at least one system of quantified causal logic has been proposed and appears to work, viz. that of Arthur W. Burks.[9]

This system consists of a standard system of truth-functional logic and quantification theory, supplemented with the following axioms and rule for the causal and modal notions:[10]

A.1 $\Box A \supset \boxed{C}A$
A.2 $\boxed{C}A \supset A$
A.3 $\Box(A \supset B) \supset . \Box A \supset \Box B$
A.4 $\boxed{C}(A \supset B) \supset . \boxed{C}A \supset \boxed{C}B$
A.5 $(x)\Box A \supset \Box(x)A$
A.6 $(x)\boxed{C}A \supset \boxed{C}(x)A$
RL   If $\vdash A$ then $\vdash \Box A$

And surely, there is no collapse of causal distinctions in Burks's system. However, the Quinean argument that I just presented was a semantic argument, relating to the *interpretation* of quantified causal logic. And important semantic points may easily remain hidden without being reflected in the syntax.

In order to bring the difficulties of causal logic into the open let us, therefore, supplement Burks's system with a standard system of identity and descriptions. This is not done by Burks, and for good reasons, for see what happens: We now become able to carry through the following disastrous argument (I will use Quine's system of natural deduction, but of course any system of quantification theory will do):

(1′) $x = x$		axiom of identity
(2′) $\Box(x = x)$		(1′) RL
(3′) $(\boxed{C}x = x)$		(2′) by A.1
*(4′) $(\imath y)(y = x . p) = x$		
*(5′) $(y)(y = x . p . \equiv . y = x)$		(4′) by contextual definition of definite description
*(6′) $x = x . p . \equiv . x = x$		(5′)

---

[9] Arthur W. Burks, 'The logic of causal propositions', *Mind*, 60 (1951), 363–82.
[10] Here, '$\Box$' stands for 'it is logically necessary that'. For convenience, Burks lets his '$\boxed{C}$' stand for 'it is causally or logically necessary that'. 'It is causally necessary that' is thus perhaps best paraphrased by '$\boxed{C}p . - \Box p$' (Burks, op. cit., pp. 374–5, 380).

*(7′) p	(6′) by axiom of identity
(8′) $(\imath y)(y = x \cdot p) = x \; . \supset p$	*(7′)
(9′) $\square((\imath y)(y = x \cdot p) = x \; . \supset p)$	(8′) RL
(10′) $\boxed{C}((\imath y)(y = x \cdot p) = x \; . \supset p)$	(9′) by A.1
*(11′) p	
*(12′) $y = x \cdot p \; . \equiv . \; y = x$	(11′)
*(13′) $(y)(y = x \cdot p \; . \equiv . \; y = x)$	(12′) y
*(14′) $(\imath y)(y = x \cdot p) = x$	(13′) by def. of description
*(15′) $\boxed{C}((\imath y)(y = x \cdot p) = x)$	(3′) (14′) by substitutivity of identity
*(16′) $\boxed{C}((\imath y)(y = x \cdot p) = x \; . \supset p)$	
$\supset . \; \boxed{C}((\imath y)(y = x \cdot p) = x) \supset \boxed{C}p$	A.4
*(17′) $\boxed{C}p$	(10′) (15′) (16′)
(18′) $p \supset \boxed{C}p$	*(17′)

That is, modal distinctions collapse. What now are we to do? One thing would be to confine ourselves to quantification theory when we do causal logic and be silent about the rest. But, if the foundations of causal logic are so muddled as they now seem to be, this is not a position to rest content with.

It we look at our proof (1′)–(18′), however, another way out might seem a natural one to take:

Line (15′) was got from lines (3′) and (14′) by the principle of substitutivity of identity. By this principle one can prove, as we did in this proof, that all identities are causally or logically necessary, and this certainly does not seem to be the case, witness our example of the man who drank from the well. He was supposedly identical with the man who was born in p at t, yet this identity was apparently neither causally nor logically necessary. Why not, therefore, forbid substitutivity of identity in causal context in order to prevent inferences like the one leading to (15′) and thereby to the fatal (18′)? This is the way taken by many working on the logical and epistemic modalities, and it has probably been most ably argued for by Jaakko Hintikka.[11]

However, again it seems to me that the problems are being covered up rather than solved.

For one thing, tampering with the substitutivity of identity may easily make the notion of identity unintelligible. Thus, e.g., Neil Wilson: 'If identity does not mean universal interchangeability, then I do not really understand identity at all.'[12]

[11] E.g., in 'Modality as referential multiplicity', *Ajatus*, 20 (1957), 49–64; *Knowledge and Belief* (Ithaca, N.Y., 1962); and 'The modes of modality', *Acta Philosophica Fennica*, 16 (1963), 65–81.

[12] Neil L. Wilson *The Concept of Language* (Toronto, 1959), p. 39.

However, it seems to me that also the interpretation of quantifiers requires unrestricted substitutivity of identity; that is, *quantification and substitutivity of identity go hand in hand.*

To see this, let us try to get some insight into what actually happens when we quantify into causal contexts:

To start with statement logic, it can be given a helpful algebraic representation by adapting Leibniz's idea of possible worlds. '$\Box p$' will simply be said to be true if 'p' is true in every 'physically possible world'. This talk about worlds is of course a purely algebraic device. The notion of a 'physically possible world' is just as much in need of clarification as the notions of physical possibility and necessity themselves. However, this device is helpful for one's intuitions and has been used frequently by modal logicians from Leibniz on. Leibniz's idea is inadequate for the representation of iterated modalities; however, in 1957 Hintikka got the idea of representing modalities algebraically by considering, instead of a set of worlds that are possible outright, a set of worlds that are, or are not, *possible with respect to* another.[13]

Iterated operators are needed in causal logic, e.g. to express that one dispositional property causes the appearance of another, or that if a certain causal law were false such-and-such would be the case, or that it is a causal law that a given kind of habit or resolution arises under certain circumstances (Burks's examples).[14] However, the problems of quantifying into causal contexts are basically the same whether these contexts are governed by several or just one causal operator. Let us therefore stick to Leibniz's worlds that are possible outright, and let us now leave statement logic and go on to examine quantified causal logic.

Consider the following simple example:

$(\exists x)\Box Fx$

Using the Leibnizean representation, this should mean that there is an object, let us call it 'a', such that not only is 'F' true of it in our actual

[13] Jaakko Hintikka, 'Quantifiers in deontic logic', *Societas Scientiarum Fennica, Commentationes Humanarum Literarum*, 23, (1957), No. 4, esp. p. 13; 'Modality as referential multiplicity', *Ajatus*, 20 (1957) esp. 61–2. The idea was anticipated in work by Jónsson and Tarski on Boolean algebra in 1951: B. Jónsson and A. Tarski, 'Boolean algebras with operators', *American Journal of Mathematics*, 73 (1951), 891–939; 74 (1952), 127–62; and was used by Stig Kanger in modal logic in 1957: Stig Kanger, *Provability in Logic*, Stockholm Studies in Philosophy I (Stockholm, 1957). Later, Saul Kripke got the idea independently, cf. his 'Semantical analysis of modal logic I: Normal modal propositional calculi', *Zeitschrift für mathematische Logik und Grundlagen der Mathematik*, 9 (1963), 69, n. 2.

[14] Arthur W. Burks, op. cit., p. 380.

world, but 'F' is true of it in every physically possible world, that is, if we use a diagram and let horizontal lines represent possible worlds:

(9) Fa
     — — — — — — —
                 .
             : Fa
     — — — — — — —
                 :
Actual   : Fa
world   — — — — — — —

What now about an identity like

(10) $x = y$

Can (10) be true in our actual world and yet false in some physically possible world? That is, can we have a situation like this:

           a' a''
     — — — — — — —
             .   .
               .   .
                 .
                 ..
Actual   .
world   — — — — — —
                 a

where to one and the same object a in our actual world there correspond two objects a' and a'' in some physically possible world: If so, what would it mean, when seeking to interpret e.g.

   $(x)\Box Fx$

one picks the object a and says that 'F' is true of *it* in every physically possible world? Apparently, this makes no sense; the pronouns of quantification, in this case 'it', make sense only when there is one and only one object that we are talking about. So, if we want to make sense of quantification into causal contexts, we apparently have to require that *no identity statement which is true in our actual world is false in any physically possible world.*

What this amounts to, is that in order to make sense of quantification, identity should be *universally substitutive*. Tampering with the substitutivity of identity prevents the derivation of undesirable results, but only at the cost of making both identity and quantification unintelligible.

We have now explored two attempts to get out of the difficulties, restrictions on our universe of discourse, which led to a collapse of modal distinctions, and restrictions on the substitutivity of identity, which led to unintelligibility. Are we then left with a choice between unintelligibility and a collapse of modal distinctions, either one of which would make quantification into causal contexts pointless?

There are surely many other steps in the derivation (1′)–(18′) which we might attempt to forbid in our efforts to prevent this fatal proof from going through.

However, not any *ad hoc* restriction will do, as we just saw in the case of identity. There are, however, restrictions which prevent derivation of undesirable results and yet avoid the difficulties we just had in making sense of the pronouns of quantification. I will now describe one of these, which appears fairly natural.

Clearly, as we saw in our Quinean argument, the root of our trouble is that objects of our universe can be described uniquely in ways that are not causally equivalent. This, however, is not a peculiarity of the objects; as we just saw, no choice of universe will prevent this. Whether we restrict our universe or not is irrelevant, nothing was presupposed about the universe of discourse in the derivation (1′)–(18′) (except that it be nonempty). Rather than looking for a solution by doing something to our objects, let us therefore direct our attention to the expressions we use to refer to these objects:

To make sense of quantification, the variables have to *keep their references as we pass from the actual world to another which is physically possible*. Now, in order to avoid trouble, all we have to require, is that *all* referring expressions do the same. But definite descriptions obviously do not do this, for if we consider our diagram (9) again, we see easily that a general term, e.g. 'man who drank from the well', which is true of a unique object in our actual world, may be true of another object in another physically possible world, of several objects in a third such world, of none at all in a fourth, and so on.

That is, definite descriptions that have a reference in our actual world may fail to have in other worlds, and even if they have one in some other world(s), their references may differ from one world to the next. Definite descriptions do therefore not in general satisfy the requirement we just found it necessary to put on our referring expressions in causal logic.

In order to avoid trouble, we should admit into our stock of singular terms *only those descriptions which keep the same descriptum in all physically possible worlds*. That is, we can admit a description '$(?x)Fx$' as a singular term if and only if the following condition is satisfied:

$$(\exists y)\Box(x)(Fx \equiv . \, x = y)$$

(Note the order of the existential quantifier and the causal operator.)

All singular terms must satisfy a condition to this effect. That is, every admissible singular term must name one and the same object in every physically possible world.

For quantification into iterated modalities, parallel reasoning leads to similar, but slightly stronger conditions.

If, with Quine, we insist on the 'primacy of predicates', an even simpler way out is possible. We simply eliminate *all* definite singular terms in favour of general terms and variables.[15]

Looking back to our fatal derivation, (1′)–(18′), we now see how our strictures on singular terms make the derivation break down. The substitution of '$(?y)(y = x \, . \, p)$' for 'x', which gave us (15′) from (3′) and (14′), is no longer legitimate, since line (14′) is not a genuine identity statement. A genuine identity sign can be flanked only by genuine singular terms, and hence not by '$(?y)(y = x \, . \, p)$'. In (14′) and the other lines in our proof where '$=$' is flanked by '$(?y)(y = x \, . \, p)$', the '$=$' indicates merely that the two expressions which flank it relate to the same object in our actual world. This relation of "co-extensiveness" will of course not be universally substitutive in non-extensional contexts, like causal contexts. To avoid ambiguity, we should perhaps not use '$=$' but a different symbol for this relation.

That undesirable results disappear from modal logic when descriptions are not treated as names, but contextually defined, was first observed by Church more than twenty years ago.[16] However, modal logicians have frequently preferred other measures to avoid difficulties, especially restrictions on the substitutivity of identity. The semantic considerations which we have just been through, indicate, however, that restrictions on singular terms, and not restrictions on the substitutivity of identity, are what we need in order to make sense of quantification into causal contexts.

[15] Cf. e.g. Quine, *Methods of Logic* (New York, 1950, 1959), pp. 218–19. By insisting on the 'primacy of predicates' and the eliminability of *all* singular terms in favour of general terms and variables, Quine thus can be said to have levelled the road for modal logic.

[16] Alonzo Church, Review of Quine, 'Whitehead and the Rise of Modern Logic', *Journal of Symbolic Logic*, 7 (1942), 100–1.

At last, a few words about the intelligibility of causal contexts and of the logical modalities.

The arguments which I have given concerning causal contexts can of course be paralleled for the logical modalities. It seems therefore that one can give no formal argument against quantification into either type of context. However, we found that substitutivity of identity and quantification go hand in hand, and this has certain philosophical consequences which many champions of quantified modal logic and quantification into causal contexts may find hard to digest.

To take the logical modalities first: In quantified modal logic one will affirm statements of the form

$\Box Fa$

Yet Carnap, Lewis, and others who are opposed to so-called Aristotelian essentialism, will deny that this commits them to the view that 'F' is essential to a. '$\Box F$' is true of the object a, yes, but only of the object *qua a*. Which properties are necessary of an object will depend on how we refer to it. If $a = b$, '$\Box F$' may be true of this object *qua a*, but false of this object *qua b*. These philosophers will reject as unintelligible the view attributed to Aristotle, that certain properties, the essential ones, are in a way inherent in the object itself, necessary of it regardless of the way we refer to it.

Now we have seen, however, that if one wants to quantify into modal contexts, identity must be universally substitutive in these contexts. But that means that if '$\Box F$' is true of an object, '$\Box F$' is true of it *regardless of the way in which this object is referred to*. That is, quantification into modal contexts commits us to essentialism.

Carnap and Lewis, who on the one side quantify into modal contexts and on the other denounce essentialism, therefore appear to be in a rather awkward position.

What now about causal contexts? Depending on exactly what one means by essentialism and what position one takes to it,[17] quantification into causal contexts leads to a similar quandary. If one rejects as incomprehensible the view that causally necessary properties are inherent in

---

[17] This qualification is important. It seems that 'causal essentialism' is better off than 'logical essentialism', since many arguments directed against the notion of logical necessity (and thereby also against logical essentialism) e.g. in Quine's 'Two Dogmas of Empiricism' (*From a Logical Point of View*, pp. 20–46), have no counterparts for the notion of causal necessity. In fact, treating dispositions as inhering structural traits of objects (cf. note 3 above) is a form of causal essentialism; dispositional properties remain properties of the object regardless of the way the object is referred to.

objects, that is that '$\boxed{C}F$', if true of an object, is true of it regardless of the way in which it is referred to, then one should better not quantify into causal contexts; one should avoid contrary-to-fact conditionals, scientific law-statements, confirmation statements, and many types of probability statements and disposition terms—if one wants to make sense.

V

SEMANTICAL CONSIDERATIONS ON MODAL LOGIC

Saul A. Kripke

THIS paper gives an exposition of some features of a semantical theory of modal logics.[1] For a certain quantified extension of S5, this theory was presented in 'A Completeness Theorem in Modal Logic',[2] and it has been summarized in 'Semantical Analysis of Modal Logic'.[3] The present paper will concentrate on one aspect of the theory—the introduction of quantifiers—and it will restrict itself in the main to one method of achieving this end. The emphasis of the paper will be purely semantical, and hence it will omit the use of semantic tableaux, which is essential to a full presentation of the theory.[4] Proofs, also, will largely be suppressed.

We consider four modal systems. Formulae A, B, C, . . . are built out of atomic formulae P, Q, R, . . ., using the connectives $\wedge$, $\sim$, and $\Box$. The system M has the following axiom schemes and rules:

A0. Truth-functional tautologies
A1. $\Box A \supset A$
A2. $\Box(A \supset B) \supset . \Box A \supset \Box B$
R1. $A, A \supset B/B$
R2. $A/\Box A$

If we add the following axiom scheme, we get S4:

$$\Box A \supset \Box\Box A$$

From *Acta Philosophica Fennica*, 16 (1963), 83–94. Reprinted by permission of the author and the publishers, Societas Philosophica Fennica, Helsinki.

[1] The theory given here has points of contact with many authors: For lists of these, see S. Kripke, 'Semantical Analysis of Modal Logic', *Zeitschrift für Mathematische Logik und Grundlagen der Mathematik*, 9 (1963), 67–96, and J. Hintikka, 'Modality and Quantification' *Theoria*, 27 (1961) 119–28. The authors closest to the present theory appear to be Hintikka and Kanger. The present treatment of quantification, however, is unique as far as I know, although it derives some inspiration from acquaintance with the very different methods of Prior and Hintikka.

[2] *Journal of Symbolic Logic*, 24 (1959), 1–15.

[3] Ibid., pp. 323–4 (Abstract).

[4] For these see 'A Completeness Theorem in Modal Logic', *Journal of Symbolic Logic*, 24 (1959), 1–15 and 'Semantical Analysis of Modal Logic', *Zeitschrift für Mathematische Logik und Grundlagen der Mathematik*, 9, 67–96.

We get the *Brouwersche* system if we add to M:

$A \supset \Box\Diamond A$

S5, if we add:

$\Diamond A \supset \Box\Diamond A$

Modal systems whose theorems are closed under the rules R1 and R2, and include all theorems of M, are called 'normal'. Although we have developed a theory which applies to such non-normal systems as Lewis's S2 and S3, we will restrict ourselves here to normal systems.

To get a semantics for modal logic, we introduce the notion of a (normal) *model structure*. A model structure (m.s.) is an ordered triple (G, K, R) where K is a set, R is a reflexive relation on K, and $G \varepsilon K$. Intuitively, we look at matters thus: K is the set of all 'possible worlds'; G is the 'real world'. If H_1 and H_2 are two worlds, $H_1 R H_2$ means intuitively that H_2 is 'possible relative to' H_1; *i.e.*, that every proposition *true* in H_2 is *possible* in H_1. Clearly, then, the relation R should indeed be reflexive; every world H is *possible* relative to itself, since every proposition *true* in H is, *a fortiori*, possible in H. Reflexivity is thus an intuitively natural requirement. We may impose additional requirements, corresponding to various 'reduction axioms' of modal logic: If R is transitive, we call (G, K, R) an S4-m.s.; if R is symmetric, (G, K, R) is a *Brouwersche* m.s.; and if R is an equivalence relation, we call (G, K, R) an S5-m.s. A model structure without restriction is also called an M-model structure.

To complete the picture, we need the notion of *model*. Given a model structure (G, K, R), a *model* assigns to each atomic formula (propositional variable) P a truth-value T or F in each world $H \varepsilon K$. Formally, a *model* φ on a m.s. (G, K, R) is a binary function $\varphi(P, H)$, where P varies over atomic formulae and H varies over elements of K, whose range is the set $\{T, F\}$. Given a model, we can define the assignments of truth-values to non-atomic formulae by induction. Assume $\varphi(A, H)$ and $\varphi(B, H)$ have already been defined for all $H \varepsilon K$. Then if $\varphi(A, H) = \varphi(B, H) = T$, define $\varphi(A \wedge B, H) = T$; otherwise, $\varphi(A \wedge B, H) = F$. $\varphi(\sim A, H)$ is defined to be F iff $\varphi(A, H) = T$; otherwise, $\varphi(\sim A, H) = T$. Finally, we define $\varphi(\Box A, H) = T$ iff $\varphi(A, H') = T$ for every $H' \varepsilon K$ such that $H R H'$; otherwise, $\varphi(\Box A, H) = F$. Intuitively, this says that A is necessary in H iff A is true in all worlds H' possible relative to H.

Completeness theorem. $\vdash A$ in M (S4, S5, the *Brouwersche* system) if and only if $\varphi(A, G) = T$ for every model φ on an M-(S4-, S5-, *Brouwersche*) model structure (G, K, R).[5]

---

[5] For a proof, see 'Semantical Analysis . . .,' *Zeitschrift* . . ., 9.

This completeness theorem equates the syntactical notion of *provability* in a modal system with a semantical notion of *validity*.

The rest of this paper concerns, with the exception of some concluding remarks, the introduction of quantifiers. To do this, we must associate with each world a domain of individuals, the individuals that exist in that world. Formally, we define a *quantificational model structure* (q.m.s.) as a model structure (G, K, R), together with a function ψ which assigns to each H ε K a set ψ(H), called the *domain* of H. Intuitively ψ(H) is the set of all individuals existing in H. Notice, of course, that ψ(H) need not be the same set for different arguments H, just as, intuitively, in worlds other than the real one, some actually existing individuals may be absent, while new individuals, like Pegasus, may appear.

We may then add, to the symbols of modal logic, an infinite list of individual variables x, y, z, . . ., and, for each nonnegative integer n, a list of n-adic predicate letters P^n, Q^n, . . ., where the superscripts will sometimes be understood from the context. We count propositional variables (atomic formulae) as '0-adic' predicate letters. We then build up well-formed formulae in the usual manner, and can now prepare ourselves to define a quantificational *model*.

To define a quantificational model, we must extend the original notion, which assigned a truth-value to each atomic formula in each world. Analogously, we must suppose that in each world a given n-adic predicate letter determines a certain set of ordered n-tuples, its *extension* in that world. Consider, for example, the case of a monadic predicate letter $P(x)$. We would like to say that, in the world H, the predicate $P(x)$ is true of some individuals in ψ(H) and false of others; formally, we would say that, relative to certain assignments of elements of ψ(H) to x, $\varphi(P(x),$ H) = T and relative to others $\varphi(P(x),$ H) = F. The set of all individuals of which P is true is called the *extension* of P in H. But there is a problem: should $\varphi(P(x),$ H) be given a truth-value when x is assigned a value in the domain of some *other* world H' and not in the domain of H? Intuitively, suppose $P(x)$ means 'x is bald'—are we to assign a truth-value to the substitution instance 'Sherlock Holmes is bald'? Holmes does not exist, but in other states of affairs, he would have existed. Should we assign a definite truth-value to the statement that he is bald, or not? Frege[6] and Strawson[7]

---

[6] G. Frege 'Uber Sinn und Bedeutung', *Zeitschrift für Philosophie und philosophische Kritik*, 100 (1892), 25–50. English translations in Geach and Black, *Translations from the Philosophical Writings of Gottlob Frege*, (Oxford: Blackwell, 1952), and in Feigl and Sellars (eds.), *Readings in Philosophical Analysis* (New York: Appleton Century Crofts, 1949).

[7] P. F. Strawson, 'On referring', *Mind*, n.s., 59 (1950), 320–44.

would not assign the statement a truth-value; Russell would.[8] For the purposes of modal logic we hold that different answers to this question represent alternative *conventions*. All are tenable. The only existing discussions of this problem I have seen—those of Hintikka[9] and Prior[10]—adopt the Frege-Strawson view. This view necessarily must lead to some modification of the usual modal logic. The reason is that the semantics for modal propositional logic, which we have already given, assumed that every formula must take a truth-value in each world; and now, for a formula $A(x)$ containing a free variable x, the Frege-Strawson view requires that it not be given a truth-value in a world H when the variable x is assigned an individual not in the domain of that world. We thus can no longer expect that the original laws of modal propositional logic hold for statements containing free variables, and are faced with an option: either revise modal propositional logic or restrict the rule of substitution. Prior does the former, Hintikka the latter. There are further alternatives the Frege-Strawson choice involves: Should we take $\Box A$ (in H) to mean that A is *true* in all possible worlds (relative to H), or just *not false* in any such world? The second alternative merely demands that A be either true or lack a truth-value in each world. Prior, in his system Q, in effect admits both types of necessity, one as 'L' and the other as 'NMN'. A similar question arises for conjunction: if A is false and B has no truth-value, should we take $A \wedge B$ to be false or truth-valueless?

In a full statement of the semantical theory, we would explore all these variants of the Frege-Strawson view. Here we will take the other option, and assume that a statement containing free variables has a truth-value in each world for every assignment to its free variables.[11] Formally, we state the matter as follows: Let $U = \underset{H \varepsilon K}{U} \; \psi(H)$. U^n is the nth Cartesian product of U with itself. We define a quantificational *model* on a q.m.s. (G, K, R) as a binary function $\varphi(P^n, H)$, where the first variable ranges over n-adic predicate letters, for arbitrary n, and H ranges

---

[8] Bertrand Russell, 'On denoting', *Mind*, n.s., 14 (1905), 479–93.

[9] 'Modality and Quantification'.

[10] A. N. Prior, *Time and Modality* (Oxford: Clarendon Press, 1957, viii+148 pp.)

[11] It is natural to assume that an *atomic* predicate should be *false* in a world H of all those individuals not existing in that world; that is, that the extension of a predicate letter must consist of actually existing individuals. We can do this by requiring semantically that $\varphi(P^n, H)$ be a subset of $[\psi(H)]^n$; the semantical treatment below would otherwise suffice without change. We would have to add to the axiom system below all closures of formulae of the form $P^n(x_1, \ldots, x_n) \wedge (y)A(y) . \supset . A(x_i)$ $(1 \leq i \leq n)$. We have chosen not to do this because the rule of substitution would no longer hold; theorems would hold for atomic formulae which would not hold when the atomic formulae are replaced by arbitrary formulae. (This answers a question of Putnam and Kalmar.)

over elements of K. If $n = 0$, $\varphi(P^n, H) = T$ or F; if $n \geq 1$, $\varphi(P^n, H)$ is a subset of U^n. We now define, inductively, for every formula A and $H \varepsilon K$, a truth-value $\varphi(A, H)$, relative to a given assignment of elements of U to the free variables of A. The case of a propositional variable is obvious. For an atomic formula $P^n(x_1, \ldots, x_n)$, where P^n is an n-adic predicate letter and $n \geq 1$, given an assignment of elements $a_1, \ldots, a_n$ of U to $x_1, \ldots, x_n$, we define $\varphi(P^n(x_1, \ldots, x_n), H) = T$ if the n-tuple $(a_1, \ldots, a_n)$ is a member of $\varphi(P^n, H)$; otherwise, $\varphi(P^n(x_1, \ldots, x_n), H) = F$, relative to the given assignment. Given these assignments for atomic formulae, we can build up the assignments for complex formulae by induction. The induction steps for the propositional connectives $\wedge$, $\sim$, $\square$, have already been given. Assume we have a formula $A(x, y_1, \ldots, y_n)$, where x and the y_i are the only free variables present, and that a truth-value $\varphi(A(x, y_1, \ldots, y_n), H)$ has been defined for each assignment to the free variables of $A(x, y_1, \ldots, y_n)$. Then we define $\varphi((x)A(x, y_1, \ldots, y_n), H) = T$ relative to an assignment of $b_1, \ldots, b_n$ to $y_1, \ldots, y_n$ (where the b_i are elements of U), if $\varphi((A(x, y_1, \ldots, y_n), H) = T$ for every assignment of $a, b_1, \ldots, b_n$ to $x, y_1, \ldots, y_n$, respectively, where $a \varepsilon \psi(H)$; otherwise, $\varphi((x)A(x, y_1, \ldots, y_n), H) = F$ relative to the given assignment. Notice that the restriction $a \varepsilon \psi(H)$ means that, in H, we quantify only over the objects actually existing in H.

To illustrate the semantics, we give counterexamples to two familiar proposals for laws of modal quantification theory—the 'Barcan formula' $(x)\square A(x) \supset \square(x)A(x)$ and its converse $\square(x)A(x) \supset (x)\square A(x)$. For each we consider a model structure (G, K, R), where $K = \{G, H\}$, $G \neq H$, and R is simply the Cartesian product K^2. Clearly R is reflexive, transitive, and symmetric, so our considerations apply even to S5.

For the Barcan formula, we extend (G, K, R) to a quantificational model structure by defining $\psi(G) = \{a\}$, $\psi(H) = \{a, b\}$, where a and b are distinct. We then define, for a monadic predicate letter P, a model φ in which $\varphi(P, G) = \{a\}$, $\varphi(P, H) = \{a\}$. Then clearly $\square P(x)$ is true in G when x is assigned a; and since a is the only object in the domain of G, so is $(x)\square P(x)$. But, $(x)P(x)$ is clearly false in H (for $\varphi(P(x), H) = F$ when x is assigned b), and hence $\square(x)P(x)$ is false in G. So we have a counterexample to the Barcan formula. Notice that this counterexample is quite independent of whether $P(x)$ is assigned a truth-value in G or not when x is assigned b, so also it applies to the systems of Hintikka and Prior. Such counterexamples can be disallowed, and the Barcan formula reinstated, only if we require a model structure to satisfy the condition that $\psi(H') \subseteq \psi(H)$ whenever HRH' (H, $H' \varepsilon K$).

For the converse of the Barcan formula, set $\psi(G) = \{a, b\}$, $\psi(H) = \{a\}$, where again $a \neq b$. Define $\varphi(P, \mathbf{G}) = \{a, b\}$, $\varphi(P, \mathbf{H}) = \{a\}$, where P is a given monadic predicate letter. Then clearly $(x)P(x)$ holds in both $\mathbf{G}$ and $\mathbf{H}$, so that $\varphi(\Box(x)P(x), \mathbf{G}) = \mathbf{T}$. But $\varphi(P(x), \mathbf{H}) = \mathbf{F}$ when x is assigned b, so that, when x is assigned b, $\varphi(\Box P(x), \mathbf{G}) = \mathbf{F}$. Hence $\varphi((x)\Box P(x), \mathbf{G})$ $= \mathbf{F}$, and we have the desired counterexample to the converse of the Barcan formula. This counterexample, however, depends on asserting that, in $\mathbf{H}$, $P(x)$ is actually *false* when x is assigned b; it might thus disappear if, for this assignment, $P(x)$ were declared to lack truth-value in $\mathbf{H}$. In this case, we will still have a counterexample if we require a necessary statement to be *true* in all possible worlds (Prior's 'L'), but not if we merely require that it never be false (Prior's 'NMN'). On our present convention, we can eliminate the counterexample only by requiring, for each q.m.s., that $\psi(\mathbf{H}) \subseteq \psi(\mathbf{H}')$ whenever $\mathbf{H}R\mathbf{H}'$.

These counterexamples lead to a peculiar difficulty: We have given countermodels, in quantified S5, to both the Barcan formula and its converse. Yet Prior appears to have shown[12] that the Barcan formula is derivable in quantified S5; and the converse seems derivable even in quantified M by the following argument:

(A) $(x)A(x) \supset A(y)$ (by quantification theory)
(B) $\Box((x)A(x) \supset A(y))$ (by necessitation)
(C) $\Box((x)A(x) \supset A(y)) \supset \Box(x)A(x) \supset \Box A(y)$ (Axiom A2)
(D) $\Box(x)A(x) \supset \Box A(y)$ (from (B) and (C))
(E) $(y)(\Box(x)A(x) \supset \Box A(y))$ (generalizing on (D))
(F) $\Box(x)A(x) \supset (y)\Box A(y)$ (by quantification theory, and (E))

We seem to have derived the conclusion using principles that should all be valid in the model-theory. Actually, the flaw lies in the application of necessitation to (A). In a formula like (A), we give the free variables the

---

[12] See 'Modality and Quantification in s5', *Journal of Symbolic Logic*, 21 (1956), 60–2.

[13] It is not asserted that the generality interpretation of theorems with free variables is the only possible one. One might wish a formula A to be provable iff, for each model φ, $\varphi(A, \mathbf{G}) = \mathbf{T}$ for every assignment to the free variables of A. But then $(x)A(x)$ $\supset A(y)$ will not be a theorem; in fact, in the countermodel above to the Barcan formula, $\varphi((x)P(x) \supset P(y), \mathbf{G}) = \mathbf{F}$ if y is assigned b. Thus quantification theory would have to be revised along the lines proposed by Hintikka (in 'Existential Presuppositions and Existential Commitments', *Journal of Philosophy*, 56 (1959), 125–37) and by H. Leblanc and T. Hailperin (in 'Nondesignating Singular Terms', *Philosophical Review*, 68 (1959), 239–43). This procedure has much to recommend it, but we have not adopted it since we wished to show that the difficulty can be solved without revising quantification theory or modal propositional logic.

generality interpretation:[13] When (A) is asserted as a theorem, it abbreviates assertion of its ordinary universal closure

(A') $(y)((x)A(x) \supset A(y))$

Now if we applied necessitation to (A'), we would get

(B') $\Box(y)((x)A(x) \supset A(y))$

On the other hand, (B) itself is interpreted as asserting

(B'') $(y)\Box((x)A(x) \supset A(y))$

To infer (B'') from (B'), we would need a law of the form $\Box(y)C(y) \supset (y)\Box C(y)$, which is just the converse Barcan formula that we are trying to prove. In fact, it is readily checked that (B'') fails in the counter-model given above for the converse Barcan formula, if we replace $A(x)$ by $P(x)$.

We can avoid this sort of difficulty if, following Quine[14] we formulate quantification theory so that only *closed* formulae are asserted. Assertion of formulae containing free variables is at best a convenience; assertion of $A(x)$ with free x can always be replaced by assertion of $(x)A(x)$.

If A is a formula containing free variables, we define a *closure* of A to be any formula without free variables obtained by prefixing universal quantifiers and necessity signs, in any order, to A. We then define the axioms of quantified M to be the closures of the following schemata:

(0) Truth-functional tautologies

(1) $\Box A \supset A$

(2) $\Box(A \supset B) . \supset . \Box A \supset \Box B$

(3) $A \supset (x)A$, where x is not free in A

(4) $(x)(A \supset B) . \supset . (x)A \supset (x)B$

(5) $(y)((x)A(x) \supset A(y))$

The rule of inference is detachment for material implication. Necessitation can be obtained as a derived rule.

To obtain quantified extensions of S4, S5, the *Brouwersche* system, simply add to the axiom schemata all closures of the appropriate reduction axiom.

The systems we have obtained have the following properties: They are a straightforward extension of the modal propositional logics, without the modifications of Prior's Q; the rule of substitution holds without restriction, unlike Hintikka's presentation; and nevertheless neither the Barcan formula nor its converse is derivable. Further, all the laws of quantification theory—modified to admit the empty domain—hold.

[14] W. Quine, *Mathematical Logic* (Cambridge, Mass.: Harvard Univ. Press, 1940; 2nd edn., rev., 1951, XII+346 pp.).

The semantical completeness theorem we gave for modal propositional logic can be extended to the new systems.

We can introduce *existence as a predicate* in the present system if we like. Semantically, existence is a monadic predicate $E(x)$ satisfying, for each model φ on a m.s. (G, K, R), the identity $\varphi(E, H) = \psi(H)$ for every $H \varepsilon K$. Axiomatically, we can introduce it through the postulation of closures of formulae of the form: $(x)A(x) \wedge E(y) \,.\, \supset \,.\, A(y)$, and $(x)E(x)$. The predicate P used above in the counter-example to the converse Barcan formula can now be recognized as simply existence. This fact shows how existence differs from the tautological predicate $A(x) \vee \sim A(x)$ even though $\square(x)E(x)$ is provable. For although $(x)\square(A(x)\vee \sim A(x))$ is valid, $(x)\square E(x)$ is not; although it is necessary that every thing exists, it does not follow that everything has the property of necessary existence.

We can introduce identity semantically in the model theory by defining $x = y$ to be true in a world H when x and y are assigned the same value and otherwise false; existence could then be defined in terms of identity, by stipulating that $E(x)$ means $(\exists y)(x = y)$. For reasons not given here, a broader theory of identity could be obtained if we complicated the notion of quantificational model structure.

We conclude with some brief and sketchy remarks on the 'provability' interpretations of modal logics, which we give in each case for propositional calculus only. The reader will have obtained the main point of this paper if he omits this section. Provability interpretations are based on a desire to adjoin a necessity operator to a formal system, say Peano arithmetic, in such a way that, for any formula A of the system, $\square A$ will be interpreted as true iff A is provable in the system. It has been argued that such 'provability' interpretations of a model operator are dispensable in favour of a provability *predicate*, attaching to the Gödel number of A; but Professor Montague's contribution to the present volume casts at least some doubt on this viewpoint.

Let us consider the formal system **PA** of Peano arithmetic, as formalized in Kleene.[15] We adjoin to the formation rules operators $\wedge$, $\sim$, and $\square$ (the conjunction and negation adjoined are to be distinct from those of the original system), operating on closed formulae only. In the model theory we gave above, we took atomic formulae to be propositional variables, or predicate letters followed by parenthesized individual variables; here we take them to be simply the closed well-formed formulae of **PA** (*not* just the atomic formulae of **PA**). We define a model structure (G, K, R), where K is the set of all distinct (non-isomorphic) countable models of

---

[15] S. C. Kleene, *Introduction to Metamathematics* (New York: D. Van Nostrand, 1952, x+550 pp.).

PA, **G** is the standard model in the natural numbers, and R is the Cartesian product $\mathbf{K}^2$. We define a model φ by requiring that, for any atomic formula P and $\mathbf{H} \, \varepsilon \, \mathbf{K}$, $\varphi(P, \mathbf{H}) = \mathbf{T}(\mathbf{F})$ iff P is true (false) in the model **H**. (Remember, P is a wff of **PA**, and **H** is a countable model of **PA**.) We then build up the evaluation for compound formulae as before.[16] To say that A is true is to say it is true in the real world **G**; and, for any atomic P, $\varphi(\Box P, \mathbf{G}) = \mathbf{T}$ iff P is provable in **PA**. (Notice that $\varphi(P, \mathbf{G}) = \mathbf{T}$ iff P is true in the intuitive sense). Since $(\mathbf{G}, \mathbf{K}, R)$ is an S5-m.s., all the laws of S5 will be valid on this interpretation; and we can show that *only* the laws of S5 are generally valid. (For example, if P is Gödel's undecidable formula, $\varphi(\Box P \mathbf{v} \Box \sim P, \mathbf{G}) = \mathbf{F}$, which is a counterexample to the 'law' $\Box A \mathbf{v} \Box \sim A$.)

Another provability interpretation is the following: Again we take the atomic formulae to be the closed wffs of **PA**, and then build up new formulae using the adjoined connectives $\wedge$, $\sim$, and $\Box$. Let **K** be the set of all ordered pairs $(\mathbf{E}, \alpha)$, where **E** is a consistent extension of **PA**, and α is a (countable) model of the system **E**. Let $\mathbf{G} = (\mathbf{PA}, \alpha_0)$, where α_0 is the standard model of **PA**. We say $(\mathbf{E}, \alpha) \, R \, (\mathbf{E}', \alpha')$, where $(\mathbf{E}, \alpha)$ and $(\mathbf{E}', \alpha')$ are in **K**, iff **E**′ is an extension of **E**. For atomic P, define $\varphi(P, (\mathbf{E}, \alpha)) = \mathbf{T}(\mathbf{F})$ iff P is true (false) in α. Then we can show, for atomic P, that $\varphi(\Box P, (\mathbf{E}, \alpha)) = \mathbf{T}$ iff P is provable in **E**; in particular, $\varphi(\Box P, \mathbf{G}) = \mathbf{T}$ iff P is provable in **PA**. Since $(\mathbf{G}, \mathbf{K}, R)$ is an S4-m.s., all the laws of S4 hold. But not all the laws of S5 hold; if P is Gödel's undecidable formula, $\varphi((\sim \Box P \supset \Box \sim \Box P), \mathbf{G}) = \mathbf{F}$. But some laws are valid which are not provable in S4; in particular, we can prove for any A, $\varphi(\Box \sim \Box(\Diamond A \wedge \Diamond \sim A), \mathbf{G}) = \mathbf{T}$, which yields the theorems of McKinsey's S4.1.[17] By suitable modifications this difficulty could be removed; but we do not go into the matter here.

Similar interpretations of M and the *Brouwersche* system could be stated; but, in the present writer's opinion, they have less interest than those given above. We mention one more class of provability interpretations, the 'reflexive' extensions of **PA**. Let **E** be a formal system containing

---

[16] It may be protested that **PA** already contain symbols for conjunction and negation, say '&' and '$\neg$'; so why do we adjoin new symbols '$\wedge$' and '$\sim$'? The answer is that if P and Q are atomic formulae, then $P \, \& \, Q$ is *also* atomic in the present sense, since it is well-formed in **PA**; but $P \wedge Q$ is not. In order to be able to apply the previous theory, in which the conjunction of atomic formulae is not atomic, we need '$\wedge$'. Nevertheless, for any $\mathbf{H} \, \varepsilon \, \mathbf{K}$ and atomic P and Q, $\varphi(P \& Q, \mathbf{H}) = \varphi(P \wedge Q, \mathbf{H})$, so that confusion of '&' with '$\wedge$' causes no harm in practice. Similar remarks apply to negation, and to the provability interpretation of s4 in the next paragraph.

[17] See J. C. C. McKinsey, 'On the Syntactical Construction of Systems of Modal Logic', *Journal of Symbolic Logic*, 10 (1945), 83–94.

PA, and whose well-formed formulae are formed out of the closed formulae of **PA** by use of the connectives &, $\neg$, and $\square$. (I say '&' and '$\neg$'
to indicate that I am using the same conjunction and negation as in **PA**
itself, not introducing new ones. See footnote 16, p. 71.) Then **E** is called a
reflexive extension of **PA** iff: (1) It is an inessential extension of **PA**; (2)
$\square A$ is provable in **E** iff A is; (3) there is a valuation α, mapping the closed
formulae of **E** into the set $\{T, F\}$, such that conjunction and negation obey
the usual truth tables, all the true closed formulae of **PA** get the value **T**,
$\alpha(\square A) = T$ iff A is provable in **E**, and all the theorems of **E** get the value
T. It can be shown that there are reflexive extensions of **PA** containing the
axioms of S4 or even S4.1, but none containing S5.

Finally, we remark that, using the usual mapping of intuitionistic
logic into S4, we can get a model theory for the intuitionistic predicate
calculus. We will not give this model theory here, but instead will mention,
for propositional calculus only, a particular useful interpretation of intuitionistic logic that results from the model theory. Let **E** be any consistent
extension of **PA**. We say a formula P of **PA** is *verified* in **E** iff it is provable
in **E**. We take the closed wffs P of **PA** as atomic, and build formulae out
of them using the intuitionistic connectives $\wedge$, $\vee$, $\neg$, and $\supset$. We then
stipulate inductively: $A \wedge B$ is verified in **E** iff A and B are; $A \vee B$ is
verified in **E** iff A or B is; $\neg A$ is verified in **E** iff there is no consistent extension of **E** verifying A; $A \supset B$ is verified in **E** iff every consistent
extension **E′** of **E** verifying A also verifies B.

Then every instance of a law of intuitionistic logic is verified in **PA**;
but, e.g., $A \vee \neg A$ is not, if A is the Gödel undecidable formula. In future
work, we will extend this interpretation further, and show that using it we
can find an interpretation for Kreisel's system FC of absolutely free choice
sequences.[18] It is clear, incidentally, that **PA** can be replaced in the provability interpretations of S4 and S5 by any truth functional system (i.e.,
by any system whose models determine each closed formula as true or
false); while the interpretation of intuitionism applies to any formal
system whatsoever.

---

[18] G. Kreisel, 'A Remark on Free Choice Sequences and the Topological Completeness' Proofs, *Journal of Symbolic Logic*, 23 (1958), 369–88.

See Addendum on p. 172

VI

ESSENTIALISM AND QUANTIFIED MODAL LOGIC[1]

Terence Parsons

PROBLEMS involving essentialism are now receiving a great deal of attention from modal logicians and philosophers. Even a cursory glance at work in this field, however, soon reveals that there are many doctrines which go by this title. I will isolate and discuss one such doctrine. In particular, after isolating one version of essentialism (Sections I and II), I will argue that work in quantified modal logic can be and is independent of the acceptance of the truth of this doctrine (Sections III–V). In the last section (Section VI) I will attempt to show, on the basis of facts established in Sections III–V, just why this particular form of essentialism is a philosophically suspect doctrine. I will also argue that work in quantified modal logic need not even presuppose the *meaningfulness* of essentialist claims *in any objectionable sense.*

My arguments aim at (a) a clarification of one sort of essentialism, and (b) a partial vindication of quantified modal logic.

I. PRELIMINARY CLARIFICATION

To begin, let us dichotomize essentialist doctrines into two kinds. One kind has to do with what I shall call *individual* essences and the other with what I shall call *general* essences. The former doctrine makes some claim to the effect that some or all objects have characteristics (or properties) which are so intimately associated with the object that nothing else *could* (with emphasis on the 'could') have precisely those characteristics without being that object. This is meant to be a stronger thesis than the Identity of Indiscernibles, which holds merely that no two objects can simultaneously exist while sharing all properties. It is stronger in two ways: (1) it prohibits the simultaneous existence of two objects which share the same individual essence (even when they could differ in other of their properties), and (2) it makes a claim about what *might have been*: had

From *The Philosophical Review*, LXXVIII. 1 (January 1969), 35–52. Reprinted by permission of the author and *The Philosophical Review*.

[1] In addition to the authors cited in the paper, I am particularly indebted to John Vickers and to Kathryn Pyne Parsons for comments on earlier drafts, and to the referee of *The Philosophical Review* for help in improving the final draft.

the world been different, and had there been an object, b, in it, where b had the individual essence which object a has in this world, then b (in the world which might have been) would have *been* object a. This doctrine of individual essences comes in for discussion in modal logic in the problem of identifying objects in one possible world with objects in other possible worlds.[2]

The doctrine of *general* essences, on the other hand, simply singles out certain characteristics as being necessarily true of certain objects. Distinct objects are not prohibited from sharing the same general essence, as is the case with individual essences. While individual essences completely individuate their bearers, general essences do not (although they may help). The doctrine of general essences is a natural, though not inevitable, extension of the metaphysical doctrine of natural kinds (where natural-kind properties and properties definitional to them are taken as the general essences).

My discussion is concerned wholly with the doctrine of general essences. This doctrine also may take many forms, and the next section is devoted to an exposition of one such form.

II. FORMULATING THE 'TROUBLESOME' KIND OF ESSENTIALISM

Part of the motivation for studying essentialism is a suspicion that two claims about it are true:

(A) that quantified modal logic is committed to essentialism, and
(B) that essentialism is a false, or at least philosophically suspect, doctrine.

If both (A) and (B) are true, they constitute a strong argument against the significance of quantified modal logic. This argument is mainly due to Quine.[3] It is intended to apply specifically to *quantified* modal logic— that is, the kind of essentialism involved is supposed to arise *only* when

---

[2] Roughly, an object in one world is identified with an object in another world just in case they have the same individual essence. Cf. J. Hintikka, *Knowledge and Belief* (Ithaca: Cornell Univ. Press, 1962); R. Chisholm, 'Identity Through Possible Worlds: Some Questions', *Nous*, I (1967). This issue was also the central topic of a symposium sponsored jointly by the Western Division A.P.A. and the Association for Symbolic Logic in May, 1967, with D. Kaplan (principal speaker), J. Hintikka, and T. Parsons.

[3] W. Quine, 'Two Dogmas of Empiricism' and 'Reference and Modality' (esp. pp. 143–56), in *From a Logical Point of View* (New York: Harper & Row, 1961) [See Essay I, above]; also 'Three Grades of Modal Involvement', *The Ways of Paradox* (New York, 1966).

quantifiers are added to modal logic and allowed to intermingle with modal operators.[4]

In fact, there are many different forms of essentialism and many different forms of modal logic, and until these are made specific, the argument implicit in (A) and (B) cannot be evaluated. Previous attempts to find a precise formulation of a form of essentialism which would make both (A) and (B) true (for some interesting modal logic) have ended with negative conclusions[5]—the forms of essentialism to which quantified modal logic is committed are the forms which are most innocuous. This article is in part another step in that search.

Previous searching has been for a purely syntactical characterization of essentialism. In particular, it has been a search for a schema, S, such that any quantified modal logic endorsing any instance of S would be committed to a suspect version of essentialism. Two interesting schemata were these:

(1) $(\exists x_1)...(\exists x_n)(\Box F \ \& \ -\Box G)$

and

(2) $(\exists x_1)...(\exists x_n)(\Box F) \ \& \ (\exists x_1)...(\exists x_n)(-\Box F).$[6]

Definition (1), which is essentially due to Quine,[7] is not intrinsically more suspect than is the division of closed sentences into necessary and contingent. That a system of modal logic is essential in sense (1) does not entail that it will endorse controversial claims like 'something is necessarily greater than seven'. It may only endorse 'essential' claims like 'something is necessarily either-bald-or-not-bald,' claims whose truth-conditions can be made perfectly precise.[8]

---

[4] i.e., it applies specifically to Quine's *third* grade of modal involvement. Cf. 'Grades of Modal Involvement', Section III.

[5] Cf. R. Marcus, 'Essentialism in Modal Logic', *Nous*, I (1967); also T. Parsons, 'Grades of Essentialism in Quantified Modal Logic', *Nous*, I (1967).

[6] In each case F and G are to be formulas whose only free variables are among $x_1 . . . x_n$. We also assume that F and G contain no constants. If they contain constants, a more detailed formulation is necessary; see Parsons, op. cit., for details. It should be stressed that schemata (1) and (2) provide a 'syntactic' characterization of forms of essentialism only on the assumption that the quantifiers are interpreted to range over individuals, and not over individual concepts or descriptions. For interpretations of the latter sort, see footnote 12.

[7] 'Grades of Modal Involvement', p. 174. Quine adds an additional clause within the scope of the quantifiers, the clause 'Gx'. The point is that G is a property which objects have, but have contingently. The assumption that some objects have some properties contingently is shared by *all* views under discussion. This particular assumption is not an issue here—cf. footnote 8.

[8] See Parsons, op cit., for a way to do this for one system. The important point is that the 'essentialist' difficulties at issue are supposed to be difficulties *in addition to* the difficulties encountered in making sense of modal operators preceding closed sentences.

Version (2), roughly due to Marcus,[9] is an attempt to formulate a more troublesome kind of essentialism. While version (1) merely says (for case $n = 1$) that an object has some properties necessarily and some contingently, version (2) says that an object has a property necessarily, which other objects *do not* have necessarily. Version (1) will be true as soon as properties are divided into contingent ones and necessary ones, a division that can be made with no more difficulty than the division of propositions (or sentences) into necessary and contingent; but for version (2) to be satisfied we need a more complex categorization. Properties cannot be just necessary or not necessary; they must be necessary *for* this object and not necessary *for* that one.

This notion—that properties can be necessary for some objects but not necessary for others—seems to be precisely that doctrine which is responsible for the troublesomeness of the examples which Quine offers. What worries us about some things being necessarily two-legged[10] is that other things are *not* necessarily two-legged, and thus we cannot attribute the necessity of the two-leggedness to the predicate or property in question. There must be something about the *object* which gives rise to the necessity. But what could this be? The lack, so far, of a satisfactory answer to this question is what makes this version of essentialism a real source of philosophical perplexity.

Unfortunately, version (2), *as stated*, is not a completely adequate syntactic formulation of the 'suspect' version of essentialism. For there are a *few* instances of version (2), which are as untroublesome as instances of version (1). For example, consider the following instance of schema (2):

$$(\exists x)\,(\exists y)\,\Box(Fx \lor -Fy) \quad \& \quad (\exists x)\,(\exists y)-\Box(Fx \lor -Fy).$$

Whenever there exists more than one object, this sentence will be true.[11] It will be true because the two quantifiers in the first conjunct can range over the same objects. Keeping this in mind, it is clear that this instance of schema (2) is true, and unobjectionably so, and thus 'being an instance of (2)' cannot be taken as a criterion for being essential in a clearly troublesome sense.

[9] Op. cit., p. 93.

[10] Cf. 'Two Dogmas of Empiricism', p. 22.

[11] i.e., the sentence will be true in most interesting modal logics; for example, in the systems in S. Kripke, 'Semantic Considerations on Modal Logics', *Acta Philosophica Fennica*, 16 (1963) [V above]. Another sentence which illustrates the same point is (given one usual treatment of '='):

$$(\exists x)(\exists y)\,\Box(x = y) \quad \& \quad (\exists x)(\exists y)-\Box(x = y)$$

which will be true in any domain of more than one individual.

Nor is the general schema (2) an adequate formalization of the troublesome doctrine discussed above in rough terms. We have discussed only essential properties, but (2) treats relations as well as properties. And here is where the special examples arise. For (2) treats a relation as essential even if it applies necessarily to a single object in relation to itself, while not applying necessarily to distinct objects in relation to each other.

I propose, then, to modify (2) so as to rule out these special cases. I think the following formulation does it: I shall call a sentence *essential* (in the sense under discussion hereafter) if it is an instance of the schema:

(3) $(\exists x_1)...(\exists x_n)(\pi_n x_n$ & $\Box F)$ &
   $(\exists x_1)...(\exists x_n)(\pi_n x_n$ & $-\Box F)^{12}$

where F is an open formula whose free variables are included in $x_1, \ldots,$ x_n, and where $\pi_n x_n$ is any conjunction of formulas of the form $x_i = x_j$ or $x_i \neq x_j$ for every $1 \leq i < j \leq n$, but not including both $x_i = x_j$ and $x_i \neq x_j$ for any i, j.

Schema (3) differs from schema (2) only in the insertion of the clause '$\pi_n x_n$' following the quantifiers; this (hopefully) rules out exactly the trivial and unobjectionable instances of schema (2), and leaves us with only examples of the *troublesome* essentialist doctrine we have been trying to characterize. (In most cases the additional complexity of schema (3) can be ignored—that is, except for the 'special' cases, schema (2) is an adequate formulation.)

III. A NONESSENTIAL MODAL LOGIC

Having isolated a notion of essentialism which qualifies for the title 'philosophically suspect' (this will be argued in more detail in Section VI), let me turn to question (A) above: *is* quantified modal logic committed to this doctrine? The answer, of course, will depend both on which version of modal logic is at issue, and on what 'commitment' means.

Taking the latter issue first, there seem to be three relevant notions of

---

[12] Again the assumption is that the variables are to range over individuals and not over individual concepts or descriptions. In some of these other systems, equivalent formulations can be given. In particular, suppose that $x_1, x_2, \ldots$ range over individuals, and $\alpha_1, \alpha_2, \ldots$ range over individual concepts. Suppose also that $\alpha_i \, \Delta x_j$ means 'α_i is a concept of x_j'. We also suppose that we quantify into modal contexts by use of variables $\alpha_1, \alpha_2, \ldots$ but not with variables $x_1, x_2, \ldots$ (otherwise (3) is adequate as it stands). We can now define an essential sentence as any instance of:

(3′) $(\exists x_1) \ldots (\exists x_n)(\pi_n x_n$ & $(\alpha_1) \ldots (\alpha_n)(\alpha_1 \Delta x_1$ & $\ldots$ & $\alpha_n \Delta x_n \supset \Box F))$ &
   $(\exists x_1) \ldots (\exists x_n)(\pi_n x_n$ & $-(\alpha_1) \ldots (\alpha_n)(\alpha_1 \Delta x_1$ & $\ldots$ & $\alpha_n \Delta x_n \supset \Box F))$
(note that F will contain some of $\alpha_1, \ldots, \alpha_n$ but none of $x_1, \ldots, x_n$).

commitment to essentialism. We will say that a system of quantified modal logic is committed to essentialism if

(*i*) it has some essential sentence as a theorem,

or

(*ii*) it has no essential sentence as a theorem, but nevertheless requires that some essential sentence be true—in the sense that the system, together with some obvious and uncontroversial non-modal facts, entails that some such sentence be true,[13]

or

(*iii*) the system allows the formulation of (and thus presupposes the *meaningfulness* of) some essential sentence.

I will discuss (*i*) and (*ii*) in Sections III–V; discussion of (*iii*) is postponed until Section VI.

As for the particular version of quantified modal logic, I will treat the class of systems discussed by S. Kripke (op. cit.). These systems have come in for considerable discussion recently, and the results presented here will extend to a great deal of related work.

The idea behind Kripke's analysis is this: we begin with the notion of a set of *possible worlds* (or a set of *possible states of affairs*, or of *ways the world might have been*). Such a set is called a *model structure*.[14] We can remain neutral among various conceptions of the nature of possible worlds; for the purpose of modal semantics the only facts about possible worlds that are relevant are (*i*) which things exist in each possible world, and (*ii*) what the extensions of the predicates of the language are in each world. Given a *domain* for each world (i.e., given the set of things which exist in that world), and given an assignment of extensions to predicates of the language for each world, the truth values of formulas can be defined for each world. For a closed sentence, *A*, the definition of *necessity* is:

$\Box A$ is true in world *H* if and only if *A* is true in every alternative possible world H'.[15]

---

[13] I have in mind situations like the following. Essentialism of form (2) above is such that no essential sentence (of form (2)) is a theorem, but some modal logics (e.g., Kripke's) have the consequence that some essential sentence is true *whenever there exists more than one individual* (this is the 'obvious and uncontroversial non-modal fact').

[14] For complete details see Appendix A.

[15] I have omitted discussion of the alternativeness relation (of one world's being *possible relative to* another) for simplicity, and because it is irrelevant to the present issue. This relation enters into modal semantics in the following way: for some interpretations of the modal system we suppose that not all worlds are possible relative to

A sentence is a *theorem* of quantified modal logic just in case it is true in every world in every model structure no matter how extensions are assigned to the predicates of the language. Let us call a model structure plus an assignment of extensions to the predicates of the language (for each world) a *model*. Then we can also state that a sentence is a theorem of quantified modal logic just in case it is true in every world in every model.

Now the following fact can be proved concerning Kripke's system:

Theorem 1: There are certain models, called *maximal models*, in which no essential sentence is true in any world in the model.

The exact statement of this theorem is given in Appendix A. Part of the significance of this theorem is that it shows conclusively that no essential sentence is a *theorem* of quantified modal logic, and therefore that Kripke's version of quantified modal logic is *not* committed to essentialism in the first sense defined above (in sense (*i*)).

But the theorem also has significance for evaluating commitment to essentialism in the second sense—that is, for deciding whether 'the facts' force some essential sentence to be true (according to the system). For, given any set of non-modal facts expressible in our symbolism (i.e., expressible in sentences without modal signs), these facts must be expressible by a *consistent* set of sentences.[16] And a maximal model is, by definition, a model that will contain, for every consistent set of non-modal sentences, a possible world in which they are all true. Thus, whatever the facts are, the sentences expressing them must all be true in some possible world in some maximal model. But no essential sentence is true in any world in any maximal model (Theorem 1). Thus there is a world in which all the 'facts' of this world hold, and in which no essential sentence is true. And therefore we are also free of commitment to essentialism in the second sense defined above.

IV. NONESSENTIALISM IN APPLIED MODAL LOGIC

The results of the preceding section have to do only with a relatively austere notion of necessity, roughly equivalent to Quine's notion of 'logical

a given world. For example, if we were to interpret '$\Box$' as physical necessity, rather than logical necessity, then we might require that a world not be possible relative to another unless all physical laws which hold in the latter also hold in the former. A world which *is* possible relative to a given world, *H*, is called an *alternative* to *H*. The formal structure of this alternativeness relation corresponds to the logical behaviour of iterations of modal operators (e.g., '$\Box A \supset \Box\Box A$' is valid if and only if the alternativeness relation is transitive). In the maximal models discussed in the text, every world is considered to be an alternative to every other world; this is the most general case (see also footnote 28).

[16] By 'consistent' here I simply mean consistent in the ordinary first-order predicate logic sense.

truth'.[17] The essentialism question re-arises when one goes on to 'apply' the modal logic. There are two natural ways in which this is frequently done. One is to extend the class of necessary sentences to include the truths of some a priori discipline—for example, mathematics. A second is to extend the class to include sentences which are analytic (but not theorems of logic).

First, what happens when we attempt to extend the interpretation of '$\square$' to precede, say, truths of arithmetic as well as truths of logic? Will we *then* be stuck with essentialism? We are especially bothered by classic examples like:

$$\square(9 > 7) \quad \& \quad -\square(7 > 9)$$

which seem to lead to truths of the form:

$$(\exists x)(\exists y)(\square(x > y)) \quad \& \quad (\exists x)(\exists y)(-\square(x > y))$$

that is, to essentialism.[18]

The claim of this section is that in certain widespread and well-defined situations, essentialism *can* always be avoided. To be precise: suppose we wish to extend the range of the '$\square$' sign by choosing a certain consistent set of sentences as axioms, and interpreting '$\square F$' to be true just in case 'F' is true in every world in which the axioms hold. Then two requirements suffice to guarantee that we will find ourselves endorsing no essential sentences: (*i*) that the axioms all be closed and contain no constants, and (*ii*) that the axioms contain no modal operators, except on the front. Theorem 2, which shows this, is stated in Appendix B. We know that (*i*) is no real restriction, since any theory formulated with constants is replaceable by an equivalent theory without constants. Also, requirement (*ii*) can sometimes be relaxed (for example, in cases where modal operators appear within the sentence but only preceding closed formulas).

We might look at an example of an application of this theorem to arithmetic. What happens to

(a) Necessarily $9 > 7$

---

[17] Cf. Quine, 'Two Dogmas of Empiricism', p. 22.
[18] Strictly speaking, it is truths of the form

$$9 \neq 7 \ \& \ \square(9 > 7) \ \& \ 7 \neq 9 \ \& \ -\square(7 > 9)$$

which seem to lead to

$$(\exists x)(\exists y)(x \neq y \ \& \ \square x > y) \ \& \ (\exists x)(\exists y)(x \neq y \ \& \ -\square x > y),$$

i.e., our form of essentialism. I've omitted the non-identity clause for simplicity.

if we take this line? Formulated without constants, (a) has at least two plausible representations:

(b) $\Box(\exists x)(\exists y)(x$ is nine   & y is seven   & $x > y)$

or

(c) $(\exists x)(\exists y)(x$ is nine   & y is seven   & $\Box(x > y)).$[19]

In terms of the 'possible world' approach, the difference between (b) and (c) is this: (b) only requires that in each possible world there be some things or other such that the first 'is nine' and the second 'is seven' and the first is greater than the second. On the other hand, (c) requires that there be things, nine and seven, such that in every possible world *these* things are such that the first is greater than the second. Thus (c) requires that certain specific objects reappear in every world, retaining certain properties and relations in every world, while (b) does not.

Now if most of the motivation for accepting essentialism is that *some* analogue of (a) remain true, then that motivation is misguided. For (b) is such an analogue and is nonessential. (c), on the other hand, entails essentialism, and thus will be treated as false if we add axioms only in the manner indicated above. None of this proves that (c) *should* be false; only if it is to be true (i.e., if we are to accept essentialism) it cannot be because we are *forced* to, either by general considerations, or by examples like (a).

This nonessentialist option, incidentally, yields an *alternative* to Smullyan's escape from Quine's 'paradox'[20] based on (a) above. Quine suggests that both:

(d) Necessarily 9 > 7

and

(e) —Necessarily (the number of planets > 7)

are true. But since 9 = the number of planets, (a) and (b) seem to contradict one another. Smullyan objects that if we rephrase (e) as

(e') $-(\exists x)(x$ is the number of planets   & $\Box(x > 7))$

---

[19] Actually there are many other analogues of (a) as well; for example, we might include uniqueness claims, or in (c) the necessity sign might immediately follow the quantifiers. Or we might avoid the 'necessary existence' claim of (b) by altering it to

$(b')\Box(x)(y)(x$ is nine   & y is seven $\supset x > y).$

(b) and (c) constitute one illustration among many of the *important* choice between essentialism and nonessentialism.

[20] Cf. the paragraph beginning at the bottom of p. 154 in 'Reference and Modality' [Essay I, above, p. 30].

we no longer have any reason to assert (e) (so construed)—that is, it is just obviously *true* that

$(\exists x)(x$ is the number of planets   & $\square(x > 7))$.

Thus Quine's 'paradox' for quantified modal logic is avoided.

I think we *do* have reason to assert (e′)—for (e′) is a denial of an instance of essentialism. And thus, any serious objections to essentialism (see Sections v and vi) will carry over to Smullyan's 'way out'.

But, contrary to claims by Quine,[21] there is *another* escape from the paradox, and one which avoids essentialism altogether. Consider both the essentialist and nonessentialist construals of (d) and (e) (where 'Px' stands for 'x, is the number of planets'):

(d′) $(\exists x)(\exists y)(x$ is nine   & y is seven   & $\square x > y)$
(d″) $\square(\exists x)(\exists y)(x$ is nine   & y is seven   & $x > y)$
(e′) $-(\exists x)(\exists y)(Px$ & y is seven   & $\square x > y)$
(e″) $-\square(\exists x)(\exists y)(Px$ & y is seven   & $x > y)$.

Maintaining a nonessentialist line, we can deny (d′), while accepting (d″), (e′), and (e″). The 'paradox' now has two construals, both of which are non-paradoxical. When construed as having (d′) and (e′) as premises, it simply has a false premise. On the other hand, when construed as having (d″) and (e″) as premises, no contradiction follows—for the familiar reason that interchanging contingently co-extensive predicates within modal contexts does not guarantee a preservation of truth value.

Thus there is an alternative to Smullyan's solution—an alternative which is consistent with nonessentialism, as Smullyan's is not. (This solution, again in distinction to Smullyan's, does not depend on a distinction between genuinely proper names and [overt and covert] descriptions; cf. Quine's discussion, footnote 20.)

What about analyticity? Well, Theorem 2 also shows that we can extend the interpretation of '$\square$' to something like 'analytically true' in Quine's sense,[22] just provided that we do so by taking as axioms only synonymy relations which are closed non-modal sentences.

Thus even when '$\square$' is extended so as to include arithmetical and non-logical analytic truths, commitment to essentialism in both senses (*i*) and (*ii*) can be avoided.

---

[21] The specific claim to which I take issue is '*The only hope lies in* accepting the situation illustrated by (32) and (33) and *insisting*, despite it, *that the object x in question is necessarily greater than* 7.' (Italics mine.) From p. 135, 'Reference and Modality' (I, above, p. 30].

[22] 'Two Dogmas of Empiricism', p. 22.

v. THE INDEPENDENCE OF *DE DICTO* AND
DE RE MODALITIES

What is the relation between *de dicto* and *de re* modalities?[23]

Since essential sentences are paradigm cases of *de re* modalities, we have a partial answer to that question in the last section: some *de re* modalities (namely, all essential sentences) are not entailed by some *de dicto* modalities (namely, those which lack constants and which lack internal *de re* modalities). A converse result also holds; certain sorts of essential sentences do not entail any *de dicto* modalities of a certain sort.

Let us call a sentence S a *simple essential sentence* if S is an essential sentence—that is, of the form:

$$(\exists x_1)...(\exists x_n)(\pi_n x_n \quad \& \quad \Box F) \quad \& \quad (\exists x_1)...(\exists x_n)(\pi_n x_n \quad \& \quad -\Box F)$$

where F is non-modal, quantifier-free, and neither tautologous nor contradictory.

Let R be any non-modal closed sentence such that $\Box R$ is not already provable in our system. Then we can show:

Theorem 3: $\Box R$ is not entailed by any simple essential sentence.[24]

That is, accepting certain essential sentences (the *simple* ones) cannot force us to accept new *de dicto* modalities of the sort indicated.

Theorems 2 and 3 provide a partial independence of *de dicto* and *de re* modalities. A complete independence of *de dicto* and *de re* modalities is prevented by trivial counterexamples; for example, the essential sentence:

$$(\exists x)\Box(Fx \quad \& \quad G) \quad \& \quad (\exists x)-\Box(Fx \quad \& \quad G)$$

where G is closed and nonessential, entails the nonessential *de dicto* sentence:

$$\Box G;$$

Conversely, the nonessential *de dicto* sentence:

$$-\Box G$$

entails the *de re* sentence:

$$-[(\exists x)\Box(Fx \quad \& \quad G) \quad \& \quad (\exists x)-\Box(Fx \quad \& \quad G)].$$

---

[23] I take a *de re* sentence to be one in which quantifiers outside of a modal context bind variables within. A *de dicto* sentence is a sentence without individual constants which is not *de re*. The classification of sentences which contain individual constants within modal contexts depends on the logical behaviour of the constants.

[24] T. Parsons, xeroxed, Chicago Circle, June, 1967.

These logical interrelations are of a trivial kind, however. I think there is an important sense in which essential and non-essential (or *de dicto* and *de re*) sentences are logically independent. This independence is partially formulated by Theorems 2 and 3; a fuller formulation of this independence (one which clearly distinguished the 'trivial' from the 'non-trivial' cases) would be desirable.[25]

VI. THE STATUS OF ESSENTIALISM; COMMITMENT IN SENSE (*iii*)

Given the logical independence of essential and nonessential sentences (as qualified above), we are now in a position to evaluate the status of essentialism—the view that some instances of schema (3) are true. I think two things begin to emerge. One is that if there are to be objections to essentialism, they cannot be made on the basis of claims that any essential sentence must deny facts which we normally regard as well established. Epistemologically, it seems that ordinary contingent truths, together (possibly) with certain nonessential *de dicto* truths, are basic; these are the truths for which we have evidence in the straightforward sense. And one thing that has been shown is that essentialism does not contradict *these*. Thus, I suggest that this general doctrine of essentialism is not the kind of doctrine for which (or against which) we can collect empirical evidence (or *one* sort of logical evidence; but see below).

The same logical independence, however, which frees essentialism from one kind of objection (an objection to its *truth*) opens the door to another: the claim that the truth-conditions of essential sentences are so indeterminate as to leave them devoid of any significance.

The consequence for quantified modal logic is this: although a system of quantified modal logic can assert, deny, or be neutral with respect to the *truth* of essentialism, it cannot be neutral concerning the *meaningfulness* of essentialism, for quantified modal logic simply *is* that symbolism within which essential sentences are formulable. Thus, in order to guarantee that all of its formulas are meaningful, any system of quantified modal logic must provide a meaning for each essential sentence. In short, quantified modal logic *is* committed, in the third sense, to essentialism—it is committed to the meaningfulness of essential sentences. But how bad is this?

Here is where prior discussion of the first two sorts of commitment is relevant. Suppose that a modal logician believes that essentialism is

---

[25] Theorems 2 and 3 are by no means maximal; that is, neither exhausts the categories of essential and nonessential sentences which fail to entail one another, nor the categories of *de dicto* and *de re* sentences which fail to entail one another.

true—that is, that some essential sentences are true. He must then face the problem of providing such sentences with a clear meaning. And although it is by no means obvious that this cannot be done in a clear and natural way, it is obvious that this is a *problem*, and that it is a problem *added on to* the problem of giving truth-conditions for nonessential sentences.

Suppose, however, that the modal logician disbelieves all essential sentences. He then has a simple method of assigning determinate (and natural) truth-conditions to all essential sentences. That is to make them all false in all possible worlds. In other words, freedom of commitment to essentialism in the first two senses *allows* a freedom of any *objectionable* commitment in the third sense.

Further, making essential sentences false in all possible worlds is not an *ad hoc* device adopted merely to avoid Quinean criticisms; it has an independent and natural motivation. As we mentioned earlier (Section II), it seems natural to locate the source of necessities in the logical character of predicates (on a conventionalist view) or properties (on a 'naturalist' view), *rather* than in the objects of which these are predicated. Yet essential sentences cannot be verified on such a view. So far Quine and I are in agreement. But while Quine wishes to infer from this that essential sentences are somehow deficient in meaning, it seems equally natural to conclude simply that they are false (and false 'for semantical reasons', and thus necessarily false).

In summary, there are an easy way and a hard way to free modal logic from any objectionable kind of commitment to essentialism. The easy way is to add the negation of schema (3) to the axioms for quantified modal logic—that is, to accept as *logically true* the schema:

(4) $(\exists x_1)...(\exists x_n)(\pi_n x_n \quad \& \quad \Box F) \supset (x_1)...(x_n)(\pi_n x_n \supset \Box F)$.

The hard way is to provide and justify some *other* truth-conditions for essential sentences. One or the other of these ways must be chosen, in order for a system of quantified modal logic to be unobjectionable.[26]

---

[26] There is a stronger kind of essentialism than the one I have discussed in this paper. Instead of just requiring that an object have a property necessarily which other objects do not have necessarily, it requires that an object have a property necessarily which other objects *have*, although not necessarily. In symbols, it is given by the schema:

(3') $(\exists x_1)...(\exists x_n)(\pi_n x_n \quad \& \quad \Box F) \quad \&$
$(\exists x_1)...(\exists x_n)(\pi_n x_n \quad \& \quad F \quad \& \quad -\Box F)$

Theorems 1 and 2 hold for (3') as well as for (3); further, determining truth-conditions for essentialism of kind (3) would also determine truth-conditions for essentialism of kind (3'), so the formulability of (3') in quantified modal logic adds no new problems.

APPENDIX A[27]

We define a *model structure* as a triple $\langle G, K, R \rangle$ together with a function, ψ, where K is a set (the set of 'possible worlds'), R a reflexive relation on K, G (the 'actual world') a member of K, and $\psi(H)$ a set for each $H \in K$. Intuitively, $\psi(H)$ represents the set of things which exist in world H. Now let $U = \cup_{H \, \varepsilon \, K} \, \psi(H)$, and let U^n be the nth Cartesian product of U with itself.

A *model* on a model structure $\langle G, K, R \rangle$ is a binary function $\phi(P^n, H)$, where the first variable ranges over n-adic predicate letters, H ranges over members of K, and $\phi(P^n, H) \subseteq U^n$. For the identity predicate, '=', we add the condition that $\phi(=, H) = \{\langle u, u \rangle : u \in U\}$ for every $H \in K$. We now extend ϕ to give a truth value for each formula A in each world H, relative to a given assignment of members of U to the free variables of A:

(*i*) For atomic A:

$\phi(P^n(x_1, \ldots, x_n), H) = T$ with respect to an assignment of $u_1, \ldots, u_n$ to $x_1, \ldots, x_n$ if and only if $\langle u_1, \ldots, u_n \rangle \in \phi(P^n, H)$.

(*ii*) $\phi(-A(x_1, \ldots, x_n), H) = T$ with respect to an assignment of $u_1, \ldots, u_n$ to $x_1, \ldots, x_n$ if and only if $\phi(A(x_1, \ldots, x_n), H) \neq T$ with respect to that assignment.

(*iii*) $\phi(A(x_1, \ldots, x_n)$ & $B(y_1, \ldots, y_m), H) = T$ with respect to an assignment of $u_1, \ldots, u_n$ to $x_1, \ldots, x_n$, and of $v_1, \ldots, v_m$ to $y_1, \ldots, y_m$ if and only if both $\phi(A(x_1, \ldots, x_n), H) = T$ and $\phi(B(y_1, \ldots, y_m), H) = T$ with respect to that assignment.

(*iv*) $\phi((\exists x)A(x, y_1, \ldots, y_n), H) = T$ with respect to an assignment of $u_1, \ldots, u_n$ to $y_1, \ldots, y_n$ if and only if there is some $u \in \psi(H)$ such that $\phi(A(x, y_1, \ldots, y_n), H) = T$ with respect to an assignment of $u, u_1, \ldots, u_n$ to $x, y_1, \ldots, y_n$.

(*v*) $\phi(\Box A(x_1, \ldots, x_n), H) = T$ with respect to a given assignment if and only if $\phi(A(x_1, \ldots, x_n), H') = T$ with respect to that assignment, for every H' such that HRH'.

The informal terminology used earlier can now be made precise: a closed sentence S is true in a given possible world H in the model ϕ on $\langle G, K, R \rangle$ just in case $\phi(S, H) = T$. A sentence S is a theorem of this system of modal logic just in case $\phi(S, H) = T$ for every world H in every model ϕ on every model structure $\langle G, K, R \rangle$.

---

[27] The following is a paraphrase of portions of pp. 84–7 of Kripke, op. cit. [Essay V above, pp. 64–67].

We are now in a position to define the sort of model referred to above as a 'maximal model':

We call ϕ a maximal model if ϕ is a model on a quantificational model structure $\langle G, K, R \rangle$ such that:

(i) $R = K \times K^{28}$

(ii) $U = \cup_{H \varepsilon K} \psi(H)$ and $U \neq O$

(iii) For every function χ which maps the predicate symbols P^n of the language onto subsets of U^n, and for every subset U^* of U, there is an $H \in K$ such that $\psi(H) = U^*$ and such that $\phi(P^n, H) = \chi(P^n)$ for all P^n of the language other than $=$.

(iv) If $\psi(H_1) = \psi(H_2)$ and $\phi(P^n, H_1) = \phi(P^n, H_2)$ for all P^n of the language, then $H_1 = H_2$.

(Note: clause [iv] is added merely for technical reasons.) It is easy to verify that there are maximal models, and that the actual world is represented in each. The following theorem can be proved by straightforward model-theoretic reasoning:

Theorem 1: Every essential sentence is false in every world in every maximal model.[29]

APPENDIX B

Suppose ϕ is a maximal model on $\langle G, K, R \rangle$, and suppose that Δ is a consistent set of closed formulas with no modal operators (Δ is our set of axioms). Let K^Δ be the set of $H \in K$ such that $\phi(\Gamma, H) = T$ for every $\Gamma \in \Delta$. And let ϕ^Δ be the result of restricting ϕ to K^Δ. Then:

Theorem 2: Every essential sentence is false in every world in ϕ^Δ.[30]

[28] This clause requires that a maximal model be a model on an S_5 model structure. However, any S_5 model structure is also an S_4, Br-, and an M-model structure, so both of our conclusions, (i) that no essential sentence is a theorem, and (ii) that no essential sentence is entailed by any consistent set of non-modal sentences, carry over to these other systems automatically.

[29] T. Parsons, xeroxed, Chicago Circle, May, 1967. A similar theorem for a language including constants is given in T. Parsons, *The Elimination of Individual Concepts* (Stanford: Ph.D. Dissertation, 1966), p. 193.

[30] T. Parsons, xeroxed, Chicago Circle, May, 1967.

VII

REFERENCE, ESSENTIALISM, AND MODALITY

Leonard Linsky

I

GIVEN the truth of 'Socrates is the teacher of Plato' and 'The teacher of Plato is the husband of Xantippe', the *principle of substitutivity* yields the truth of 'Socrates is the husband of Xantippe'. The principle states that '*given a true statement of identity, one of its two terms may be substituted for the other in any true statement and the result will be true*,'[1] or, equivalently, '*two terms of a true identity statement are everywhere intersubstitutive, salva veritate*'. This is different from the principle formulated in *Principia Mathematica*[2] which identifies identity with indiscernibility as follows:

(1) $(x = y) = {}_{df}(\varphi)(\varphi x \equiv \varphi y)$

Wittgenstein, in the *Tractatus*, objects to this equation of identity with indiscernibility. The objection is that 'Russell's definition of "=" is inadequate, because according to it we cannot say that two objects have all their properties in common. (Even if this proposition is never correct, it still has sense).'[3] (1) says not only that if x and y are identical, they share all their properties; it provides for the converse as well: that objects cannot, in Leibniz's phrase, differ *solo numero*. Wittgenstein's objection is to *this* implication of Russell's definition. The idea of objects' differing only numerically has been introduced solely that it may be set aside. It is not at issue in the *principle of the indiscernibility of identicals*, which states that identical objects do not differ qualitatively. One may agree with Wittgenstein that qualitative identity does not entail numerical identity, but one cannot coherently think that numerical identity does not entail the qualitative sort.

From *Journal of Philosophy* LXVI, 20 (1969), 687–700. Reprinted by permission of the author and the *Journal of Philosophy*.

[1] W. Quine, 'Reference and Modality', in *From A Logical Point of View* (Cambridge, Mass.: Harvard University Press, 1961), p. 139 [Essay I, above, p. 17]. Parenthetical page references to Quine will be to this essay, 1961 edition, and to the present volume.

[2] See *13.01 (Cambridge: University Press, 2nd edn., 1925), p. 169. A complication in the definition deriving from the ramified theory of types is here ignored.

[3] *Tractatus Logico-Philosophicus*, D. F. Pears and B. F. McGuinness, trans. (London: Routledge & Kegan Paul; New York: Humanities, 1961), 5.5302, p. 105.

The principle of substitutivity appears to be merely a formal-mode version of the indiscernibility of identicals, but it lacks the self-evidence of the latter; its justification turns on semantical considerations. Logic teaches us to analyse statements as arising from predicates by binding of their free variables or by replacement of these by singular terms. Predicates are expressions that are true of certain objects and false of others. For example, a true statement results from the predicate 'x is a Greek' when some name, or other designation, for some object of which the predicate is true replaces the variable 'x'.

Given this semantical analysis, together with some further details, we see why the principle of substitutivity has been accepted; for that the terms of a true identity statement are everywhere inter-substitutive, *salva veritate*, is merely explicative of the idea of singular terms' having singular reference. The reasoning is as follows. By replacing, with an appropriate variable, any singular term in one or more of its occurrences in each statement containing at least one singular term, we construct a class of (one-place) predicates. Any singular term thus replaced in a true statement refers to an object that satisfies the predicate thus constructed. An object satisfies such a predicate only if (but not if) replacing the predicate's free variable by *any* singular term making reference to the object turns the predicate into a true statement. (The converse of this conditional is not correct because it is not assumed that every object in our domain of discourse is designated by some term. The conditional itself holds for all objects in the domain, albeit vacuously of those without designations.) Consequently, the result of replacing a singular term in a true statement by any other singular term referring to the same object leaves the truth value of the host statement unchanged. Terms of a true identity statement refer to the same thing. And with this we have a proof of the principle of substitutivity.

II

The principle of substitutivity is explicative of the concept of singular reference; so is it also of the idea of quantification. '$(\exists x)F(x)$' is true if and only if there is at least one object in the domain of discourse that satisfies the open sentence '$F(x)$'. If it be granted that '$F(a)$' is true (where 'a' is a singular term) and that it remains true under substitution of co-referential terms for 'a', then, by the semantical account already given, we have our satisfying object in a. Consequently, '$(\exists x)F(x)$' is also true. The inference by existential generalization is justified because in performing it we are merely abstracting from the particular mode of designating an object in a true statement where *no particular* mode of designation is relevant to the truth of that statement. Failure of the inference from '$F(a)$' to '$(\exists x)F(x)$' occurs if and only if 'a' fails of singular reference in '$F(a)$'. For example, the inference from 'Pegasus does not exist' to '$(\exists x)(x$ does not exist)' fails because nothing satisfies the open sentence 'x does not exist'. Failure of substitutivity for a term in a given context entails failure of reference for that term in that context. For this reason, by the present argument, it entails failure of existential generalization on that term as well. Contexts productive of failure of substitutivity are for this reason called by Quine 'referentially opaque'. Our argument shows that we cannot sensibly quantify into referentially opaque contexts.

III

The principle of substitutivity has now come to be seen as an integral part of the semantics of classical quantification theory. From the vantage point of this semantical account we are left with no choice about what we are to make of the notorious purported counter-examples to the principle. It is a true contingent statement that

(2) 9 = the number of the planets

It is further true that

(3) N(9 > 7)

But replacement of '9' in (3) by 'the number of the planets' in virtue of (2) yields

(4) N(the number of the planets > 7)

which is false. Since the principle of substitutivity is analytic of the idea of singular reference, we are left with no alternative but to conclude that '9' in '$N(9 > 7)$' does not make singular reference to 9. We cannot, on our semantics, make the view coherent that '9' refers to the object 9 in (3), in view of the truth of (2) and (3) and the falsity of (4). This is Quine's view of the matter (pp. 139–44) [pp. 17–22 above]. He distinguishes between purely referential and non-purely referential occurrences of singular terms. Failure of substitutivity for a term in a given occurrence is merely symptomatic of the term's failure to perform its purely referential function in that occurrence. Quine leaves us to suppose that, in some unexplained fashion, such terms in such occurrences still manage to refer, only non-purely. But this part of the theory is never developed.

Referential opacity poses a problem because our semantics is inapplicable to opaque contexts. '$N(9 > 7)$' does not, on analysis, yield a predicate '$N(x > 7)$' from which it results by replacement of 'x' by '9'. '$N(x > 7)$'

cannot, coherently, be taken as a predicate; for, given a predicate and an object for which it is defined, either the predicate is true or it is false of that object. Is our purported predicate true of the object 9? Since the number of the planets *is* 9, an affirmative answer is incompatible with the falsity of (4), and a negative answer is incompatible with the truth of (3). Thus, '$N(x > 7)$' is not a predicate at all. But if the numeral '9' does not name a subject of predicates in '$N(9 > 7)$', what role is it performing there? Our inability to answer this question reveals that we do not know the logical form of such statements.

IV

We have assumed that, if '9' names a subject of predicates in '$N(9 > 7)$', what it names is 9. By abandoning the assumption that in opaque contexts names stand for their ordinary references, Frege was able to provide an analysis that did not take these contexts as productive of reference failure.[4] From a Fregean point of view, such contexts are incorrectly characterized as 'referentially opaque'. For Frege, they are producers of reference shift rather than reference failure, and he calls them 'oblique'. The references of names in oblique contexts are what, in ordinary contexts, are their senses. For Frege, it is false that '9' in (2) and '9' in (3) have the same reference; there is a fallacy of ambiguity in passing from (2) and (3) to (4). So, for Frege, there is no such thing as referential opacity, where the criterion for this is failure of substitutivity. In (2), '9' has the same reference as 'the number of the planets' but a different sense. This sense is the (oblique) reference of '9' in (3).

In an early paper,[5] Quine exploits a distinction between *meaning* and *designation* which is very like Frege's between sense and reference. It we pursue the similarity and adopt, for Quine's pair of concepts, the Fregean principle that in oblique contexts the designations of names are their meanings, we have a proof at hand that there are no opaque contexts. On our Fregean assumption, the principle of substitutivity allows replacement of names in oblique contexts only by synonymous names; and reference now is taken as context-relative. Hence the principle of substitutivity is recast so as to affirm the replaceability of any term in a given context by any other term having the same reference as the first *in that context*.

---

[4] 'Sense and Reference', in M. Black and P. Geach, eds., *Translations from the Philosophical Writings of Gottlob Frege* (Oxford: Blackwell, 1952), pp. 56–78. Frege never discusses alethic modality in this connection. What is presented here is therefore an application to these cases.

[5] 'Notes on Existence and Necessity', in my anthology *Semantics and the Philosophy of Language* (Urbana: Illinois Univ. Press, 1952), pp. 83–4.

Since we cannot change the meaning of a statement, ordinary or oblique, by replacing any of its constituents by a synonym, such substitution cannot change truth values. If, with Quine, we take failure of substitutivity as a criterion of referential opacity (p. 140, fn.) [p. 18 n. above], there are no longer any referentially opaque contexts. By shifting the domain of discourse, we retain our semantics, and the old analysis continues its applicability to the misnamed opaque contexts.

V

If we assume, with Frege, that the reference of a complex name is a function of the references of its constituent names and that the reference of a (declarative) sentence is its truth value, we have a proof that 'N(9 > 7)' remains true under every replacement of '9' by a name having the same ordinary sense as '9', provided that '9' is assumed to name that sense in that sentence. Under this last assumption, 'N($x > 7$)' may be treated as a predicate true of this sense. Failure of substitutivity in oblique contexts reveals that the relevant names differ in their ordinary senses. To defend his thesis that numbers are objects, Frege thought it necessary to provide a sense for statements of identity between numbers, and between numbers and other objects.[6] If, now, we take senses to be objects, we must also provide them with identity conditions. It is somewhat surprising that Frege himself made no attempt to do this. Lacking an independent identity condition for senses, the principle that coreferential terms are everywhere intersubstitutive tells us only that names may replace each other, *salva veritate*, wherever they can. Senses as *objects* become idle wheels turning nothing. In Quine's phrase, 'No entity without identity.'[7]

But, far from paving the way for the happy marriage of quantification and modality, Frege's theory of reference makes the union inevitably barren. On Frege's view, what can we make of statements in which names appear both inside and outside the scope of opacity-inducing operators? Consider

(5) 9 is greater than 7, and necessarily 9 is greater than 7.

According to Frege, the object here said to be greater than 7 is not the same as the object said to be necessarily greater than 7. But this is not what is intended in (5). (5) is intended as synonymous with

(6) 9 is greater than 7, and necessarily it is greater than 7.

<hr />

[6] *Foundations of Arithmetic*, J. L. Austin, trans. (Oxford: Blackwell, 1959), p. 73.

[7] Cited by Charles Parsons in 'Frege's Theory of Number', in *Philosophy in America*, ed. Max Black (Ithaca, N.Y.: Cornell, 1965), p. 182.

The difficulty is that, for Frege, (6) must be sheer nonsense because the pronoun 'it' inside the scope of the modal operator cannot pick up the reference of the numeral '9' outside the scope of that operator. If the pronoun did pick up the reference of the numeral, it would refer to the object 9 rather than a sense, and this Frege denies. Pronouns being the equivalents of bound variables in ordinary language, we see that Frege's theory is incapable of reflecting the interplay between occurrences of terms both inside and outside the scopes of modal operators that statements of modality are ordinarily taken to express.

VI

The rationale behind the recourse to intensions as values for the variables of quantified modal logic was the consideration that intensions have the right sort of names for their job. Names for intensions were supposed to satisfy the condition that any two of them naming the same intension would be terms of a necessarily true statement of identity. A modal logic that confines its domain of discourse to intensions would thus be free of referentially opaque contexts.

Intensions, with the obscurity of their identity conditions, may be, as Quine says, 'creatures of darkness'. But if the above-stated condition on their names is taken as analytic of them, it can be shown that they do not exist at all. The argument is Quine's: 'For, where A is any intensional object, say an attribute, and 'p' stands for an arbitrarily true sentence, clearly,

$$(35) \quad A = (\imath x)[p \, . \, (x = A)].$$

Yet, if the true statement represented by "p" is not analytic, then neither is (35), and its sides are no more interchangeable in modal contexts than are "Evening Star" and "Morning Star", or "9" and "the number of the planets"' (152–3 [pp. 28 above]; Quine's numbering). Objection might arise to this argument on the Russellian grounds that Quine's (35) is not an identity statement since it contains a definite description. One might maintain that Quine has given an overly liberal interpretation to the condition on designations for intensions. It is not required that *any* designations for the same intension be terms of a necessarily true identity statement; this is required only of proper names. One might argue even more radically that all of Quine's difficulties in interpreting modal logic, together with the recourse to intensions, could have been avoided by scrupulous attention to the distinction between proper names and definite descriptions together with the scope distinctions attendant upon the latter. We turn now to consideration of this view.

VII

The view was first put forth by A. F. Smullyan.[8] According to Smullyan, sentence (3) is unambiguous, it is analysed simply as $N(F(y))$; and the identity premise (2) has the form $y = (\imath x)(\varphi x)$. But the conclusion (4) is ambiguous, for it can be understood as according the description a primary occurrence, i.e. as being of the form

(7) $[(\imath x)(\varphi x)]N\{F(\imath x)(\varphi x)\}$

or (4) can be understood as according the description a secondary occurrence, i.e., as being of the form

(8) $N\{[(\imath x)(\varphi x)]F(\imath x)(\varphi x)\}$

The distinction is the same as that between as assertion of the form

(9) The so-and-so satisfies the condition that it is necessary that $F(x)$

and an assertion of the form

(10) It is necessary that the so-and-so satisfied the condition that $F(x)$

Here is Smullyan's illustration of the difference. 'I will ask the reader to believe that James is now thinking of the number 3. If, now, someone were to remark "there is one and only one integer which James is now thinking of and that integer is necessarily odd", then he would be stating a contingent truth. For that there is just one integer James now thinks of, is only an empirical fact. This fact could just as well be expressed in the form (9) "The integer, which James is now thinking of, satisfies the condition that it is necessarily odd." In contrast, the statement, "It is necessary that James's integer is odd", which is of the form (10), is an impossible statement and not a contingent one. If not necessary then necessarily not necessary: at least, so we assume.'[9]

Quine's mistake, according to Smullyan, is to ignore the ambiguity of (4). Quine assumes it to be of the form (8), for he assumes that (4) is false. But understood as exemplifying the form (8), (4) does not follow from the premises. Understood as being of the form (7), (4) does follow by substitutivity; and there is no paradox in this, for, thus understood, (4) is true. But is this last contention as clearly true as Smullyan thinks it to be? When the description is eliminated, (7) becomes

(11) $(\exists c)(x)\{(\varphi x \equiv x = c)$　&　$N(Fc)\}$

[8] 'Modality and Description', *Journal of Symbolic Logic*, 13. 1 (March 1948), 31–7 [Essay II, above].

[9] Ibid., p. 31. I have inserted my own numbering here to maintain conformity with earlier text. [See p. 35 above.]

Smullyan totally by-passes the problem of making sense of such constructions as this. Has Quine not shown that the attempt to bind a variable in a
referentially opaque context by a quantifier outside the context produces
nonsense? According to Quine, (11) is nonsense, so it cannot represent a
possible sense of (4). Thus Smullyan's argument from ambiguity is des-
troyed. Friends of Smullyan's viewpoint will be quick to answer that
Quine's *argument* for the unintelligibility of constructions such as (11)
rests on the fallacy of ambiguity exposed by Smullyan. Quine's argument
against quantifying into modal contexts assumes the unintelligibility
of such constructions as (11), so it begs the question. Smullyan's argument
against Quine assumes the intelligibility of these quantifications, but no
attempt is made to explain them. Thus it is apparent that what is required
in order to defeat Quine's *challenge* (not *argument*) is a clear semantics for
quantified modal logic.

VIII

In view of the total eliminability of singular terms, it is of importance
for Quine that the difficulties connected with quantification into modal
contexts can be demonstrated without appeal to the irregular behaviour
of such terms in such contexts. Quine tries to do this as follows: 'Whatever is greater than 7 is a number, and any given number x greater than
7 can be uniquely determined by any of various conditions, some of which
have "$x > 7$" as a *necessary* consequence and some of which do not.
One and the same number x is uniquely determined by the condition:

(32) $x = \sqrt{x} + \sqrt{x} + \sqrt{x} \neq \sqrt{x}$

and by the condition:

(33) There are exactly x planets,

but (32) has "$x > 7$" as a necessary consequence while (33) does not.
Necessary greaterness than 7 makes no sense as applied to a *number*
x; necessity attaches only to the connection between "$x > 7$" and the
particular method (32), as opposed to (33), of specifying x' (149 [p. 25
above]; original numbering of the formulas).

Quine's view seems to be that we can make tolerable sense of modal
statements, so long as we interpret them relative to particular modes of
designating the objects referred to in them. Thus (3) is true of the object 9
relative to its specification by '9', but (4), though it attributes the same
property to that object, is false relative to the specification of 9 as 'the
number of the planets'. The attempt to attribute necessary properties to

objects *an sich* aborts into nonsense. But quantification, ordinarily understood, *abstracts* from the mode in which objects are designated.[10] '$(\exists x)F(x)$' is true or false according to whether or not at least one object satisfies the open sentence following the quantifier; but whether or not an object satisfies an open sentence is quite independent of how we refer to it, or even whether we have the means of referring to it at all. Thus, there is a fundamental conflict between modality and quantification.

The only (dim) hope for modal logic, Quine thinks, lies in a reversion to 'Aristotelian essentialism'. He explains, 'This means adopting an invidious attitude toward certain ways of uniquely specifying x, for example (33), and favouring other ways, for example (32), as somehow better revealing the 'essence' of the object. Consequences of (32) can, from such a point of view be looked upon as necessarily true of the object which is 9 (and is the number of the planets), while some consequences of (33) are rated still only contingently true of that object' (155) [p. 30 above].[11] What is required of 'Aristotelian essentialism' is that, despite examples like (3) and (4), it provide a sense for the idea of an object, *an sich* and by any name (or none), having some of its properties necessarily and some contingently regardless of the fact that the former properties follow analytically for that object from certain modes of specifying it just as the latter properties do from other modes of specification. Quantification, in modal logic, must receive an interpretation that abstracts from the ways in which the values of variables are designated, on pain of not really being quantification at all.

IX

Ruth Barcan Marcus proposes to avoid Quine's difficulties by interpreting quantification substitutionally rather than ontologically with Quine.[12] She sees nothing problematic in the passage, by existential generalization, from

(12) N(the evening star = the evening star)

to

(13) $(\exists x)$N(x = the evening star)

for what the latter means, for her, is merely that there is a substitution instance of 'N(x = the evening star)' which is true; (12) itself provides

---

[10] I owe this formulation to my student, Mr. John Tienson.
[11] The numbers refer to the expressions of the last quotation from Quine.
[12] 'Modalities and Intensional Languages', *Synthese*, 27 (1962), reprinted in I. M. Copi and J. A. Gould, eds., *Contemporary Readings in Logical Theory* (New York: Macmillan, 1967); see especially pp. 287–9.

the required instance. For her, it does not matter that 'N (the morning star = the evening star)' is false in spite of the identity of the evening star and the morning star; for it is not claimed in (13) that *more* than one substitution instance of the quantified matrix is true. Presumably, Mrs. Marcus interprets universal quantifications as asserting the truth of all substitution instances of the relevant matrices.

Quine's objection to this substitutional interpretation is that 'it abstracts from reference altogether. Quantification ordinarily so-called is purely and simply the logical idiom of objective reference. When we reconstrue it in terms of substituted expressions rather than real values, we waive reference.'[13] But there is a difficulty about this. For Quine, the variables of quantification are the sole channel of extralinguistic references, because he invisages the total elimination of the singular terms that usually share this burden. But, of course, we cannot *both* eliminate singular terms and reinterpret quantification substitutionally, for then all universal quantifications would be true and all existential quantifications false merely for the lack of any substitution instances of open sentences at all. But it we retain singular terms in order to provide substitution instances, they will *a fortiori* provide for extralinguistic reference as well.[14]

How much real comfort can the friends of modal logic hope for from the reinterpretation of quantification? It does get them out of the fire, perhaps, but only to land them in the frying pan. Quantifications such as (13) are, according to the substitutional view, no more problematic than their unquantified sources such as (12); and they are no *less* problematic either. The positions occupied by 'the evening star' in (12) are 'referentially opaque'. To say that is to say they lack a certain logical form, but it is not to say what their logical form is. Mrs. Marcus follows the line of Smullyan and Fitch[15] in her treatment of definite descriptions in modal settings, so if we follow her here we will be led to the conclusion already reached. The success of the treatment of the puzzle about the morning star and the evening star and its ilk along this line is predicated upon a clear semantics for quantified modal logic.

X

From different directions, our considerations converge upon the conclusion that these various claims and counterclaims can be properly

[13] 'Reply to Mrs. Marcus', *Synthèse*, 27 (1962), in Copi and Gould, op. cit., p. 298.

[14] A precise account of this interpretation of quantification is to be found in J. M. Dunn and N. D. Belnap 'The Substitution Interpretation of Quantification', *Nous*, II.2 (May 1968), 177–85.

[15] Cf. 'The Problem of the Morning Star and the Evening Star', in Copi and Gould, op. cit., pp. 273–8.

assessed only within the framework of a clear semantics. In recent years, impressive attempts by Jaakko Hintikka,[16] Stig Kanger,[17] Saul Kripke,[18] Richard Montague,[19] and others, have been made to fill this need. In what follows, familiarity is presupposed with Kripke's 'Semantical Considerations on Modal Logic'[18] as perhaps the most widely known representative of this group. We begin with an illustration of Kripke's semantics. Consider a model structure $\langle G, K, R \rangle$, where $K = \{G, H\}$, $G \neq H$, and $R = K^2$. We obtain a quantificational model structure by defining $\psi(G) = \{a\}$, $\psi(H) = \{a, b\}$, where $a \neq b$. For a monadic predicate letter 'P', we define a model φ such that $\varphi(P, G) = \{a\}$, $\varphi(P, H) = \{a\}$. Then $\Box P(x)$ is true in G when x is assigned a; but, since a is the only element of $\psi(G)$, $(x) \Box P(x)$ is also true in G. When x is assigned b, $\varphi(P(x), H) = F$; consequently $(x)P(x)$ is false in H, and $\Box(x)P(x)$ is false in G as well. The Barcan formula is rejected.

Notice that $\Box P(x)$ is true in G when x is assigned a because $P(x)$ is true in both G and H under this assignment. Intuitively, this is to say that a falls under the extension of P in H and in G, i.e., in all possible worlds. Thus our intuitive interpretation of Kripke's semantics makes crucial use of the idea of one and the same individual existing in different possible worlds. If quantified modal logic is to be of interest, there must be a distinction between necessary properties, properties that an object has in all possible worlds, and contingent properties, which it has in some but not all possible worlds.

How then is an object to be identified *across* possible worlds? The problem arises because the properties of objects change from possible world to possible world. But not all of them change. It seems that we have no alternative but to fall back on some variety of essentialism; for if objects have essential properties they cannot lack them in any possible world in which those objects exist. Perhaps then, objects can be identified across possible worlds by some of their essential properties. Further, it is only by their essential properties, if at all, that such identifications can be made; for no matter how similar two objects in different possible worlds may be, we cannot conclude that they are identical if they differ in their essential properties at all. But not any necessary property will serve here, supposing that all necessary properties are essential. The essential properties needed for transworld identification must be individuating; i.e.,

---

[16] 'Modality and Quantification', *Theoria*, 27.2 (1961), 119–28.

[17] *Provability in Logic* (Stockholm: Almquist & Wiksell, 1957).

[18] 'Semantical Considerations on Modal Logic', *Acta Philosophica Fennica*, 16 (1963), 83–94. [See Essay V, above.]

[19] 'Logical Necessity, Physical Necessity, Ethics, and Quantifiers', *Inquiry*, III. 4 (1960), 259–69.

they must be properties an object has in all possible worlds in which it exists and which only that object has. But not all such properties will serve either; a property may be too individuating to be of help here. Every object a has the necessary property of being identical with itself, and no other object is identical with a. It is fatuous, however, to suppose that one can identify a across possible worlds by finding the object that is identical with a in each possible world; for our problem is how to do that.

The problem of how an object's essential properties can be made to yield a criterion of transworld identification is not a problem that we propose here to solve; nor was it part of Kripke's undertaking. It is not a logical problem but a metaphysical one. We can, however, fairly maintain that, in the absence of its solution, we lack a clear, explicit, intuitive, understanding of a semantics such as Kripke's. In this way, modal logic is committed to essentialism. Quine, of course, never posed the problem of essentialism in this way; his work on the topic antedates that of Kripke. Nevertheless, the work of Kripke and the others mentioned above has, in a sense, vindicated Quine's claim that modal logic is committed to essentialism; only in one sense, of course, for essentialism and commitment are, in this context, vague. Terence Parsons,[20] following Ruth Marcus,[21] has sought the essentialist commitments of modal logic elsewhere, among its theorems (valid sentences). He distinguishes between grades of essentialist involvement; vicious from benign essentialism, and he shows that the more vicious the essentialism the less the commitment; but again, he is concerned only with the *theorems* of modal logic. But we have no quarrel with him; for his findings are completely compatible with our own.

Having found a sense in which modal logic is committed to essentialism, need we accept Quine's conclusion: 'so much the worse for quantified modal logic' (156) [p. 31 above]? Having concluded that quantified modal logic entails essentialism, Quine rejects modal logic, because, for him, essentialism is a nonsensical metaphysical doctrine. But we must distinguish between the claim that we are unable to state a satisfactory explicit criterion for identifying individuals across possible worlds and the claim that we are unable to make sense of such identifications. The latter claim is not entailed by the former, and it is false. Further, it is not at all clear what a 'criterion' is supposed to be. Just so, our inability to articulate a clear, explicit, criterion (whatever exactly that is) for the reidentification of individuals through time in the actual world does not entail our inability to make such reidentifications successfully. And it is a

[20] 'Grades of Essentialism in Quantified Modal Logic', *Nous*, I.2 (May 1967), 181–91.
[21] 'Essentialism in Modal Logic', ibid., I.1 (March 1967), 91–6.

plain matter of fact that we do succeed in making reidentifications of
both kinds.

Suppose someone tells us 'I did not miss this morning's lecture, but I
might have'. The intelligibility to us of this statement depends upon our
ability to make sense of the idea that the subject of the statement is
identical with an individual in another possible world: one in which he
misses this morning's lecture. Indeed, the statements, 'I did not miss
this morning's lecture, but I might have' and 'I did not miss this morning's
lecture, but there is a possible world in which I did,' are full paraphrases of
each other. The latter statement explicitly identifies its subject with an
individual in another possible world; if this makes no sense to us, neither
does the former statement. But the former statement does make perfect
sense. To the extent that we understand such assertions we are able to
make sense of the idea of identical individuals in different possible worlds;
and we may exploit this understanding to give intuitive meaning to the
statements of quantified modal logic. So much the better for quantified
modal logic; for this is good enough for modal logicians to be going on
with.

VIII

QUANTIFIERS AND PROPOSITIONAL ATTITUDES[1]

W. V. O. QUINE

I

THE incorrectness of rendering 'Ctesias is hunting unicorns' in the fashion:

$(\exists x)(x$ is a unicorn. Ctesias is hunting $x)$

is conveniently attested by the non-existence of unicorns, but is not due simply to that zoological lacuna. It would be equally incorrect to render 'Ernest is hunting lions' as:

(1) $(\exists x)(x$ is a lion . Ernest is hunting $x)$,

where Ernest is a sportsman in Africa. The force of (1) is rather that there is some individual lion (or several) which Ernest is hunting; stray circus property, for example.

The contrast recurs in 'I want a sloop'. The version:

(2) $(\exists x)(x$ is a sloop . I want $x)$

is suitable in so far only as there may be said to be a certain sloop that I want. If what I seek is mere relief from slooplessness, then (2) gives the wrong idea.

The contrast is that between what may be called the *relational* sense of lion-hunting or sloop-wanting, viz. (1)–(2), and the likelier or *notional* sense. Appreciation of the difference is evinced in Latin and Romance languages by a distinction of mood in subordinate clauses; thus '*Procuro un perro que habla*' has the relational sense:

$(\exists x)(x$ is a dog . x talks . I seek $x)$

as against the notional '*Procuro un perro que hable*':

I strive that $(\exists x)(x$ is a dog . x talks . I find $x)$.

From *The Ways of Paradox*, by W. Quine (New York: Random House, 1966), pp. 183–94. Reprinted by permission of the author and the *Journal of Philosophy*.

[1] This paper appeared in the *Journal of Philosophy*, 53 (1956), summing up some points which I had made in lectures at Harvard and Oxford from 1952 onwards. It is reprinted here minus fifteen lines.

Pending considerations to the contrary in later pages, we may represent the contrast strikingly in terms of permutations of components. Thus (1) and (2) may be expanded (with some violence to both logic and grammar) as follows:

(3) $(\exists x)(x$ is a lion . Ernest strives that Ernest finds $x)$,

(4) $(\exists x)(x$ is a sloop . I wish that I have $x)$,

whereas 'Ernest is hunting lions' and 'I want a sloop' in their notional senses may be rendered rather thus:

(5) Ernest strives that $(\exists x)(x$ is a lion . Ernest finds $x)$,

(6) I wish that $(\exists x)(x$ is a sloop . I have $x)$.

The contrasting versions (3)–(6) have been wrought by so paraphrasing 'hunt' and 'want' as to uncover the locutions 'strive that' and 'wish that', expressive of what Russell has called *propositional attitudes*. Now of all examples of propositional attitudes, the first and foremost is *belief*; and, true to form, this example can be used to point up the contrast between relational and notional senses still better than (3)–(6) do. Consider the relational and notional senses of believing in spies.

(7) $(\exists x)($Ralph believes that x is a spy$)$,

(8) Ralph believes that $(\exists x)(x$ is a spy$)$.

Both may perhaps be ambiguously phrased as 'Ralph believes that someone is a spy', but they may be unambiguously phrased respectively as 'There is someone whom Ralph believes to be a spy' and 'Ralph believes there are spies'. The difference is vast; indeed, if Ralph is like most of us, (8) is true and (7) false.

In moving over to propositional attitudes, as we did in (3)–(6), we gain not only the graphic structural contrast between (3)–(4) and (5)–(6) but also a certain generality. For we can now multiply examples of striving and wishing, unrelated to hunting and wanting. Thus we get the relational and notional senses of wishing for a president:

(9) $(\exists x)($Witold wishes that x is president$)$,

(10) Witold wishes that $(\exists x)(x$ is president$)$.

According to (9), Witold has his candidate; according to (10) he merely wishes the appropriate form of government were in force. Also we open other propositional attitudes to similar consideration—as witness (7)–(8).

However, the suggested formulations of the relational senses—viz.

(3), (4), (7), and (9)—all involve quantifying into a propositional-attitude idiom from outside. This is a dubious business, as may be seen from the following example.

There is a certain man in a brown hat whom Ralph has glimpsed several times under questionable circumstances on which we need not enter here; suffice it to say that Ralph suspects he is a spy. Also there is a grey-haired man, vaguely known to Ralph as rather a pillar of the community, whom Ralph is not aware of having seen except once at the beach. Now Ralph does not know it, but the men are one and the same. Can we say of this *man* (Bernard J. Ortcutt, to give him a name) that Ralph believes him to be a spy? If so, we find ourselves accepting a conjunction of the type:

(11) w sincerely denies '. . .' . w believes that . . .

as true, with one and the same sentence in both blanks. For, Ralph is ready enough to say, in all sincerity, 'Bernard J. Ortcutt is no spy'. If, on the other hand, with a view to disallowing situations of the type (11), we rule simultaneously that

(12) Ralph believes that the man in the brown hat is a spy,

(13) Ralph does not believe that the man seen at the beach is a spy,

then we cease to affirm any relationship between Ralph and any man at all. Both of the component 'that'-clauses are indeed about the man Ortcutt; but the 'that' must be viewed in (12) and (13) as sealing those clauses off, thereby rendering (12) and (13) compatible because not, as wholes, about Ortcutt at all. It then becomes improper to quantify as in (7); 'believes that' becomes, in a word, referentially opaque.[2]

No question arises over (8); it exhibits only a quantification *within* the 'believes that' context, not a quantification *into* it. What goes by the board, when we rule (12) and (13) both true, is just (7). Yet we are scarcely prepared to sacrifice the relational construction 'There is someone whom Ralph believes to be a spy', which (7) as against (8) was supposed to reproduce.

The obvious next move is to try to make the best of our dilemma by distinguishing two senses of belief: *belief$_1$*, which disallows (11), and *belief$_2$*, which tolerates (11) but makes sense of (7). For belief$_1$, accordingly, we sustain (12)–(13) and ban (7) as nonsense. For belief$_2$, on the other hand, we sustain (7); and for *this* sense of belief we must reject (13) and acquiesce in the conclusion that Ralph believes$_2$ that the man at the beach is a

---

[2] See *From a Logical Point of View*, pp. 142–59 [pp. 19–34 above]; also 'Three grades of modal involvement', Essay 13, *The Ways of Paradox*.

spy even though he *also* believes$_2$ (and believes$_1$) that the man at the beach is not a spy.

II

But there is a more suggestive treatment. Beginning with a single sense of belief, viz., belief$_1$ above, let us think of this at first as a relation between the believer and a certain *intension*, named by the 'that'-clause. Intensions are creatures of darkness, and I shall rejoice with the reader when they are exorcised, but first I want to make certain points with the help of them. Now intensions named thus by 'that'-clauses, without free variables, I shall speak of more specifically as intensions of degree 0, or propositions. In addition I shall (for the moment) recognize intensions of degree 1, or attributes. These are to be named by prefixing a variable to a sentence in which it occurs free; thus z (z is a spy) is spyhood. Similarly we may specify intensions of higher degrees by prefixing multiple variables.

Now just as we have recognized a dyadic relation of belief between a believer and a proposition, thus:

(14) Ralph believes that Ortcutt is a spy,

so we may recognize also a triadic relation of belief among a believer, an object, and an attribute, thus:

(15) Ralph believes z(z is a spy) of Ortcutt.

For reasons which will appear, this is to be viewed not as dyadic belief between Ralph and the proposition *that* Ortcutt has z(z is a spy), but rather as an irreducibly triadic relation among the three things Ralph, z(z is a spy), and Ortcutt. Similarly there is tetradic belief:

(16) Tom believes yz(y denounced z) of Cicero and Catiline,

and so on.

Now we can clap on a hard and fast rule against quantifying into propositional-attitude idioms; but we give it the form now of a rule against quantifying into names of intensions. Thus, though (7) as it stands becomes unallowable, we can meet the needs which prompted (7) by quantifying rather into the triadic belief construction, thus:

(17) $(\exists x)$(Ralph believes z(z is a spy) of x).

Here then, in place of (7), is our new way of saying that there is someone whom Ralph believes to be a spy.

Belief$_1$ was belief so construed that a proposition might be believed when an object was specified in it in one way, and yet not believed when the same object was specified in another way; witness (12)–(13). Hereafter we can adhere uniformly to this narrow sense of belief, both for the dyadic case and for triadic and higher; in each case the term which names the intension (whether proposition or attribute or intension of higher degree) is to be looked on as referentially opaque.

The situation (11) is thus excluded. At the same time the effect of belief$_2$ can be gained, simply by ascending from dyadic to triadic belief as in (15). For (15) does relate the men Ralph and Ortcutt precisely as belief$_2$ was intended to do. (15) does remain true of Ortcutt under any designation; and hence the legitimacy of (17).

Similarly, whereas from:

Tom believes that Cicero denounced Catiline

we cannot conclude:

Tom believes that Tully denounced Catiline,

on the other hand we can conclude from:

Tom believes $y(y$ denounced Catiline) of Cicero

that

Tom believes $y(y$ denounced Catiline) of Tully,

and also that

(18) $(\exists x)$(Tom believes $y(y$ denounced Catiline) of x).

From (16), similarly, we may infer that

(19) $(\exists w)(\exists x)$(Tom believes $yz(y$ denounced z) of w and x).

Such quantifications as:

$(\exists x)$(Tom believes that x denounced Catiline),

$(\exists x)$(Tom believes $y(y$ denounced x) of Cicero)

still count as nonsense, along with (7); but such legitimate purposes as these might have served are severed by (17)–(19) and the like. Our names of intensions, and these only, are what count as referentially opaque.

Let us sum up our findings concerning the seven numbered statements about Ralph. (7) is now counted as nonsense, (8) as true, (12)–(13) as true, (14) as false, and (15) and (17) as true. Another that is true is:

(20) Ralph believes that the man seen at the beach is not a spy,

which of course must not be confused with (13).

The kind of exportation which leads from (14) to (15) should doubtless be viewed in general as implicative. Under the terms of our illustrative story, (14) happens to be false; but (20) is true, and it leads by exportation to:

(21) Ralph believes $z(z$ is not a spy) of the man seen at the beach.

The man at the beach, hence Ortcutt, does not receive reference in (20), because of referential opacity; but he does in (21), so we may conclude from (21) that

(22) Ralph believes $z(z$ is not a spy) of Ortcutt.

Thus (15) and (22) both count as true. This is not, however, to charge Ralph with contradictory beliefs. Such a charge might reasonably be read into:

(23) Ralph believes $z(z$ is a spy . z is not a spy) of Ortcutt,

but this merely goes to show that it is undesirable to look upon (15) and (22) as implying (23).

It hardly needs be said that the barbarous usage illustrated in (15)–(19) and (21)–(23) is not urged as a practical reform. It is put forward by way of straightening out a theoretical difficulty, which, summed up, was as follows: Belief contexts are referentially opaque; therefore it is *prima facie* meaningless to quantify into them; how then to provide for those indispensable relational statements of belief, like 'There is someone whom Ralph believes to be a spy'?

Let it not be supposed that the theory which we have been examining is just a matter of allowing unbridled quantification into belief contexts after all, with a legalistic change of notation. On the contrary, the crucial choice recurs at each point: quantify if you will, but pay the price of accepting near-contraries like (15) and (22) at each point at which you choose to quantify. In other words: distinguish as you please between referential and non-referential positions, but keep track, so as to treat each kind appropriately. The notation of intensions, of degree one and higher, is in effect a device for inking in a boundary between referential and non-referential occurrences of terms.

III

Striving and wishing, like believing, are propositional attitudes and referentially opaque. (3) and (4) are objectionable in the same way as (7), and our recent treatment of belief can be repeated for these propositional attitudes. Thus, just as (7) gave way to (17), so (3) and (4) give way to:

(24) $(\exists x)(x$ is a lion . Ernest strives z(Ernest finds z) of x),

(25) $(\exists x(x$ is a sloop . I wish z(I have z) of x),

a certain breach of idiom being allowed for the sake of analogy in the case of 'strives'.

These examples came from a study of hunting and wanting. Observing in (3)–(4) the quantification into opaque contexts, then, we might have retreated to (1)–(2) and forborne to paraphrase them into terms of striving and wishing. For (1)–(2) were quite straightforward renderings of lion-hunting and sloop-wanting in their relational senses; it was only the notional senses that really needed the breakdown into terms of striving and wishing, (5)–(6).

Actually, though, it would be myopic to leave the relational senses of lion-hunting and sloop-wanting at the unanalyzed stage (1)–(2). For, whether or not we choose to put these over into terms of wishing and striving, there are other relational cases of wishing and striving which require our consideration anyway—as witness (9). The untenable formulations (3)–(4) may indeed be either corrected as (24)–(25) or condensed back into (1)–(2); on the other hand we have no choice but to correct the untenable (9) on the pattern of (24)–(25), viz., as:

$(\exists x)$(Witold wishes y(y is president) of x).

The untenable versions (3)–(4) and (9) all had to do with wishing and striving in the relational sense. We see in contrast that (5)–(6) and (10), on the notional side of wishing and striving, are innocent of any illicit quantification into opaque contexts from outside. But now notice that exactly the same trouble begins also on the notional side, as soon as we try to say not just that Ernest hunts lions and I want a sloop, but that *someone* hunts lions or wants a sloop. This move carries us, ostensibly, from (5)–(6) to:

(26) $(\exists w)(w$ strives that $(\exists x)(x$ is a lion . w finds x)),

(27) $(\exists w)(w$ wishes that $(\exists x)(x$ is a sloop . w has x)),

and these do quantify unallowably into opaque contexts.

We know how, with help of the attribute apparatus, to put (26)–(27) in order; the pattern, indeed, is substantially before us in (24)–(25). Admissible versions are:

$(\exists w)(w$ strives $y(\exists x)(x$ is a lion . y finds x) of w),

$(\exists w)(w$ wishes $y(\exists x)(x$ is a sloop . y has x) of w), or briefly:

(28) $(\exists w)(w$ strives $y(y$ finds a lion) of $w)$,

(29) $(\exists w)(w$ wishes $y(y$ has a sloop) of $w)$.

Such quantification of the subject of the propositional attitude can of course occur in belief as well; and, if the subject is mentioned in the belief itself, the above pattern is the one to use. Thus 'Someone believes he is Napoleon' must be rendered:

$(\exists w)(w$ believes $y(y =$ Napoleon) of $w)$.

For concreteness I have been discussing belief primarily, and two other propositional attitudes secondarily: striving and wishing. The treatment is, we see, closely parallel for the three; and it will pretty evidently carry over to other propositional attitudes as well—e.g., hope, fear, surprise. In all cases my concern is, of course, with a special technical aspect of the propositional attitudes: the problem of quantifying in.

IV

There are good reasons for being discontent with an analysis that leaves us with propositions, attributes, and the rest of the intensions. Intensions are less economical than extensions (truth values, classes, relations), in that they are more narrowly individuated. The principle of their individuation, moreover, is obscure.

Commonly logical equivalence is adopted as the principle of individuation of intensions. More explicitly: if S and S' are any two sentences with $n(\geqq 0)$ free variables, the same in each, then the respective intensions which we name by putting the n variables (or 'that', if $n = 0$) before S and S' shall be one and the same intension if and only if S and S' are logically equivalent. But the relevant concept of logical equivalence raises serious questions in turn.[3] The intensions are at best a pretty obscure lot.

Yet it is evident enough that we cannot, in the foregoing treatment of propositional attitudes, drop the intensions in favour of the corresponding extensions. Thus, to take a trivial example, consider 'w is hunting unicorns'. On the analogy of (28), it becomes:

w strives $y(y$ finds a unicorn) of w.

Correspondingly for the hunting of griffins. Hence, if anyone w is to hunt unicorns without hunting griffins, the attributes

$y(y$ finds a unicorn),

$y(y$ finds a griffin)

---

[3] See my 'Two Dogmas of Empiricism', in *From a Logical Point of View*; also 'Carnap and logical truth', which is Essay 10 in *The Ways of Paradox*.

must be distinct. But the corresponding classes are identical, being empty. So it is indeed the attributes, and not the classes, that were needed in our formulation. The same moral could be drawn, though less briefly, without appeal to empty cases.

But there is a way of dodging the intensions which merits serious consideration. Instead of speaking of intensions we can speak of sentences, naming these by quotation. Instead of:

w believes that . . .

we may say:

w believes-true '. . .'.

Instead of:

(30) w believes y(. . . y . . .) of x

we may say:

(31) w believes '. . . y . . .' satisfied by x.

The words 'believes satisfied by' here, like 'believes of' before, would be viewed as an irreducibly triadic predicate. A similar shift can be made in the case of the other propositional attitudes, of course, and in the tetradic and higher cases.

This semantical reformulation is not, of course, intended to suggest that the subject of the propositional attitude speaks the language of the quotation, or any language. We may treat a mouse's fear of a cat as his fearing true a certain English sentence. This is unnatural without being therefore wrong. It is a little like describing a prehistoric ocean current as clockwise.

How, where, and on what grounds to draw a boundary between those who believe or wish or strive that p, and those who do not quite believe or wish or strive that p, is undeniably a vague and obscure affair. However, if anyone does approve of speaking of belief of a proposition at all and of speaking of a proposition in turn as meant by a sentence, then certainly he cannot object to our semantical reformulation 'w believes-true S' on any special grounds of obscurity; for, 'w believes-true S' is explicitly definable in his terms as 'w believes the proposition meant by S'. Similarly for the semantical reformulation (31) of (30); similarly for the tetradic and higher cases; and similarly for wishing, striving, and other propositional attitudes.

Our semantical versions do involve a relativity to language, however, which must be made explicit. When we say that w believes-true S, we need to be able to say what language the sentence S is thought of as belonging to; not because *w* needs to understand *S*, but because *S* might by coincidence exist (as a linguistic form) with very different meanings in two languages.[4] Strictly, therefore, we should think of the dyadic 'believes-true *S*' as expanded to a triadic '*w* believes-true *S* in *L*'; and correspondingly for (31) and its suite.

As noted two paragraphs back, the semantical form of expression:

(32) *w* believes-true '. . .' in *L*

can be explained in intensional terms, for persons who favour them, as:

(33) *w* believes the proposition meant by '. . .' in *L*,

thus leaving no cause for protest on the score of relative clarity. Protest may still be heard, however, on a different score: (32) and (33), though equivalent to each other, are not strictly equivalent to the '*w* believes that . . .' which is our real concern. For, it is argued, in order to infer (33) we need not only the information about *w* which '*w* believes that . . .' provides, but also some extraneous information about the language *L*. Church[5] brings the point out by appeal to translations, substantially as follows. The respective statements:

w believes that there are unicorns,
w believes the proposition meant by 'There are unicorns' in English

go into German as:

(34) *w glaubt, dass es Einhörne gibt,*

(35) *w glaubt diejenige Aussage, die* „There are unicorns" *auf Englisch bedeutet,*

and clearly (34) does not provide enough information to enable a German ignorant of English to infer (35).

The same reasoning can be used to show that 'There are unicorns' is not strictly or analytically equivalent to:

'There are unicorns' is true in English.

Nor, indeed, was Tarski's truth paradigm intended to assert analytic equivalence. Similarly, then, for (32) in relation to '*w* believes that . . .'; a systematic agreement in truth value can be claimed, and no more. This limitation will prove of little moment to persons who share my scepticism about analyticity.

---

[4] This point is made by Church in 'On Carnap's analysis' [Essay XI below].
[5] Ibid., with an acknowledgement to Langford.

What I find more disturbing about the semantical versions, such as (32), is the need of dragging in the language concept at all. What is a language? What degree of fixity is supposed? When do we have one language and not two? The propositional attitudes are dim affairs to begin with, and it is a pity to have to add obscurity to obscurity by bringing in language variables too. Only let it not be supposed that any clarity is gained by restituting the intensions.

IX

QUANTIFYING IN[1]
DAVID KAPLAN

I

EXPRESSIONS are used in a variety of ways. Two radically different ways in which the expression 'nine' can occur are illustrated by the paradigms:

(1) Nine is greater than five,

(2) Canines are larger than felines.

Let us call the kind of occurrence illustrated in (1) a *vulgar* occurrence, and that in (2) an *accidental* occurrence (or, following Quine, an orthographic accident). For present purposes we need not try to define either of these notions; but presumably there are no serious logical or semantical problems connected with occurrences of either kind. The first denotes, is open to substitution and existential generalization, and contributes to the meaning of the sentence which contains it. To the second, all such concerns are inappropriate.

There are other occurrences of the word 'nine', illustrated in

(3) 'Nine is greater than five' is a truth of Arithmetic,

(4) It is necessary that nine is greater than five,

(5) Hegel believed that nine is greater than five.

These diverge from the paradigm of vulgar occurrence (they fail the substitution test, the existential generalization test, and probably others

From *Words and Objections: Essays on the Work of W. V. Quine*, edited by D. Davidson and J. Hintikka (Dordrecht-Holland: D. Reidel Publishing Co., 1969), pp. 178–214. Reprinted by permission of the publishers.

[1] This paper is intended as a commentary on Quine's 'Quantifiers and Propositional Attitudes' [Essay VIII, above]. Quine's article was first published in 1956 and I have been thinking about it ever since. Quine has not been idle while I have been thinking, but his subsequent writings do not seem to have repudiated any part of 'Quantifiers and Propositional Attitudes' which remains, to my mind, the best brief introduction to the field. The first half of my reflections was read to the Harvard Philosophy Colloquium in January 1966. Its writing was aided by conversations with Montgomery Furth. The present ending has been influenced by a number of different persons, most significantly by Saul Kripke and Charles Chastain. But they should not be held to blame for it. Furth, who also read the penultimate version, is responsible for any remaining deficiencies aside from Section IX about which he is sceptical. My research has been partially supported by N.S.F. Grant GP-7706.

as well), but they are not, at least to the untutored mind, clearly ortho-graphic accidents either: for in them, the meaning of 'nine' seems, some-how, relevant. Let us call them *intermediate occurrences* and their contexts *intermediate contexts.*

These intermediate occurrences have come in for considerable discussion lately. Two kinds of analyses which have been proposed can be conve-niently characterized as: (a) assimilating the intermediate occurrences to the accidental occurrences, and (b) assimilating the intermediate occur-rences to the vulgar occurrences.

The former view, that the intermediate occurrences are to be thought of like accidental ones, I identify with Quine. Such a charge is slightly inaccurate; I make it chiefly for the sake of dramatic impact. My evidence, carefully selected, is that he has proposed in a few places that quotation contexts, as in (3), be thought of as single words and that 'believes that nine is greater than five' be thought of as a simple predicate. And that after introducing a dichotomous classification of occurrences of names into those which he terms 'purely referential' (our vulgar—his criterion is substitutivity) and those which he terms 'non-referential' (our inter-mediate and accidental) he writes, 'We are not unaccustomed to passing over occurrences that somehow "do not count"—"mary" in "summary", "can" in "canary"; and we can allow similarly for all non-referential occur-rences of terms, once we know what to look out for.' Further, his very terminology: 'opaque' for a context in which names occur non-refer-entially, seems to suggest an indissoluble whole, unarticulated by semanti-cally relevant components.[2] But be that as it may, I shall put forward this analysis—the assimilation of intermediate occurrence to accidental ones—primarily in order to contrast its defeatist character with the sanguine view of Frege (and his followers) that we can assimilate the intermediate occurrences to vulgar ones.

II

The view that the occurrences of 'nine' in (3), (4), and (5) are accidental may be elaborated, as Quine has done, by contrasting (3), (4), and (5) with:

(6) Nine is such that the result of writing it followed by 'is greater than five' is a theorem of Arithmetic,

---

[2] The quotation is from *Word and Object* (New York: Wiley and Sons, 1960), p. 144, wherein the inspiration for 'opaque' is explicitly given. The assimilation of intermediate occurrences to accidental ones might fairly be said to represent a *tendency* on Quine's part. The further evidence of *Word and Object* belies any simplistic charac-terization of Quine's attitudes toward intermediate occurrences.

(7) Nine is such that necessarily it is greater than five,

(8) Nine is such that Hegel believed it to be greater than five,

in which we put, or attempt to put, 'nine' into purely referential position. Quine would still term the occurrences of 'five' as non-referential; thus, the 'necessarily it is greater than five' in (7) might be thought of as an atomic predicate expressing some property of the number of baseball positions (assuming (7) to be true). And similarly for (6) and (8). I am not trying to say how we would 'ordinarily' understand (6)–(8). I merely use these forms, in which the occurrence of 'nine' does not stand within the so-called opaque construction, as a kind of canonical form to express what must be carefully explained, namely that here we attribute a property to a certain number, and that the correctness of this attribution is independent of the manner in which we refer to the number. Thus (6), (7), and (8) are to be understood in such a way that the result of replacing the occurrence of 'nine' by any other expression denoting that number would not affect the truth value of the sentence. This includes replacement by a variable, thus validating existential generalization. In these respects (6)–(8) do indeed resemble (1).

But (3)–(5), which are to be understood in the natural way, are such that the result of substituting 'the number of planets' for the occurrences of 'nine' would lead from truth to falsehood (didn't Hegel 'prove' that the number of planets = 5?). Thus, for Quine, these contexts are opaque, and the result of replacing the occurrences of 'nine' by the variable 'x' and prefixing '$\exists x$' would lead from truth to formulas of, at best, questionable import. In fact, Quine deems such quantification into an opaque context flatly 'improper'.[3] In these respects (3)–(5) resemble (2). Although the impropriety of substituting or quantifying on the recurrence of 'nine' in (2) is gross compared with that involved in applying the corresponding operations to (3)–(5), the view I am here characterizing would make this difference a matter of degree rather than of kind.

I will not expatiate on the contrast between (3)–(5) and (6)–(8), since

---

[3] In 'Three Grades of Modal Involvement', in *The Ways of Paradox* (New York: Random House, 1966), p. 172, and other places. An intriguing suggestion for notational efficiency at no loss (or gain) to Quine's theory is to take advantage of the fact that occurrences of variables within opaque contexts which are bindable from without are prohibited, and use the vacated forms as 'a way of indicating, selectively and changeably, just what positions in the contained sentence are to shine through as referential on any particular occasion' (*Word and Object*, p. 199). We interpret, 'Hegel believed that x is greater than five' with bindable 'x', as 'x is such that Hegel believed it to be greater than five' which is modelled on (8). Similarly, 'Hegel believed that x is greater than y' is now read as, 'x and y are such that Hegel believed the former to be greater than the latter'. (8) itself could be rendered as, '$\exists x[x =$ nine & Hegel believed that x is greater than five]', and still not be a logical consequence of (5).

Quine and others have made familiarity with this contrast a part of the conventional wisdom of our philosophical times. But note that (6)–(8) are not introduced as defined forms whose non-logical apparatus is simply that of (3)–(5), in the way in which

Exactly one thing is greater than five

can be defined in terms of the non-logical apparatus of (1). Instead (6)–(8) are introduced as new primitive forms.

Earlier I said that (3)–(5) should be understood in the natural way, whereas careful explanation was required for (6)–(8). But will careful explanation suffice? Will anything suffice? What we have done, or rather what we have sketched, is this: a certain skeletal language structure has been given, here using fragments of English, so of course an English reading is at once available, and then certain logical transformations have been pronounced valid. Predicate logic was conducted in this way before Gödel and Tarski, and modal logic was so conducted before Carnap and others began to supply semantical foundations. The earlier method, especially as applied to modal logic (we might call it the run-it-up-the-axiom-list-and-see-if-anyone-deduces-a-contradiction method), seems to me to have been stimulated more by a compulsive permutations-and-combinations mentality than by the true philosophical temperament.

Thus, it just is not enough to describe the form (6) and say that the predicate expresses a property of numbers so that both Leibniz's law, and existential generalization apply. What property of numbers is this? It makes no sense to talk of the result of writing a number. We can write numerals and various other names of numbers but such talk as (6), in the absence of a theory of standard names, is surely based on confusion of mention and use.[4] One is tempted to make the same remark about (7), but in this case an alternative explanation is possible in a metaphysical tradition connected with so-called 'Aristotelian essentialism'. It is claimed that among the properties of a thing, e.g. being greater than 5, and numbering the planets, some hold of it necessarily, others only contingently. Quine has ably expounded the inevitability of this view of (7).[5]

---

[4] The reader will recognize that I have incorporated, without reference, many themes upon which Quine has harped, and that I have not attempted to make my agreement with him explicit at each point at which it occurs. Suffice it to say that the agreements far outweigh the disagreements, and that in both the areas of agreement and of disagreement I have benefited greatly from his writings.

[5] See especially the end of 'Three Grades of Modal Involvement'. I am informed by scholarly sources that Aristotelian essentialism has its origin in 'Two Dogmas of Empiricism', *The Philosophical Review*, 60 (1951), 20–43. It reappears significantly in 'Reply to Professor Marcus', *Synthèse*, 13 (1961), 323–30, where essential properties of numbers are discussed, and in *Word and Object*, p. 199, where essential properties of persons are discussed. I will later argue that the two cases are unlike.

In contrast to (6) and (7), we can put a strong prima facie case for the sensicalness of (8) by way of illustrative examples which indicate important uses of the form exemplified in (8) as compared with that of the form exemplified in (5). Russell mentions, in a slightly different context, the man who remarked to an acquaintance 'I thought that your yacht was longer than it is'. The correct rendering here is clearly in the style of (8), viz:

The length of your yacht is such that I thought that your yacht was longer than that.

not in the style of (5);

I thought that your yacht was longer than the length of your yacht.

In 'Quantifiers and Propositional Attitudes', Quine supports the use of (8) as against (5) by an ingenious use of existential quantification. He contrasts:

(9) Ralph believes that someone is a spy,

in which the quantifier occurs within the opaque construction, as does the term in (5), with:

(10) Someone is such that Ralph believes that he is a spy,

which is an existential generalization of a formula of the form (8). After pointing out that (9) may be rephrased as:

Ralph believes that there are spies,

Quine remarks, 'The difference is vast; indeed, if Ralph is like most of us, [(9)] is true and [(10)] is false.' In this connection recall that according to Quine's theory of referential opacity, (10) cannot be obtained by existential generalization directly from a formula of the form (5) say,

Ralph believes that Ortcutt is a spy,

since the occurrence of the term to be generalized on is here assimilated to that of the orthographic accident and thus is not immediately open to such a move.

Let me sum up what I have called Quine's elaboration of the view that intermediate occurrences are to be assimilated to accidental ones. For those cases in which it is desired to make connections between what occurs within the opaque construction and what occurs without, a special new primitive form is introduced, parallel to the original, but containing one (or more than one) of the crucial terms in a purely referential position.

Quine refers to the new form as expressing the *relational* sense of belief. The possibility of introducing such forms always exists and the style of their introduction seems uniform, but since they are primitive each such introduction must be supplied with an ad hoc justification (to the effect that the predicate or operator being introduced makes sense).

III

Let me turn now to the Fregean view that assimilates intermediate occurrences to vulgar ones. The brilliant simplicity of Frege's leading idea in the treatment of intermediate occurrences has often been obscured by a failure to separate that idea from various turgid details involved in carrying the programme through in particular interesting cases. But theory must be served.

Frege's main idea, as I understand it, was just this. There are no *real* intermediate occurrences; the appearance of intermediacy created by apparent failures of substitutivity and the like is due to confusion about what is denoted by the given occurrence. Frege here calls our attention to an implicit assumption made in testing for substitutivity and the like. Namely, that a denoting expression must *always* have its usual denotation, and, *a fortiori*, that two expressions must have the same denotation in a given context if they usually (i.e. in most contexts) have the same denotation.

But we are all familiar with many counter-examples to the assumption that a name always has its usual denotation. Consider:

(11) Although F.D.R. ran for office many times, F.D.R. ran on television only once.

The natural analysis of (11) involves pointing out that the name 'F.D.R.' is ambiguous, and that in the second clause it denotes a television show rather than a man. Substitutions or any other logical operations based on the assumption that the name has here its usual denotation are pointless and demonstrate nothing. But transformations based on a *correct* analysis of the name's denotation *in this context* will reveal the occurrence to be vulgar. I call this the natural analysis, but it is of course possible for a fanatical mono-denotationalist to insist that his transformations have shown the context:

. . . ran on television only once

to be opaque, and so to conclude that the second occurrence of 'F.D.R.' in (11) is not purely referential. This view may be expressed moderately, resulting only in an insistence that (11) is improper unless the second clause is rewritten as:

the television show named 'F.D.R.' ran on television only once.

Often when there is a serious possibility of confusion, we conform to the practice (even if not the theory) of the fanatical mono-denotationalist and do introduce a new word, add a subscript, or put the original in bold face, italics, or quotation marks. It is often good practice to continue to so mark the different uses of an expression, even when there is little possibility of confusion. Discovering and marking such ambiguities plays a considerable and useful role in philosophy (some, not I, would say it is the essence of philosophy), and much of what has proved most engaging and at the same time most fruitless in logical theory might have been avoided had the first 25 years of this century not seen a lapse from Frege's standards of mention and use. It would be unwary of us to suppose that we have now caught all such ambiguities. Thus, we should not leap to conclusions of opacity.

I indicated in the case of the fanatical mono-denotationalist how it is possible to trade a finding of opacity for one of ambiguity. Frege attempts his assimilation of intermediate occurrences to vulgar ones by indicating (some would say, postulating) ambiguities where others have seen only opacity. It is not denied that the ambiguities involved in the Fregean analysis are far more subtle than that noted in (11), but on his analysis the difference is seen as a matter of degree rather than of kind.

Frege referred to intermediate occurrences as *ungerade* (indirect, oblique). And the terminology is a natural one, for on his conception such an occurrence does not refer directly to its usual denotation but only, at best, indirectly by way of some intermediate *entity* such as a sense or an expression, I will return to this subject later. For now just notice that occurrences which Quine would call purely referential, Frege might call standardly referential; and those in contexts Quine would call referentially opaque, Frege might call non-standardly referential, but in either case for Frege the occurrences are fully referential. So we require no special non-extensional logic, no restrictions on Leibniz' law, on existential generalization, etc., except those attendant upon consideration of a language containing ambiguous expressions. And even these can be avoided if we follow the practice of the fanatical mono-denotationalist and require linguistic reform so that distinct uses of expressions are marked by some distinction in the expressions themselves. This feature of a development of Frege's doctrine has been especially emphasized by Church.[6]

This then is Frege's treatment of intermediate contexts—obliquity indicates ambiguity. This doctrine accounts in a very natural way for the well-known logical peculiarities of intermediate contexts, such as the failure of substitutivity, existential generalization, etc.

IV

The difficulties in Frege's treatment appear in attempting to work out the details—details of the sort: exactly what *does* 'nine' denote in (3)–(5)? Frege's treatment of oblique contexts is often described as one according to which expressions in such contexts denote their ordinary sense or meaning or intension (I here use these terms interchangeably). But this is a bad way of putting the matter for three reasons. (1) It is, I believe, historically inaccurate. It ignores Frege's remarks about quotation marks (see below) and other special contexts. (2) It conflates two separate principles: (a) expressions in oblique contexts don't have their ordinary denotation (which is true), and (b) expressions in oblique contexts denote their ordinary sense (which is not, in general, true). And (3) in focusing attention too rapidly on the special and separate problems of intensional logic, we lose sight of the beauty and power of Frege's general method of treating oblique contexts. We may thus lose the motivation that that general theory might provide for an attack on the problems of the special theory. My own view is that Frege's explanation, by way of ambiguity, of what appears to be the logically deviant behaviour of terms in intermediate contexts is so theoretically satisfying that if we have not yet discovered or satisfactorily grasped the peculiar intermediate objects in question, then we should simply continue looking.

There is, however, a method which may assist in the search. Look for something denoted by a compound, say, a sentence, in the oblique context. (In ordinary contexts sentences are taken to denote their own truth values and to be intersubstitutable on that basis.) And then using the fundamental principle: the denotation of the compound is a function of the denotation of the parts, look for something denoted by the parts. It was the use of this principle which, I believe, led to Carnap's discovery of individual concepts,[7] and also led Frege to the view that quotation

---

[6] In 'A Formulation of the Logic of Sense and Denotation', in *Structure, Method and Meaning*, ed. P. Henle, M. Kallen, and S. K. Langer (New York: Liberal Arts Press, 1951).

[7] See *Meaning and Necessity* (Chicago, Ill.: Univ. of Chicago Press, 1947), Section 9, for the discovery of the explicandum, and Section 40 for the discovery of the explicans.

marks produce an oblique context within which each component expression denotes itself[8] (it is clear in quotation contexts what the whole compound denotes).

Frege's view of quotation contexts would allow for quantification into such contexts, but of course we would have to quantify over expressions (since it is expressions that are denoted in such contexts), and we would have to make some provision to distinguish when a given symbol in such a context is being used as a variable and when it is being used as a constant, i.e. to denote itself. This might be done by taking some distinctive class of symbols to serve as variables.

Let us symbolize Frege's understanding of quotation marks by using forward and backward capital F's. (Typographical limitations have forced elimination of the centre horizontal bar of the Capital F's.) Then, using Greek letters for variables ranging over expressions we can express such truths as:

(12) $\exists \alpha [\ulcorner \alpha$ is greater than five$\urcorner$ is a truth of arithmetic].[9]

Such is Frege's treatment of quotation marks: it seems to me more interesting and certainly much more fruitful (for the development of any theory in which quotation contexts are at all common) than the usual orthographic accident treatment according to which the quotation marks seal off the context, which is treated as a single indissoluble word. And it is well known that for serious theoretical purposes, quotation marks (under the conventional treatment) are of little use.

The ontological status of meanings or senses is less well settled than that of expressions. But we can again illustrate the principle involved in searching for the intermediate entities, and perhaps even engender an illusion of understanding, by introducing some symbolic devices. First, in analogy to the conventional use of quotation marks, I introduce meaning marks. Their use is illustrated in the following:

(13) The meaning of 'brother' = ^{m}male sibling^{m}.

Now we can adapt the idea used in producing (12) to meaning marks, so as to produce a Fregan interpretation of them. The context produced by the meaning marks will then not be thought of as referentially opaque but rather such that each expression in such a context will denote its own meaning. Quantification in is permitted, but restricted of course to

---

[8] See 'On Sense and Reference' pp. 58, 59 in *Translations from the Philosophical Writings of Gottlob Frege*, ed. Geach and Black (Oxford: Blackwell, 1952).

[9] The acute reader will have discerned a certain similarity in function, though not in foundation, between the Frege quotes and another familiar quotation device.

quantification over meanings. Following the earlier pattern, let us symbolize the new meaning marks with forward and backward capital M's. Using italic letters for variables ranging over meanings, we can express such truths as:

(14) $\exists a \exists b [^{\mathrm{M}}a$ kicked $b^{\mathrm{M}} = {}^{\mathrm{M}}b$ was kicked by $a^{\mathrm{M}}]$

I leave to the reader the problem of making sense of (12)–(14).

This comparison of meaning marks with quotation marks also allows me to make another point relevant to Quine's 'Quantifiers and Propositional Attitudes'. In his section IV, Quine suggests that by a harmless shift in idiom we can replace talk of meanings by talk of expressions, thus achieving ontological security. I agree, but the parallel can be exploited in either direction: as suggested by the introduction of meaning marks, we might also try to replace talk of expressions by talk of meanings, thus achieving ontological insight. These structural parallels are most helpful in constructing a logic of intensions.[10]

V

We have finished comparing the treatments of (3)–(5) with respect to the two main analyses of intermediate occurrences: assimilation to orthographic accident versus assimilation to vulgar occurrence. The forms involved in (6)–(8) were introduced in connection with what I called Quine's elaboration of the first line. Now what can be done in this direction following Frege's line? The purpose of the new forms in (6)–(8) is to get an expression out from an accidental position to a vulgar one; or, in Quine's terminology, to move a term from an opaque context to a purely referential position. There should be no problem here on Frege's theory, because what is opaque for Quine is already fully referential for Frege. Thus the term is in a fully referential position in the first place. But this will not quite satisfy the demands of (6)–(8), because the term in question does not denote the right thing.

At this point it will be useful to reformulate (3)–(8) (or at least (4), (5), (7), and (8)) so as to make explicit what the objects of belief and necessity are. In so doing we take a step along Frege's path, for the non-substitutability of one true sentence for another in such contexts would indicate to Frege an ambiguity in both of them: the sentences lack their usual denotation, a truth value, and instead denote some other entity. Before saying what, note that the necessity symbol will stand for a property—of something or other—and the belief symbol will stand for a

---

[10] These parallels are exhibited at some length in my dissertation *Foundations of Intensional Logic* (University Microfilms, Ann Arbor, 1964).

two-place relation—between a person and something or other. (This in contrast to treating the necessity symbol simply as a 1-place referentially opaque sentential connective and similarly for belief.) Quine takes the step in Frege's direction in the article under discussion and favours it in the sister article 'Three Grades of Modal Involvement'. So I take it here. Now what shall the sentences denote? For my present purposes it will suffice to take the ontologically secure position and let them denote expressions, in particular, themselves.[11] Making this explicit, we rewrite (4) and (5) as:

(15) N 'nine is greater than five'
(16) Hegel B 'nine is greater than five'

On the usual reading of quotation marks, (15) and (16) still basically formulate the non-Fregean view, with the referential opacity now charged against the quotes. Keeping in mind that the shift to (7) and (8) was for the purpose of moving 'nine' to a purely referential position, we can rewrite (7) and (8) as:

(17) Nec ('x is greater than five', nine)

(which may be read: 'x is greater than 5' is necessarily true of nine), and

(18) Hegel Bel ('x is greater than five', nine).

Here the symbol for necessity becomes a two-place predicate and that for belief a three-place predicate. 'x is greater than five' stands for a compound predicate, with the bold face letter 'x' used only as a *place holder* to indicate subject position. The opacity of quotation marks deny such place holders a referential position in any Nec or Bel context. 'Nec' and 'Bel' are intended to express Quine's relational sense of necessity and belief.[12]

Frege would reformulate (15) and (16) as:

(19) N ⌜nine is greater than five⌝.
(20) Hegel B ⌜nine is greater than five⌝.

---

[11] A drawback to this position is that the resulting *correct* applications of Leibniz Law are rather unexciting. More interesting intermediate entities can be obtained by taking what Carnap, in *Meaning and Necessity* calls 'intensions'. Two expressions have the same intension, in this sense, if they are logically equivalent. Other interesting senses of 'intension' might be obtained by weakening the notion of logical equivalence to logical equivalence within sentential logic, intuitionistic logic, etc. Church suggests alternatives which might be understood along these lines.

[12] I have approximately followed the notational devices used by Quine in 'Quantifier and Propositional Attitudes'. Neither of us recommend the notation for practical purposes, even with the theory as is. An alternative notation is suggested in note 3 above.

Notice that we can use the same predicates as in (15) and (16) since

⌜nine is greater than five⌝ = 'nine is greater than five'

just as

$(3 \times 10^2) + (6 \times 10^1) + (8 \times 10^0) = 368$.

It should now be clear that although the occurrences of 'nine' in (19) and (20) are fully referential, (19) and (20) won't do for the purposes of (17) and (18), because the occurrences of 'nine' in (17) and (18) refer to quite a different entity. Combining (17) with:

(21) Nine numbers the planets,

we derive:

(22) $\exists y[y$ numbers the planets & **Nec** ('x is greater than five', $y)]$.

But (19) and (21) seem to yield only:

$\exists y[y$ number the planets & N ⌜nine is greater than five⌝],

in which the quantifier binds nothing in the necessity contexts, or:

$\exists \alpha[\alpha$ numbers the planets & N ⌜α is greater than five⌝],

which is false because the planets are not numbered by an expression (recall our conventions about Greek variables).

Thus the Fregean formulations appear to lack the kind of recurrence of a variable both within and without the necessity context that is characteristic of quantified modal logic and that appears in (22). But this difficulty can be considerably mitigated by taking note of the fact that though the number nine and the expression 'nine' are distinct entities, there is an important relationship between them. The second denotes the first. We can follow Church[6] by introducing a denotation predicate, 'Δ', into our language, and so restore, at least in an *indirect* way (recall Frege's indirect reference by way of intermediate entities) the connection between occurrences of an expression within and without the modal context, as in:

(23) $\exists y[y$ numbers the planets & $\exists \alpha(\Delta(\alpha, y)$ &
  N ⌜α is greater than five⌝)].

I propose (23), or some variant, as Frege's version of (22); and

(24) $\exists \alpha[\Delta(\alpha, \text{nine})$ & N ⌜α is greater than five⌝),

or some variant, as Frege's version of (17). (We shall return later to the variants.) (23) and (24) may not be as exciting as (22) and (17), but neither do they commit us to essentialism. It may well be that (24), and its variants supply all the connection between occurrences of expressions within and without modal contexts as can sensibly be allowed.

When I summed up Quine's elaboration of the orthographic accident theory of intermediate occurrences I emphasized the fact that to move an expression in an opaque construction to referential position, a new *primitive* predicate (such as 'Nec' and 'Bel' of (17) and (18)) had to be introduced and supplied with an interpretation. In contrast, the same effect is achieved by Frege's method using only the original predicate plus logical signs, including ' Δ ', and of course the ontological decomposition involved in the use of the Frege quotes.

Turning now to belief I propose:

(25) $\exists \alpha [\Delta(\alpha, \text{nine}) \ \& \ \text{Hegel } \mathbf{B} \ulcorner \alpha \text{ is greater than five} \urcorner]$,

or some variant, as Frege's version of Quine's (18).

VI

If we accept (25) as the interpretation of Quine's (18), we can justify a crucial form of inference he seems to consider valid and explain certain seemingly paradoxical results which he accepts.

Quine recites the following story.

There is a certain man in a brown hat whom Ralph has glimpsed several times under questionable circumstances on which we need not enter here; suffice it to say that Ralph suspects he is a spy. Also there is a grey-haired man, vaguely known to Ralph as rather a pillar of the community, whom Ralph is not aware of having seen except once at the beach. Now Ralph does not know it, but the men are one and the same.

Quine then poses the question, 'Can we say of this *man* (Bernard J. Ortcutt, to give him a name) that Ralph believes him to be a spy?' The critical facts of the story are summarized in what we would write as:

(26) Ralph **B** 'the man in the brown hat is a spy',

(27) Ralph **B** 'the man seen at the beach is not a spy',

(28) the man in the brown hat = the man seen at the beach = Ortcutt

Quine answers his own query by deriving what we would write as:

(29) Ralph **Bel** ('x is a spy', the man in the brown hat)

from (26). He says of this move, 'The kind of exportation which leads from [(26)] to [(29)] should doubtless be viewed in general as implicative.'[13] Now our versions of (26) and (29) are:

(30) Ralph **B** ⌜the man in the brown hat is a spy⌝,

(31) ∃α[Δ(α, the man in the brown hat) & Ralph **B** ⌜α is a spy⌝].

And (31) certainly is implied by (30) and the nearly analytic truth:

Δ('the man in the brown hat', the man in the brown hat).[14]

We thus justify exportation.

In discussing a seeming paradox Quine notes that exportation will also lead from (27) to:

Ralph **Bel** ('x is not a spy', the man seen at the beach)

and hence, by (28), to:

(32) Ralph **Bel** ('x is not a spy', Ortcutt).

Whereas (29) and (28) yield:

(33) Ralph **Bel** ('x is a spy', Ortcutt).

Thus, asserts Quine,

[(32)] and [(33)] both count as true. This is not, however, to charge Ralph with contradictory beliefs. Such a charge might reasonably be read into:

[(34) Ralph **Bel** ('x is a spy and x is not a spy', Ortcutt),]

but this merely goes to show that it is undesirable to look upon [(32)] and [(33)] as implying [(34)].

At first blush it may appear that avoidance of that undesirable course (looking upon (32) and (33) as implying (34)) calls for the most intense

---

[13] Also, see *Word and Object*, p. 211, for an implicit use of exportation.

[14] The 'nearly' of 'nearly analytic' is accounted for by a small scruple regarding the logic of singular terms. If a language L containing the name '$\imath y F y$' is extended to a metalanguage L' containing the predicate 'Δ' for denotation-in-L and also containing the logical particles, including quotes, in their usual meaning, then I regard

[∃$x x = \imath y F y \rightarrow \Delta$('$\imath y F y$', $\imath y F y$)]

as fully analytic in L'.

My reasons for thinking so depend, in part, on my treatment of quotation names as standard names, for which see Section VIII below. I am being careful, because Quine suggests disagreement in an impatient footnote to 'Notes on the Theory of Reference' (in *From a Logical Point of View*; I am grateful to Furth, who recalled the footnote.) I do not know whether our disagreement, if a fact, is over quotation or elsewhere. The whole question of analyticity is less than crucial to my line of argument.

kind of concentration and focus of interest. In fact one may be pessimisti-
cally inclined to take the easy way out and simply dispose of (32), (33),
(34) and any other assertions involving **Bel** as nonsense. But, as Quine
says, 'How then to provide for those indispensable relational statements
of belief, like "There is someone whom Ralph believes to be a spy"?'

Fortunately our versions of **Bel** again conform to Quine's intuitions.
(32), (33) and (34) go over respectively into:

(35) $\exists\alpha[\Delta(\alpha, \text{Ortcutt}) \,\&\, \text{Ralph } \mathbf{B} \ulcorner\alpha \text{ is not a spy}\urcorner]$,

(36) $\exists\alpha[\Delta(\alpha, \text{Ortcutt}) \,\&\, \text{Ralph } \mathbf{B} \ulcorner\alpha \text{ is a spy}\urcorner]$,

(37) $\exists\alpha[\Delta(\alpha, \text{Ortcutt}) \,\&\, \text{Ralph } \mathbf{B} \ulcorner\alpha \text{ is a spy and } \alpha \text{ is not a spy}\urcorner]$

which clearly verify Quine's claims, even in the presence of the suppressed
premise:

$\forall\alpha\forall\beta[\text{Ralph } \mathbf{B} \ulcorner\alpha \text{ is a spy}\urcorner \,\&\, \text{Ralph } \mathbf{B} \ulcorner\beta \text{ is not a spy}\urcorner \rightarrow$
$\text{Ralph } \mathbf{B} \ulcorner\alpha \text{ is a spy and } \beta \text{ is not a spy}\urcorner]$

VII

So far so good. But further exploration with our version of **Bel** suggests
that the rule of exportation fails to mesh with the intuitive ideas that
originally led Quine to the introduction of **Bel**. And I believe that our
version will also allow us to see more clearly exactly what problems lay
before us if we are to supply a notion answering to these motivating
intuitions. As I hope later developments will show, there are a number of
different kinds of counter-cases which could be posed. I will only develop
one at this point.

Suppose that the situation is as stated in (9). We would now express (9)
as:

(38) Ralph **B** '$\exists y\ y$ is a spy'.

Believing that spies differ widely in height, Ralph believes that one among
them is shortest. Thus,

(39) Ralph **B** 'the shortest spy is a spy'.

Supposing that there is in fact one shortest spy, by exportation (39) yields:

(40) Ralph **Bel** ('x is a spy', the shortest spy)

which, under the same supposition, by existential generalization yields:

(41) $\exists y$ Ralph **Bel** ('x is a spy', y).

And (41) currently expresses (10). But (10) was originally intended to express a fact which would interest the F.B.I. (recall Quine's comment that if Ralph is like most of us, (10) is false), and we would not expect the interest of that organization to be piqued by Ralph's conviction that no two spies share a size.

Two details of this case can be slightly improved. First, the near analyticity of Ralph's crucial belief, as expressed in (39), can be eliminated by taking advantage of Ralph's belief that all members of the C.P.U.S.A. (none of which are known to him) are spies. Second, we can weaken the assumption of Ralph's special ideas about spy sizes by using only the well-known fact that two persons cannot be born at exactly the same time at exactly the same place (where the place of birth is an interior point of the infant's body). Given any four spatial points a, b, c, d not in a plane, we can use the relations: t_1 is earlier than t_2, and p_1 is closer to $a(b, c, d)$ than p_2 is, to order all space time points. We can then form such names as 'the least spy' with the meaning: ^{m}that spy whose spatio-temporal location at birth precedes that of all other spies^m.

Details aside, the point is that exportation, as represented in our current version of **Bel**, conflicts with the intention that there be a 'vast' difference between (9) and (10). Still, I am convinced that we are on the right track. That track, roughly speaking, is this: instead of trying to introduce a new primitive relation like Quine's **Bel**, we focus on trying to define it (or something as close to it as we can sensibly come, remember modal logic) using just the dyadic **B** plus other logical and semi-logical apparatus such as quantifiers, Δ, etc., and also possibly other seemingly more fundamental epistemological notions.

Some years ago I thought that this task was hopeless and took basically the same attitude towards such quantified belief contexts as Quine takes towards quantified modal logic.[15] At that earlier time I used to argue with my colleague, Montgomery Furth, who shares my attitude toward Frege's theory, about the meaningfulness of such quantifications in as in (10). (This was after noticing the difficulty, indicated above, in our current analysis.[16]) Furth suggested that a solution might lie in somehow picking out certain kinds of names as being required for the exportation. But this just seemed essentialism all over again and we gave up. Although still uncertain that (10) makes sense, I think I can show that it comes to something like what Furth had in mind. Indeed, the analogies between the relational senses of belief and necessity are so strong that I have often

---

[15] For a recent expression see *Word and Object*, Section 41.
[16] The same difficulty was noticed, independently, by John Wallace and reported in a private communication.

wondered why Quine's scepticism with regard to **Nec** did not extend to **Bel**.

There is even an inadequacy in our proposed analysis, (24), of **Nec** parallel to that displayed for our proposed analysis, (25), of **Bel**. Although our analysis of **Nec** avoids essentialism, it also avoids rejecting:

(42) **Nec** ('x = the number of planets', nine),

which comes out true on the understanding:

(43) $\exists \alpha (\Delta(\alpha, \text{nine}) \ \& \ N^\ulcorner \alpha = \text{the number of planets}^\urcorner)$

in view of the facts that

$N^\ulcorner$the number of planets = the number of planets$^\urcorner$

and

Δ('the number of planets', nine).

In a sense, we have not avoided essentialism but only inessentialism, since so many of nine's properties become essential. Small consolation to know of our essential rationality if each blunder and error is equally ingrained.

The parallel inadequacies of our versions of **Nec** and **Bel** are now apparent. Our analyses credit nine with an excess of essence and put Ralph *en rapport* with an excess of individuals.

VIII

What is wanted is 'a frankly inequalitarian attitude towards various ways of specifying the number [nine]'.[17] This suggests to me that we should restrict our attention to a smaller class of names; names which are so intimately connected with what they name that they could not but name it. I shall say that such a name *necessarily denotes* its object, and I shall use 'Δ_N' to symbolize this more discriminating form of denotation.

Such a relation is available; based on the notion of a *standard name*. A standard name is one whose denotation is fixed on logical, or perhaps I should say linguistic, grounds alone. Numerals and quotation names are

---

[17] Quoted from the end of Quine's 'Reply to Professor Marcus'. I fully agree with Quine's characterization of the case, though not with the misinterpretation of Church's review of 'Notes on Existence and Necessity' (*Journal of Philosophy*, XL (1943), 113–27: review in *Journal of Symbolic Logic*, 8 (1943), 45–7), from which Quine's characterization springs.

prominent among the standard names.[18] Such names do, in the appropriate sense, necessarily denote their denotations.

Russell and some others who have attempted to treat proper names of persons as standard names have emphasized the purely referential function of such names and their apparent lack of descriptive content. But consideration of the place value system of arabic numerals and our conventions for the construction of quotation names of expressions should convince us that what is at stake is not pure reference in the absence of any descriptive structure, but rather reference free of *empirical* vicissitudes. Numbers and expressions, like every other kind of entity, can be named by names which are such that empirical investigation is required to determine their denotations. 'The number of planets' and '9' happen to denote the same number. The former might, under other circumstances or at some other time, denote a different number, but so long as we hold constant our conventions of language, '9' will denote the same number under all possible circumstances. To wonder what number is named by the German 'die Zahl der Planeten' may betray astronomical ignorance, but to wonder what number is named by the German 'Neun' can indicate only linguistic incompetence.[19]

$\Delta_N(\alpha, x)$ cannot be analysed in terms of the analyticity of some sentence of the form $\Delta(---, ...)$;
since:

Δ('the number of planets', the number of planets)

is analytic, but 'the number of planets' is not a standard name of the number of planets (viz: nine), and

Δ('9', the number of planets)

is not analytic, although '9' is a standard name of that number. We have in Δ_N a relation that holds between the standard name and the number itself, independent of any particular way of specifying the number. Thus there is a certain intimacy between '9' and 9, lacking between 'the number of planets' and the number of planets, which allows '9' to go proxy for 9 in assertions of necessity.

[18] See the discussion of what Carnap calls *L-determinate individual expressions* in *Meaning and Necessity*, Section 18, and also Tarski's discussion of what he calls *structural descriptive names* in 'The Concept of Truth in Formalized Languages', Section 1. (This article was originally pub. in Polish in *Projecie Bzawdy W. Jezybach Nauk Dedukcyjnych*, Travaux de La Société des Sciences et des Lettres de Varsovie, Classe III, no. 34 (1933), pp. viii+116; trans. J. Woodger in A. Tarski, *Logic Semantics Metamathematics* (Oxford: Clarendon Press, 1956), pp. 152–278.)

[19] The latter wonder is not to be confused with an ontological anxiety concerning the nature of nine, which is more appropriately expressed by dropping the word 'number' in the wonder description.

There is a sense in which the finite ordinals (which we can take the entities here under discussion to be) find their essence in their ordering. Thus, names which reflect this ordering in an *a priori* way, as by making true statements of order analytic, capture all that is essential to these numbers. And our careless attitude towards any intrinsic features of these numbers (e.g. whether zero is a set, and if so whether it has any members) suggests that such names may have captured all there is to these numbers.[20] I am less interested in urging an explanation of the special intimacy between 'nine' and nine, than in noting the fact. The phenomenon is widespread, extending to expressions, pure sets of finite rank, and others of their ilk. I would require any adequate explanation to generalize so as to handle all such cases, and I should hope that such an explanation would also support the limitations which I suggest below on the kinds of entities eligible for standard names.[21]

The foregoing considerations suggest simple variants for our current Fregean versions of (17) and (42). We replace (24) with:

$$\exists \alpha (\Delta_N(\alpha, \text{nine}) \ \& \ N^\ulcorner \alpha \text{ is greater than five}^\urcorner)$$

as our analysis of (17), and we replace (43) with:

$$\exists \alpha (\Delta_N(\alpha, \text{nine}) \ \& \ N^\ulcorner \alpha = \text{the number of planets}^\urcorner)$$

as our analysis of (42). According to the reformed analyses, (17) and (42) come out respectively as true and false, which accords much better with our intuitions and may even satisfy the essentialist.[22] All, it is hoped, without a lapse into irreducible (though questionable) metaphysical assumptions.

There are, however, limitations on the resort to standard names. Only abstract objects can have standard names, since only they (and not all of them) lack that element of contingency which makes the rest of us liable to failures of existence. Thus, Quine can have no standard name, for he might not be. And then what shall his standard name name? Quine's singleton, {Quine}, though abstract, is clearly no better off.

Numerals are reliable; they always pick out the same number. But to suppose a standard name for Quine would presuppose a solution to the more puzzling problem of what features to take into account in determining that an individual of one possible world is 'the same person' as that

[20] Benacerraf so concludes in 'What Numbers Could Not Be', *The Philosophical Review*, 74 (1965), 47–73.

[21] The present discussion of standard names is based on that in the more technical environment of my dissertation, pp. 55–7.

[22] Given this understanding of Nec, it is interesting to note that on certain natural assumptions '$\Delta_n(\alpha, y)$' is itself expressed by 'Nec($^\ulcorner \alpha = x^\urcorner$, y)'.

of another. Often when the worlds have a common part, as when we consider alternative futures to the present, the individual(s) can be traced back to the common part by the usual continuity conditions and there compared. But for individuals not extant during an overlap such techniques are unavailing. It seems that such radically disjoint worlds are sometimes contemplated by modal logicians. I am not here passing final judgment but only remarking the relevance of a second difference between Quine and Nine: namely, that he presents a very real problem of trans-world identification while it does not.

Thus the device of using standard names, which accounts nicely for my own intuitions regarding the essential properties of numbers, appears to break down when set to discriminating essential properties of persons. I am consoled by the fact that my own intuitions do not assign essential properties to persons in any broad metaphysical sense, which is not to say that quantified modal logic can have no interesting interpretation when trans-world identifications are made from the point of view of a frankly special interest.

IX

All this on Nec was aimed towards analogy with **Bel** and a charge of inconsistent scepticism against Quine. We have patched our first version of Nec with a more discriminating sense of denotation. The same trick would work for **Bel**, if Ralph would confine his cogitations to numbers and expressions. If not, we must seek some other form of special intimacy between name and object which allows the former to go proxy for the latter in Ralph's cognitive state.

I believe that the fundamental difficulty with our first version of **Bel** is that Δ gave us a relation between name and object in which Ralph played no significant role. Supposing all speakers of English to have available approximately the same stock of names (i.e. singular terms), this puts us all *en rapport* with the same persons. But the interesting relational sense of belief, and the one which I suppose Quine to have been getting at with (10), is one which provides Ralph with access to some but not all persons of whom he can frame names. What we are after this time is a three-place relation between Ralph, a name (which I here use in the broad sense of singular term) α, and a person x. For this purpose I will introduce two special notions: that of a name α being *of* x for Ralph, and that of a name being *vivid*, both of which I will compare with the notion of a name *denoting* x.

Let us begin by distinguishing the *descriptive content* of a name from the *genetic character* of the name as used by Ralph. The first goes to user-independent features of the name, the second to features of a particular user's acquisition of certain beliefs involving the name. It is perhaps easiest to make the distinction in terms not of names but of pictures, with consideration limited to pictures which show a single person. Those features of a picture, in virtue of which we say it resembles or is a likeness of a particular person, comprise the picture's descriptive content. The genetic character of a picture is determined by the causal chain of events leading to its production. In the case of photographs and portraits we say that the picture is *of* the person who was photographed or who sat for the portrait. The same relation presumably holds between a perception and the perceived object.[23] This relation between picture and person clearly depends entirely on the genetic character of the picture. Without attempting a definition, we can say that for a picture to be *of* a person, the person must serve significantly in the causal chain leading to the picture's production and also serve as object for the picture. The second clause is to prevent all of an artist's paintings from being *of* the artist. I will shortly say a bit more about how I understand this relation, which I designate with the italicized '*of*'.

The 'user-independence' of the descriptive content of a picture lies in the fact that 'identical' pictures, such as two prints made from a single negative, will resemble all the same persons. In this sense, the descriptive content of a picture is a function of what we might call the picture-type rather than the picture-token. The 'user-dependent' nature of the genetic character of a picture lies in the fact that 'identical' paintings can be such that they are *of* different persons (e.g. twins sitting separately for portraits). Thus the genetic character of a picture is a function only of the picture-token. In order to accommodate genesis, I use 'picture' throughout in the sense of 'picture-token'.

Armed with *resemblance* and *of*-ness, let me recite just a few of the familiar facts of portraiture. First, not all pictures *of* a person resemble that person. Of two recent pictures taken of me, one resembles Steve Allen and the other resembles nothing on earth. Secondly, not all pictures which resemble a person are *of* that person. It is obvious that a picture *of* one twin will, if it resembles the twin it is *of*, also resemble the other twin. What is more interesting is that a picture which resembles a person may not be *of* any person at all. My camera may have had a hallucination due to light leaks in its perceptual system. Similarly, if I have drawn my

---

[23] Note that an attempt to identify the object perceived in terms of resemblance with the perception rather than in terms of the causal chain leading to the perception would seriously distort an account of misperception.

conception of how the typical man will look in one million years, even if a man looking like that now exists, my picture is not *of* him (unless he sat as a model or played some other such role). Thirdly, a picture may be *of* more than one person, as when, by the split mirror technique, we obtain a composite photograph showing one man's head on another man's body. Indeed, in summary, a single picture may be *of* no one, one person, or many persons, while resembling no one, one person, or many persons, with any degree of overlap between those whom it is *of* and those whom it resembles. Of course, if photographs did not frequently, indeed usually, resemble their subjects, they could not serve many of the purposes for which we use them. Still, on occasion, things can and do go awry, and a bad photograph of one is yet a photograph *of* one.

I turn now to cases in which the causal chain from object to picture is relatively indirect. If one or several witnesses describe the criminal to a police artist who then constructs a picture, I shall say that it is a picture *of* the criminal, even when after such a genesis the resulting picture has quite ceased to resemble the criminal. Similarly, had a photograph of Julius Caesar been xeroxed, and the xerox copy televised to a monastery, where it was copied by a monk, and so was reproduced down through the ages, I would call the resulting copy, no matter how distorted, no matter who, if anyone, it resembled, a picture *of* Julius Caesar.[24]

A police artist's reconstruction of Santa Claus, based on a careful reading of the poem *The Night Before Christmas*, is not a picture *of* anyone no matter how many people make themselves up so that it exactly resembles them, and no matter whether the artist regards the poem as fact or fiction. Even if in combining facial features of known statistical

---

[24] The corresponding principle for determining who it is that a given proper name, as it is used by some speaker, names, was first brought to my attention by Saul Kripke. Kripke's examples incorporated both the indirect path from person named to person naming and also the possible distortions of associated descriptions.

The existence of a relatively large number of persons with the same proper name gives urgency to this problem even in mundane settings. In theoretical discussions it is usually claimed that such difficulties are settled by 'context'. I have recently found at least vague recognition of the use of genetic factors to account for the connection between name and named in such diverse sources as Henry Leonard: 'Probably for most of us there is little more than a vaguely felt willingness to mean . . . whatever the first assigners of the name intended by it.' (*An Introduction to Principles of Right Reason* New York: Holt, Rinehart & Winston, 1957 section 30.2), and P. F. Strawson: '[T]he identifying description . . . may include a reference to another's reference to that particular . . . So one reference may borrow the credentials . . . from another; and that from another.' (*Individuals* (London: Methuen, 1959) footnote 1, page 182). Though in neither case are genetic and descriptive features clearly distinguished.

Kripke's insights and those of Charles Chastain, who has especially emphasized the role of *knowledge* in order to establish the desired connection between name and named, are in large part responsible for the heavy emphasis I place on genetic factors.

frequencies the artist correctly judges that the resulting picture will resemble someone or other, that person has no special causal efficacy in the production of the picture and so it still will not be a picture *of* anyone. And if the story of Medusa originated in imagination or hallucination (as opposed to misperception or misapprehension), then a rendering based on that legend is *of* no one, notwithstanding the existence of any past, present, or future snake-haired women.

In addition to the link with reality provided by the relation of resemblance the descriptive content of a picture determines its *vividness*. A faded picture showing the back of a man wearing a cloak and lurking in shadow will lack vividness. A clear picture, head on, full length, life size, showing fingerprinst etc., would be counted highly vivid. What is counted as vivid may to some extent depend on special interests. To the clothier, nude portraits may be lacking in detail, while to the foot fetishist a picture showing only the left big toe may leap from the canvas. Though special interests may thus weight detail, I would expect that increase in detail always increases vividness. It should be clear that there are no necessary connections between how vivid a picture is and whether it is *of* anyone or whether it resembles anyone.

Returning now to names, it is their descriptive content that determines what if anything they denote. Thus, denotation is the analogue for names to resemblance for pictures. The genetic character of a name in a given person's usage will account for how he *acquired* the name, that is how he heard of such a thing and, if he believes that such a thing exists, how he came to believe it. It is the genetic character of the name that determines what if anything it is a name *of*. (I here use the same nomenclature, '*of*', for names as for pictures.) The user-dependence of this notion is required by the fact that Ralph and Fred may each have acquired the name 'John Smith', but in such a way that for Ralph it is a name *of* one John Smith while for Fred it is a name *of* another John Smith.

I would suppose that students of rhetoric realize that most of the lines of argument traditionally classified as 'informal fallacies' (*ad hominem*, *ad vericundiam*, etc.) are commonly considered relevant or even determinative by reasonable men.[25] Cases such as that of the two John Smiths, which emphasize the importance of genetic features in language use,

---

[25] Although it is useful for scholarly purposes to have a catalogue of such 'fallacies' (such as that provided in Carney and Scheer, *Fundamentals of Logic*, New York: Macmillan, 1964), the value of such discussions in improving the practical reasoning of rational beings seems to me somewhat dubious. A sensitive discussion of a related form of argument occurs in Angell, *Reasoning and Logic* (New York: Appleton-Century-Crofts, 1963), especially pp. 422–3.

indicate limitations that must be placed on the traditional dichotomy
between *what* we believe (assert, desire, etc.) and *how* we came to believe it.

Let us attempt to apply these considerations to the case of proper
names. Proper names denote each of the usually many persons so dubbed.
Ralph may acquire a proper name in a number of different ways. He may
have attended a dubbing with the subject present. I reconstruct such
dubbings as consisting of a stipulative association of the name with a
perception *of* the subject. Thus, the name becomes a name *of* the subject,
and as it passes from Ralph to others retains this feature in the manner
of the picture *of* Julius Caesar. We may of course dub on the basis of a
hallucination, in which case the name is a name *of* nothing, though it will
still denote each actual person, if any, that may be so dubbed. Dubbings
sometimes take place with the subject absent, in which case some other
name (usually a description) stands in for the perception, and the stipula-
tively introduced proper name takes its genetic character from the stand-in
name. If the latter only denotes the subject (and is not a name *of* the subject for the user in question), the proper name can do no better. This
having a name *of* x, I shall later take to be essential to having a belief
about x, and I am unwilling to adopt any theory of proper names which
permits me to perform a dubbing in absentia, as by solemnly declaring
'I hereby dub the first child to be born in the twenty-second century
"Newman 1" ', and thus grant myself standing to have beliefs about that
as yet unborn child. Another presumably more common way to acquire
a proper name is in casual conversation or reading, e.g. from the headline,
'Mayor Indicted; B. J. Ortcutt sought by F.B.I.'. In such cases we retrace
the causal sequence from Ralph back through his immediate source to
its immediate source and so on. An especially difficult case of this sort
arises when someone other than Ortcutt, say Wyman, is introduced to
Ralph as Ortcutt. Suppose that the introduction took place with intent to
deceive and that Fred, who made the introduction, acquired the name
'Ortcutt' as a name *of* Ortcutt. Clearly we should count 'Ortcutt' as a name
of Wyman for Ralph, but also, through Fred, as a name *of* Ortcutt. The
situation is analogous to the composite photograph made by the split
mirror technique. But here the much greater vividness of the perceptual
half of the equation may outweigh the dim reflection of Ortcutt.

I leave to the reader the useful exercise of constructing cases of names
(not necessarily proper) which are analogues to each of the cited cases of
pictures.

The notion of a vivid name is intended to go to the purely internal
aspects of individuation. Consider typical cases in which we would be
likely to say that Ralph knows x or is acquainted with x. Then look only

at the conglomeration of images, names, and partial descriptions which
Ralph employs to bring x before his mind. Such a conglomeration, when
suitably arranged and regimented, is what I call a vivid name. As with
pictures, there are degrees of vividness and the whole notion is to some
degree relative to special interests. The crucial feature of this notion is
that it depends only on Ralph's current mental state, and ignores all links
whether by resemblance or genesis with the actual world. If the name is
such, that on the assumption that there exists some individual x whom it
both denotes and resembles we should say that Ralph knows x or is
acquainted with x, then the name is vivid.

The vivid names 'represent' those persons who fill major roles in that
inner story which consists of all those sentences which Ralph believes. I
have placed 'represent' here in scarequotes to warn that there may not
actually exist anything which is so 'represented'. Ralph may enjoy an
inner story totally out of contact with reality, but this is not to deny it a
cast of robust and clearly delineated characters. Life is often less plausible
than art. Of course a vivid name should make an existence *claim*. If
Ralph does not believe that there is a Santa Claus, I would not call any
Santa Claus name vivid, no matter how lively it is in other respects.

There are certain features which may contribute strongly to vividness
but which I feel we should not accept as absolute requirements. It is
certainly too much to require that a vivid name must provide Ralph with
a means of recognizing its purported object under all circumstances, for
we do not follow the careers of even those we know best that closely.
There are always gaps. We sometimes even fail to recognize ourselves in
early photographs or recent descriptions, simply because of gaps in our
self-concept.[26] It also seems to me too much to require that Ralph believes
himself to have at some time perceived the purported object of a vivid
name since a scholar may be better acquainted with Julius Caesar than
with his own neighbour. Some have also suggested that the appropriate
kind of name must provide Ralph with the means of locating its purported
object. But parents and police are frequently unable to locate persons
well known to them. Also, a vivid biography of a peasant somewhere in
Asia, may involve none but the vaguest spatio-temporal references.

One might understand the assertion, 'Ralph has an opinion as to who
Ortcutt is' as a claim that Ralph can place Ortcutt among the leading
characters of his inner story, thus that Ralph believes some sentence of the
form $\ulcorner\alpha = \text{Ortcutt}\urcorner$ with α vivid. This, I believe, is the view of Hintikka.
Hintikka institutionalizes the sense of 'represents' with usual quotes by

---

[26] Such failures may also be due to self-deception, an inaccurate self-concept, but
then the purported object does not exist at all.

allowing existential generalization on the leading character or inner individual 'represented' by a vivid name. Although his symbolism allows him to distinguish between those inner individuals which are actual and those which are not, a central role is assigned to something close to what I call a vivid name.[27] In emphasizing this conceptual separation of vividness, which makes a name a *candidate* for exportation, from those features depending on genesis and resemblance, which determine what actual person, if anyone, the name really represents (without quotes), Hintikka (if I have him right) and I are in agreement.

It is a familiar fact of philosophy that no idea, description, or image can insure itself against non-natural causes. The most vivid of names may have had its origin in imagination or hallucination. Thus, to freely allow exportation a name must not only be vivid but must also be a name *of* someone, and indeed a name *of* the person it denotes. This last is an accuracy requirement which no doubt is rarely satisfied by the most vivid names we use. Our most vivid names can be roughly characterized as those elaborate descriptions containing all we believe about a single person. Such names will almost certainly contain inaccuracies which will prevent them from actually denoting anyone. Also such names are often not *of* a single person but result from conflation of information about several persons (as in Fred's prevaricating introduction of Wyman to Ralph).

One proposal for handling such difficulties would be to apply the method of best fit to our most vivid names, i.e. to seek the individual who comes closest to satisfying the two conditions: that the name denotes him and is *of* him. But it seems that this technique would distort the account of conflations, never allowing us to say that there are two persons whom Ralph believes to be one. There is an alternate method which I favour. Starting with one of our most vivid names, form the largest core, all of

---

[27] In so far as I understand Hintikka's 'Individuals, Possible Worlds, and Epistemic Logic', *Nous* I (1967), pp. 32–62, the domain of values of the bound variables fluctuates with the placement of the bound occurrences of the variables. If, in a quantifier's matrix, the occurrences of the variable bound to the quantifier fall only within uniterated epistemological contexts, then the variables range over possible (?) individuals 'represented' by vivid names. If, on the other hand, no occurrences of the variable fall within epistemological (or other opaque) contexts, then the variables range over the usual actual individuals. And if the variable occurs both within and without an epistemological context, then the values of the variables are inner individuals which are also actual. Thus if Ralph believes in Santa Claus, and σ is Ralph's vivid Santa Claus description, Hintikka would treat '⌜Ralph believes that σ = Santa Claus⌝, as true and as implying '∃x Ralph believes that x = Santa Claus', but would treat '∃$x[x$ = Santa Claus & Ralph believes that x = Santa Claus]' and presumably '∃$x[∃y \ y = x$ & Ralph believes that x = Santa Claus]' as false, and not as consequences of '⌜σ = Santa Claus & Ralph believes that σ = Santa Claus⌝.

which is *of* the same person and which denotes that person. A vivid name resulting from conflation may contain more than one such core name. The question is whether such a core, remaining after excision of inaccuracy, is yet vivid. If so, I will say that the core name *represents* the person whom it both denotes and is *of* to Ralph.

Our task was to characterize a relation between Ralph, a name, and a person, which could replace Δ in a variant analysis of Bel. For this I will use the above notion of representation. To repeat, I will say α *represents* x *to* Ralph (symbolized: 'R(α, x, Ralph)') if and only if (i) α denotes x, (ii) α is a name *of* x for Ralph, and (iii) α is (sufficiently) vivid. Our final version of (33) is the following variant of (36):

(44) ∃α[R(α, Ortcutt, Ralph) & Ralph **B** ⌜α is a spy⌝].

x

Part of our aim was to restrict the range of persons with whom Ralph is *en rapport* (in the sense of Bel). This was done by means of clauses (ii) and (iii). Clause (ii) excludes all future persons such as Newman 1[28] and indeed any person past, present, or future who has not left his mark on Ralph. The addition of clause (iii) excludes any person who has not left a vivid mark on Ralph.

The crucial exportation step for the case of the shortest spy is now blocked, because in spite of Ralph's correct belief that such a person exists, 'the shortest spy' is not, for Ralph, a name *of* him.[29]

Clause (iii) takes account of the desire to allow Ralph beliefs *about* (again in the sense of Bel) only those persons he 'has in mind', where the mere acquisition of, say, a proper name *of* x would not suffice to put x in mind. Furthermore, if we were to drop clause (iii), and allow any name which both denotes x and is a name *of* x to represent x to Holmes, then after Holmes observed the victim, 'the murderer' would represent the murderer to him. And thus we would have:

∃y∃α[R(α, y, Holmes) & Holmes **B** ⌜α = the murderer⌝],

which is our present analysis of:

∃y Holmes **Bel** ('x = the murderer', y),

which is, roughly, Quine's translation of:

There is someone whom Holmes believes to be the murderer.

---

[28] I disregard precognition explained by a reverse causal chain.

[29] We might say in such cases that the name *specifies* its denotation, in the sense in which a set of specifications, though not generated by the object specified, is written with the intention that there is or will be an object so described.

But this last should presage an arrest and not the mere certification of homicide. Clause (iii) is intended to block such cases. At some point in his investigation, the slow accretion of evidence, all 'pointing in a certain direction' may just push Holmes' description over the appropriate vividness threshold so that we *would* say that there is now someone whom Holmes believes to be the murderer.

Clause (iii) could also be used to block exportation of 'the shortest spy'. But that would not eliminate the need for clause (ii) which is still needed to insure that we export to the right individual.

Although I believe that all three clauses are required to block all the anomalies of exportation, I am less interested in a definitive analysis of that particular inference than I am in separating and elucidating certain notions which may be useful in epistemological discussions. According to my analysis, Ralph must have quite a solid conception of x before we can say that Ralph believes x to be a spy. By weakening the accuracy requirements on the notion of representation we obtain in general new relational senses of belief.[30] Any such notion, based on a clearly specified variant of (36), may be worthy of investigation.

XI

A vivid name is a little bit like a standard name, but not much. It can't guarantee existence to its purported object, and although it has a kind of inner reliability by way of Ralph's use of such names to order his inner world, a crucial condition of reliability—the determinateness of standard identities—fails. A standard identity is an identity sentence in which both terms are standard names. It is corollary to the reliability of standard names, that standard identities are either true under all circumstances or false under all circumstances. But not so for identities involving vivid names. We can easily form two vivid names, one describing Bertrand Russell as logician, and another describing Russell as social critic, which are such that the identity sentence simply cannot be decided on internal evidence. In the case of the morning star and the evening star, we can even form names which allow us to locate the purported objects (if we are willing to wait for the propitious moment) without the identity sentence being determinate. Of course Ralph may believe the negation of the identity sentence for all distinct pairs of vivid names, but such beliefs

---

[30] One such weakened notion of representation is that expressed by 'Ralph Bel $\ulcorner \alpha = x \urcorner, y)$', analysed as in (44) using our current **R**, which here, in contrast to the situation for Δ_N (see reference 22 above), is not equivalent to '$R(\alpha, y, Ralph)$'. Still this new notion of representation, when used in place of our current **R** in an analysis of the form of (44), leads to the same relational sense of belief.

may simply be wrong. And the names can remain vivid even after such inaccurate non-identities are excised. It may happen that Ralph comes to change his beliefs so that where he once believed a non-identity between vivid names, he now believes an identity. And at some intermediate stage of wonder he believes neither the identity nor the non-identity. Such Monte Cristo cases may be rare in reality (though rife in fiction)[31], but they are nevertheless clearly possible. They could be ruled out only by demanding an unreasonably high standard of vividness, to wit: no gaps, or else by adding an artificial and ad hoc requirement that all vivid names contain certain format items, e.g. exact place and date of birth. Either course would put us out of *rapport* with most of our closest friends. Thus, two vivid names can represent the same person to Ralph although Ralph does not believe the identity sentence. He may simply wonder, or he may disbelieve the identity sentence and so believe of one person that he is two. Similarly two vivid names can represent different persons to Ralph although Ralph does not believe the non-identity sentence. Again, Ralph may either suspend judgment or disbelieve the non-identity and so believe of two persons that they are one. Since this last situation is perhaps more plausible than the others, it is important to see that theoretically the cases are on a par. In fact, a case where Ralph has so conflated two persons and is then disabused by his friend Fred, becomes a case of believing one person to be two simply by assuming that Ralph was right in the first place and that Fred lied.

Quine acknowledges that Ralph can believe of one person that he is two on Quine's own understanding of **Bel**, when he remarks, as mentioned in VI above, that

(32) Ralph **Bel** ('x is not a spy', Ortcutt),

and

(33) Ralph **Bel** ('x is a spy', Ortcutt),

do not express an inconsistency on Ralph's part and do not imply (34). The background story justifying (32) and (33) involves Ralph twice spotting Ortcutt but under circumstances so different that Ralph was unaware that he was seeing the same man again. Indeed he believed he was not seeing the same man again, since on the one occasion he thought, 'There goes a spy', and on the other, 'Here is no spy'. My point is that though one may quibble about whether each or either of the names of

---

[31] Note especially the 'secret identity' genre of children's literature containing Superman, Batman, etc.

Ortcutt were vivid in the particular cases as described by Quine,[32] and so question whether in those cases exportation should have been permitted, no plausible characterization of appropriate conditions for vividness can prevent analogous cases from arising.

Cases of the foregoing kind, which agree with Quine's intuitions, argue an inadequacy in his regimentation of language. For in the same sense in which (32) and (33) do not express an inconsistency on Ralph's part, neither should (33) and

(45) ~Ralph **Bel** ('x is a spy', Ortcutt)

express an inconsistency on ours. Indeed it seems natural to claim that (45) is a consequence of (32). But the temptation to look upon (33) and (45) as contradictory is extremely difficult to resist. The problem is that since Quine's **Bel** suppresses mention of the specific name being exported, he cannot distinguish between

(46) $\exists\alpha[R(\alpha, \text{Ortcutt}, \text{Ralph}) \ \& \sim \text{Ralph } \mathbf{B} \ulcorner \alpha \text{ is a spy}\urcorner]$

and

(47) $\sim\exists\alpha[R(\alpha, \text{Ortcutt}, \text{Ralph}) \ \& \ \text{Ralph } \mathbf{B} \ulcorner \alpha \text{ is a spy}\urcorner]$

If (45) is read as (46), there is no inconsistency with (32); in fact, on this intepretation (45) is a consequence of (32) (at least on the assumption that Ralph does not have contradictory beliefs). But if (45) is read as (47) (Quine's intention, I suppose), it is inconsistent with (33) and independent of (32).

So long as Ralph can believe of one person that he is two, as in Quine's story, we should be loath to make either (46) or (47) inexpressible.[33] If (33) is read as (44), we certainly must retain some way of expressing (47) since it expresses the negation of (33). Is it important to retain expression of (46)? In Quine's story, something stronger than (46) holds, namely (32), which we now read as:

(48) $\exists\alpha[R(\alpha, \text{Ortcutt}, \text{Ralph}) \ \& \ \text{Ralph } \mathbf{B} \ulcorner \alpha \text{ is not a spy}\urcorner]$

---

[32] At least one author, Hintikka, has seemed unwilling to allow Ralph a belief *about* Ortcutt merely on the basis of Ralph's few glimpses *of* Ortcutt skulking around the missile base. See his 'Individuals, Possible Worlds, and Epistemic Logic', *Nous*, I (1967), 33–62, footnote 13.

[33] Another way out is to accept the fact that two names may represent the same person to Ralph though Ralph believes the non-identity, but to put an ad hoc restriction on exportation. For example to analyse (33) as: '$\exists\alpha[R(\alpha, \text{Ortcutt}, \text{Ralph}) \ \& \ \text{Ralph } \mathbf{B} \ulcorner \alpha \text{ is a spy}\urcorner] \ \& \sim \exists\alpha[R(\alpha, \text{Ortcutt}, \text{Ralph}) \ \& \sim \text{Ralph } \mathbf{B} \ulcorner \alpha \text{ is a spy}\urcorner]$'. This prevents exportation where contradiction threatens. But again much that we would like to say is inexpressible in Quine's nomenclature.

But we can continue the story to a later time at which Ralph's suspicions regarding even the man at the beach have begun to grow. Not that Ralph now proclaims that respected citizen to be a spy, but Ralph now suspends judgment as to the man's spyhood. At this time (48) is false, and (46) is true. If we are to have the means to express such suspensions of judgment, something like (46) is required.

I have gone to some trouble here to indicate the source of the notational inadequacy in the possibility of a single person bearing distinct exportable names not believed to name the same thing, and also to argue in favour of maintaining the possibility of such names. I have done this because logicians working in this field have for the most part been in accord with Quine in adopting the simpler language form. In my view the consequence of adopting such a form is either to exclude natural interpretations by setting an impossibly high standard for vividness, and thus for exportation, or else to make such partial expressions of suspended judgment as (46) inexpressible.

XII

When earlier I argued for Frege's method—seek the intermediate entity—it was on the grounds that a clarified view of the problem was worth at least a momentary ontological risk. But now it appears that to give adequate expression to the epistemological situation requires explicit quantificational certification of the status of such entities. I am undismayed and even would urge that the conservative course so far followed of taking expressions as the intermediate entities is clearly inadequate to the task. Many of our beliefs have the form: 'The colour of her hair is ———', or 'The song he was singing went ———', where the blanks are filled with images, sensory impressions, or what have you, but certainly not words. If we cannot even *say* it with words but have to paint it or sing it, we certainly cannot believe it with words.

My picture theory of meaning played heavily on the analogy between names and pictures. I believe that the whole theory of sense and denotation can be extended to apply to pictures as well as words. (How can an identity 'sentence' with the components filled by pictures be both true and informative?) If we explicitly include such visual images among names, we gain a new perspective on the claim that we can definitively settle the question of whether Bernard J. Ortcutt is such that Ralph believes him to be a spy by confronting Ralph with Ortcutt and asking 'Is *he* a spy?' Ralph's response will depend on recognition, a comparison of current images with stored ones. And stored images are simply one more form of description, worth perhaps a thousand words, but thoroughly comparable to words. Thus Ralph's answer in such a situation is simply one more piece in the whole jigsaw of his cognitive structure. He might answer 'yes' for some confrontations (compare—'yes' for some names), 'no' for others, and withhold judgment for still others.

The suggested extension of the intermediate entities poses an interesting problem for the ontologist. Must we posit a realm of special mental entities as values for the variables used in analysing the relational sense of belief, or will a variant on the trick of taking sentences as the objects of belief also account for beliefs involving visual images, odours, sounds, etc.?[34]

XIII

There are, I believe, two rather different problem areas connected with the analysis of intermediate contexts. The first problem area, which lies squarely within what is usually called the philosophy of language, involves chiefly the more fundamental non-relational interpretation of intermediate contexts. It calls for an explanation of the seemingly logically deviant behaviour of expressions in such contexts and perhaps also for a more exact statement of just what inferences, if any, are valid for such contexts. Here I feel that Frege's method outlines a generally acceptable solution. I especially appreciate the fact that for Frege intermediate contexts are not seen as exceptions to a powerful and heretofore general logical theory but rather are seen as fully accessible to that theory with the noted anomalies explained as due to a misreading of 'initial conditions' leading to an inappropriate application of the laws. This accounting for seemingly aberrant phenomena in terms of the correct application of a familiar theory is explanation at its most satisfying. By contrast, the view I have associated with Quine—that intermediate contexts are referentially inarticulate—contents itself with a huge and unobvious class of 'exceptions to the rules'. This is shabby explanation, if explanation at all.

The second problem area specifically concerns the relational interpretation of intermediate contexts. Here I have tried to show how Frege's method, though it may provide a basis for unifying the relational and non-relational interpretation of a given intermediate context and though it immediately provides for some form of quantification in, does not by itself necessarily provide the most interesting (and perhaps indispensable) relational interpretation. Further analysis, often specific to the context

---

[34] It should be noted that in Church's 'On Carnap's Analysis of Statements of Assertion and Belief' [Essay XI, below] serious objections are raised to even the first step.

in question, may be required in order to produce an appropriately discriminating form of Δ which will yield results in conformity with our intuitive demands. Indeed, such an investigation may well lead far beyond the philosophy of language proper into metaphysics and epistemology. I know of no earlier source than 'Quantifiers and Propositional Attitudes' in which relational uses of intermediate contexts are so clearly identified throughout an area of concern more urgent than modal logic. In that article Quine early expressed his remarkable insights into the pervasiveness of the relational forms and the need for a special analysis of their structure. And in fact following Quine's outlook and attempting to refine the conditions for valid applications of exportation, one might well arrive at the same metaphysical and epistemological insights as those obtained in attempting to refine Δ. What is important is that we should achieve some form of analysis of these contexts without recourse to the very idioms we are attempting to analyse.

The problem of interpreting the most interesting form of quantification in, appears in various guises: as the problem of making trans-world identifications, as the problem of finding favoured names, and as the problem of distinguishing 'essential' from 'accidental' properties.

The present paper suggests two polar techniques for finding favoured names. It is curious and somehow satisfying that they so neatly divide the objects between them, the one applying only to objects capable of being perceived (or at least of initiating causal chains), the other applying only to purely abstract objects. I am well aware of obscurities and difficulties in my formulations of the two central notions—that of a standard name and that of a name being *of* an object for a particular user. Yet both seem to me promising and worthy of further investigation.

X

SEMANTICS FOR PROPOSITIONAL ATTITUDES

Jaakko Hintikka

I. THE CONTRAST BETWEEN THE THEORY OF REFERENCE AND THE THEORY OF MEANING IS SPURIOUS

In the philosophy of logic a distinction is often made between the *theory of reference* and the *theory of meaning*.[1] In this paper I shall suggest (*inter alia*) that this distinction, though not without substance, is profoundly misleading. The theory of reference is, I shall argue, the theory of meaning for certain simple types of language. The only entities needed in the so-called theory of meaning are, in many interesting cases and perhaps even in all cases, merely what is required in order for the expressions of our language to be able to refer in certain more complicated situations. Instead of the theory of reference and the theory of meaning we perhaps ought to speak in some cases of the theory of simple and of multiple reference, respectively. Quine has regretted that the term 'semantics', which etymologically ought to refer to the theory of meaning, has come to mean the theory of reference.[1] I submit that this usage is happier than Quine thinks, and that large parts of the theory of meaning in reality are—or ought to be—but semantical theories for notions transcending the range of certain elementary types of concepts.

It seems to me in fact that the usual reasons for distinguishing between meaning and reference are seriously mistaken. Frequently, they are formulated in terms of a first-order (i.e., quantificational) language. In such a language, it is said, knowing the mere references of individual constants, or knowing the extensions of predicates, cannot suffice to specify their meanings because the references of two individual constants or the extensions of two predicate constants 'obviously' can coincide without there being any identity of meaning.[2] Hence, it is often concluded, the theory

From *Philosophical Logic*, J. W. Davis *et al.* (ed.), (Dordrecht-Holland: D. Reidel Publishing Co., 1969), pp. 21–45. Reprinted by permission of the publishers.

[1] See e.g. W. Quine, *From a Logical Point of View* (Cambridge, Mass.: Harvard University Press, 1953, 2nd edn., 1961), pp. 130–2.
[2] For a simple recent argument of this sort (without a specific reference to first-order theories), see e.g. William P. Alston, *Philosophy of Language* (Englewood Cliffs, N.J.: Prentice-Hall, Inc., 1964), p. 13. Cf. also Quine, op. cit. pp. 21–2.

of reference for first-order languages will have to be supplemented by a theory of the 'meanings' of the expressions of these languages.

The line of arguments is not without solid intuitive foundation, but its implications are different from what they are usually taken to be. This whole concept of meaning (as distinguished from reference) is very unclear and usually hard to fathom. However it is understood, it seems to me in any case completely hopeless to try to divorce the idea of the meaning of a sentence from the idea of the *information* that the sentence can convey to a hearer or reader, should someone truthfully address it to him.[3] Now what is this information? Clearly it is just information to the effect that the sentence is true, that the world is such as to meet the truth-conditions of the sentence.

Now in the case of a first-order language these truth-conditions cannot be divested from the references of singular terms and from the extensions of its predicates. In fact, these references and estensions are precisely what the truth-conditions of quantified sentences turn on. The truth-value of a sentence is a function of the references (extensions) of the terms it contains, not of their 'meanings'. Thus it follows from the above principles that a theory of reference is for genuine first-order languages the basis of a theory of meaning. Recently, a similar conclusion has in effect been persuasively argued for (from entirely different premises and in an entirely different way) by Donald Davidson.[4] The references, not the alleged meanings, of our primitive terms are thus what determine the meanings (in the sense explained) of first-order sentences. Hence the introduction of the 'meanings' of singular terms and predicates is strictly useless: In any theory of meaning which serves to explain the information which first-order sentences convey, these 'meanings' are bound to be completely idle.

What happens, then, to our intuitions concerning the allegedly obvious difference between reference and meaning in first-order languages? If these intuitions are sound, and if the above remarks are to the point, then the only reasonable conclusion is that our intuitions do not really

---

[3] In more general terms, it seems to me hopeless to try to develop a theory of sentential meaning which is not connected very closely with the idea of the information which the sentence can convey to us, or a theory of meaning for individual words which would not show how understanding them contributes to appreciating the information of the sentences in which they occur. There are of course many nuances in the actual use of words and sentences which are not directly explained by connecting meaning and information in this way, assuming that this can be done. However, there do not seem to be any obstacles in principle to explaining these nuances in terms of pragmatic, contextual, and other contingent pressures operating on a language-user. For remarks on this methodological situation, see my paper 'Epistemic Logic and the Methods of Philosophical Analysis', *Australasian Journal of Philosophy*, 46 (1968), 37–51.

[4] Donald Davidson, 'Truth and Meaning', *Synthèse*, 17 (1967), 304–23.

pertain to first-order discourse. The 'ordinary language' which we think of when we assert the obviousness of the distinction cannot be reduced to the canonical form of an applied first-order language without violating these intuitions. How these other languages enable us to appreciate the real (but frequently misunderstood) force of the apparently obvious difference between reference and meaning I shall indicate later (see Section VI *infra*).

II. FIRST-ORDER LANGUAGES

I conclude that the traditional theory of reference, suitably extended and developed, is all we need for a full-scale theory of meaning in the case of an applied first-order language. All that is needed to grasp the information that a sentence of such a language yields is given by the rules that determine the references of its terms, in the usual sense of the word. For the purposes of first-order languages, to specify the meaning of a singular term is therefore nearly tantamount to specifying its reference, and to specify the meaning of a predicate is for all practical purposes to specify its extension. As long as we can restrict ourselves to first-order discourse, the theory of truth and satisfaction will therefore be the central part of the theory of meaning.

A partial exception to this statement seems to be the theory of so-called 'meaning postulates' or 'semantical rules' which are supposed to catch non-logical synonymies.[5] However, I would argue that whatever non-logical identities of meaning there might be in our discourse ought to be spelled out, not in terms of definitions of terms, but by developing a satisfactory semantical theory for the terms which create these synonymies. In those cases in which meaning postulates are needed, this enterprise no longer belongs to the theory of first-order logic.

In more precise terms, one may thus say that to understand a sentence of first-order logic is to know its interpretation in the actual world. To know this is to know the interpretation function ϕ. This can be characterized as a function which does the following things:

(1.1) For each individual constant a of our first-order language, $\phi(a)$ is a member of the domain of individuals l.

The domain of individuals l is of course to be thought of as the totality of objects which our language speaks of.

(1.2) For each constant predicate Q (say of n terms), $\phi(Q)$ is a set of n-tuples of the members of l.

[5] See Quine, op. cit., pp. 32–7.

If we know ϕ and if we know the usual rules holding of satisfaction (truth), we can in principle determine the truth-values of all the sentences of our-order language. This is the cash value of the statement made above that the extensions of our individual constants and constant predicates are virtually all that we need in the theory of meaning in an applied first-order language.[6]

These conditions may be looked upon in slightly different ways. If ϕ is considered as an arbitrary function in (1.1)–(1.2), instead of that particular function which is involved in one's understanding of a language, and if l is likewise allowed to vary, we obtain a characterization of the concept of interpretation in the general model-theoretic sense.

III. PROPOSITIONAL ATTITUDES

We have to keep in mind the possibility that ϕ might be only a partial function (as applied to free singular terms), i.e., that some of our singular terms are in fact empty. This problem is not particularly prominent in the present paper, however.[7] If what I have said so far is correct, then the emphasis philosophers have put on the distinction between reference and meaning (e.g. between *Bedeutung* and *Sinn*) is motivated only in so far as they have implicitly or explicitly considered concepts which go beyond the expressive power of first-order languages.[8] Probably the most important type of such concept is a propositional attitude.[9] One purpose of this paper is to sketch some salient features of a semantical theory of such concepts. An interesting problem will be the question as to what extent we have to assume entities other than the usual individuals (the members of l) in order to give a satisfactory account of the meaning of propositional attitudes. As will be seen, what I take to be the true answer to this question is surprisingly subtle, and cannot be formulated by a simple 'yes' or 'no'.

What I take to be the distinctive feature of all use of propositional attitudes is the fact that in using them we are considering more than one

---

[6] The main reason why the truth of these observations is not appreciated more widely seems to be the failure to consider realistically what the actual use of a first-order language (say for the purpose of conveying information to another person) would look like.

[7] The basic problems as to what happens when this possibility is taken seriously are discussed in my paper, 'Studies in the Logic of Existence and Necessity I', *The Monist*, 50 (1966), 55–76.

[8] This is certainly true of Frege. His very interest in oblique contexts seems to have been kindled by the realization that they cannot be handled by means of the ideas he had successfully applied to first-order logic.

[9] The term seems to go back to Bertrand Russell, *An Inquiry into Meaning and Truth* (London: George Allen and Unwin, 1940).

possibility concerning the world.[10] (This consideration of different possibilities is precisely what makes propositional attitudes propositional, it seems to me.) It would be more natural to speak of different possibilities concerning our 'actual' world than to speak of several possible worlds. For the purpose of logical and semantical analysis, the second locution is much more appropriate than the first, however, although I admit that it sounds somewhat weird and perhaps also suggests that we are dealing with something much more unfamiliar and unrealistic than we are actually doing. In our sense, whoever has made preparations for more than one course of events has dealt with several 'possible courses of events' or 'possible worlds'. Of course, the possible courses of events he considered were from his point of view so many alternative courses that the actual events might take. However, only one such course of events (at most) became actual. Hence there is a sense in which the others were merely 'possible courses of events', and this is the sense on which we shall try to capitalize.

[10] An important qualification here is that for deep logical reasons one cannot usually distinguish effectively between what is 'really' a logically possible world and what merely 'appears' on the face of one's language (or thinking) to be a possibility. This, in a sufficiently sharp analysis, is what destroys the pleasant invariance of propositional attitudes with respect to logical equivalence. Even though p and q are equivalent, i.e. even though the 'real' possibilities concerning the world that they admit and exclude are the same,

$$a \quad \begin{matrix} \text{knows} \\ \text{believes} \\ \text{remembers} \\ \text{hopes} \\ \text{strives} \end{matrix} \quad \text{that } p$$

and

$$a \quad \begin{matrix} \text{knows} \\ \text{believes} \\ \text{remembers} \\ \text{hopes} \\ \text{strives} \end{matrix} \quad \text{that } q$$

need not be equivalent, for the apparent (to a) possibilities admitted by p and q need not be identical.

I have studied this concept of an 'apparent' possibility and its consequences at some length elsewhere (especially in the second and third paper printed in *Deskription, Analytizität und Existenz*, ed. by Paul Weingartner (Salzburg and Munich: Pustet, 1966); in 'Are Logical Truths Analytic?', *The Philosophical Review*, 74 (1965), 178–203; in 'Surface Information and Depth Information', forthcoming in *Information and Inference*, ed. by K. J. J. Hintikka and P. Suppes (Dordrecht: D. Reidel Publishing Co., 1969), and in 'Are Mathematical Truths Synthetic A Priori?', *Journal of Philosophy* LXV (1968), 640–51.

It is an extremely interesting concept to study and to codify. However, it is not directly relevant to the concerns of the present paper, and would in any case break its confines. Hence it will not be taken up here, except by way of this *caveat*.

Let us assume for simplicity that we are dealing with only one propositional attitude and that we are considering a situation in which it is attributed to one person only. Once we can handle this case, a generalization to the others is fairly straightforward. Since the person in question remains constant throughout the first part of our discussion, we need not always indicate him explicitly.

IV. PROPOSITIONAL ATTITUDES AND 'POSSIBLE WORLDS'

My basic assumption (slightly oversimplified) is that an attribution of any propositional attitude to the person in question involves a division of all the possible worlds (more precisely, all the possible worlds which we can distinguish in the part of language we use in making the attribution) into two classes: into those possible worlds which are in accordance with the attitude in question and into those which are incompatible with it. The meaning of the division in the case of such attitudes as knowledge, belief, memory, perception, hope, wish, striving, desire, etc., is clear enough. For instance, if what we are speaking of are (say) a's memories, then, these possible worlds are all the possible worlds compatible with everything he remembers.

There are propositional attitudes for which this division is not possible. Some such attitudes can be defined in terms of attitudes for which the assumptions do hold, and thus in a sense can be 'reduced' to them. Others may fail to respond to this kind of attempted reduction to those 'normal' attitudes which we shall be discussing here. If there really are such recalcitrant propositional attitudes, I shall be glad to restrict the scope of my treatment so as to exclude them. Enough extremely important notions will still remain within the purview of my methods.

There is a sense in which in discussing a propositional attitude, attributed to a person, we can even restrict our attention to those possible worlds which are in accordance with this attitude.[11] This may be brought out, e.g. by paraphrasing statements about propositional attitudes in terms

---

[11] There is a distinction here which is not particularly relevant to my concerns in the present paper but important enough to be noted in passing, especially as I have not made it clear in my earlier work. What precisely are the worlds 'alternative to' a given one, say μ? A moment's reflection on the principles underlying my discussion will show, I trust, that they must be taken to be worlds compatible with a certain person's having a definite propositional attitude in μ, and not just compatible with the content of his attitude, for instance, compatible with someone's knowing something in μ and not just compatible with what he knows. I failed to spell this out in my *Knowledge and Belief* (Ithaca, N.Y.: Cornell Univ. Press, 1962), as R. Chisholm in effect pointed out in his review article, 'The Logic of Knowing', *Journal of Philosophy*, LX (1963), 773–95.

of this restricted class of all possible worlds. The following examples will illustrate these approximate paraphrases:

> *a* believes that *p* = in all the possible worlds compatible with what *a* believes, it is the case that *p*;

> *a* does not believe that *p* (in the sense 'it is not the case that *a* believes that *p*') = in at least one possible world compatible with what *a* believes it is not the case that *p*.

V. SEMANTICS FOR PROPOSITIONAL ATTITUDES

What kind of semantics is appropriate for this mode of treating propositional attitudes? Clearly what is involved is a set Ω of possible worlds or of models in the usual sense of the word. Each of them, say $\mu \in \Omega$, is characterized by a set of individuals $I(\mu)$ existing in that 'possible world'. An interpretation of individual constants and predicates will now be a two-argument function $\phi(a, \mu)$ or $\phi(Q, \mu)$ which depends also on the possible world μ in question. Otherwise an interpretation works in the same way as in the pure first-order case, and the same rules hold for propositional connectives as in this old case.

Simple though this extension of the earlier semantical theory is, it is in many ways illuminating. For instance, it is readily seen that in many cases earlier semantical rules are applicable without changes. *Inter alia*, in so far as no words for propositional attitudes occur inside the scope of a quantifier, this quantifier is subject to the same semantical rules (satisfaction conditions) as before.

VI. MEANING AND THE DEPENDENCE OF REFERENCE ON 'POSSIBLE WORLDS'

A new aspect of the situation is the fact that the reference $\phi(a, \mu)$ of a singular term now depends on μ—on what course the events will take, one might say. This enables us to appreciate an objection which you probably felt like making earlier when it was said that in a first-order language the theory of meaning is the theory of reference. What really determines the meaning of a singular term, you felt like saying, is not whatever reference it happens to have, but rather the way in which this reference is determined. But in order for this to make any difference, we must consider more than one possibility as to what the reference is, depending on the circumstances (i.e. depending on the course events will take). This dependence is just what is expressed by $\phi(a, \mu)$ when it is considered as a function of μ. (This function *is* the meaning of *a*, one is tempted to say.) Your objection thus has a point. However, it does not show that more is involved in the theory of meaning for first-order languages than the references of its terms. Rather, what is shown is that in order to spell out the idea that the meaning of a term is the way in which its reference is determined we have to consider how the reference varies in different possible worlds, and therefore go beyond first-order languages, just as I suggested above. Analogous remarks apply of course to the extensions of predicates.

Another novelty here is the need of picking out one distinguished possible world from among them all, viz. the world that happens to be actualized ('the actual world').

VII. DEVELOPING AN EXPLICIT SEMANTICAL THEORY: ALTERNATIVENESS RELATIONS

How are these informal observations to be incorporated into a more explicit semantical theory? According to what I have said, understanding attributions of the propositional attitude in question (let us assume that this is expressed by 'B') means being able to make a distinction between two kinds of possible worlds, according to whether they are compatible with the relevant attitudes of the person in question. The semantical counterpart to this is of course a function which to a given individual person assigns a set of possible worlds.

However, a minor complication is in order here. Of course, the person in question may himself have different attitudes in the different worlds we are considering. Hence this function in effect becomes a relation which to a given individual *and to a given possible world* μ associates a number of possible worlds which we shall call the *alternatives* to μ. The relation will be called the alternativeness relation. (For different propositional attitudes, we have to consider different alternativeness relations.) Our basic apparatus does not impose many restrictions on it. The obvious requirement that ensues from what has been said is the following:

(S.B.) $B_a p$ is true in a possible world μ if and only if p is true in all the alternatives to μ.

$B_a p$ may here be thought of as a shorthand for 'a believes that p'. We can write this condition in terms of an interpretation function ϕ. What understanding B means is to have a function ϕ_B which to a given possible world μ and to a given individual a associates a set of possible worlds $\phi_B(a, \mu)$, namely, the set of all alternatives to μ.[12] Intuitively, they are

---

[12] As the reader will notice, I am misusing (in the interest of simplicity) my terminology systematically by speaking elliptically of 'the person a' etc. when 'the person referred to by a' or some such thing is meant. I do not foresee any danger of confusion resulting from this, however.

the possible worlds compatible with the presence of the attitude expressed by B in the person a in the possible world μ.

In terms of this extended interpretation function, (S.B.) can be written as follows:

$$B_a p \text{ is true in } \mu \text{ if and only if } p \text{ is true in every member of } \phi_B(a, \mu).$$

VIII. RELATION TO QUINE'S CRITERION OF COMMITMENT

The interesting and important feature of this truth-condition is that it involves quantification over a certain set of possible worlds. By Quine's famous criterion, we allegedly are ontologically committed to whatever we quantify over.[13] Thus my semantical theory of propositional attitudes seems to imply that we are committed to the existence of possible worlds as a part of our ontology.

This conclusion seems to me false, and I think that it in fact constitutes a counter-example to Quine's criterion of commitment *qua* a criterion of ontological commitment. Surely we must in some sense be *committed* to whatever we quantify over. To this extent Quine seems to be entirely right. But why call this a criterion of *ontological* commitment? One's ontology is what one assumes to exist in one's world, it seems to me. It is, as it were, one's census of one's universe. Now such a census is meaningful only in some particular possible world. Hence Quine's criterion can work as a criterion of *ontological* commitment only if the quantification it speaks of is a quantification over entities belonging to some one particular world. To be is perhaps to be a value of a bound variable. But to exist in an ontologically relevant sense, to be a part of the furniture of the world, is to be a value of a special kind of a bound variable, namely one whose values all belong to the same possible world. Thus the notion of a possible world serves to clarify considerably the idea of ontological commitment so as to limit the scope of Quine's dictum.

Clearly, our quantification over possible worlds does not satisfy this extra requirement. Hence there is a perfectly good sense in which we are not ontologically committed to possible worlds, however important their role in our semantical theory may be.

Quine's distinction between *ontology* and *ideology*, somewhat modified and put to a new use, is handy here.[14] We have to distinguish between

---

[13] e.g. Quine, op. cit., pp. 1–14; W. Quine, *Word and Object* (Cambridge, Mass.: The MIT Press, and New York and London: Wiley and Sons, 1960), pp. 241–3. It is not quite clear from Quine's exposition, however, precisely how much emphasis is to be put on the word 'ontology' in his criterion of ontological commitment. My discussion which focuses on this word may thus have to be taken as a qualification to Quine's criterion rather than as outright criticism.

[14] Quine, *From a Logical Point of View*, pp. 130–2.

what we are committed to in the sense that we believe it to exist in the actual world or in some other possible world, and what we are committed to as a part of our ways of dealing with the world conceptually, committed to as a part of our conceptual system. The former constitute our ontology, the latter our 'ideology'. What I am suggesting is that the possible worlds we have to quantify over are a part of our ideology but not of our ontology.

The general criterion of commitment is a generalization of this. Quantification over the members of one particular world is a measure of ontology, quantification that crosses possible worlds is often a measure of ideology. Quine's distinction thus ceases to mark a difference between two different types of studies or two different kinds of entities within one's universe. It now marks, rather, a distinction between the object of reference and certain aspects of our own referential apparatus. Here we can perhaps see what the so-called distinction between theory of reference and theory of meaning really amounts to.

It follows, incidentally, that if we could restrict our attention to *one* possible word only, Quine's restriction would be true without qualifications. Of course, the restriction is one which Quine apparently would very much like to make; hence he has a legitimate reason for disregarding the qualifications for his own purposes.

Our 'ideological' commitment to possible worlds other than the actual one is neither surprising nor disconcerting. If what we are dealing with are the things people do—more specifically, the concepts they use—in order to be prepared for more than one eventuality, it is not at all remarkable that in order to describe these concepts fully we have to speak of courses of events other than the actual one.

IX. SINGULAR TERMS AND QUANTIFICATION IN THE CONTEXT
OF PROPOSITIONAL ATTITUDES

Let us return to the role of individual constants (and other singular terms). Summing up what was said before, we can say that what the understanding of an individual constant amounts to in a first-order language is knowing which individual it stands for. Now it is seen that in the presence of propositional attitudes this statement has to be expanded to say that one has to know what the singular term stands for in the different possible worlds we are considering.

Furthermore, in the same way as these individuals (or perhaps rather the method of specifying them) may be said to be what is 'objectively given' to us when we understand the constant, in the same way what is involved in the understanding of a propositional attitude is precisely that distinction which in our semantical apparatus is expressed by the function which serves to define the alternativeness relation. This function is what is 'objectively given' to us with the understanding of a word for a propositional attitude.

These observations enable us to solve almost all the problems that relate to the use of identity in the context of propositional attitudes. For instance, we can at once see why the familiar principle of the substitutivity of identity is bound to fail in the presence of propositional attitudes when applied to arbitrary singular terms.[15] Two such terms, say a and b, may refer to one and the same individual in the actual world ($\phi(a, \mu_0) = \phi(b, \mu_0)$ for the world μ_0 that happens to be actualized), thus making the identity '$a = b$' true, and yet fail to refer to the same individual in some other (alternative) possible world (i.e., we may have $\phi(a, \mu_1) \neq \phi(b, \mu_1)$ for some $\mu_1 \in \phi_B(c, \mu_0)$ where c is the individual whose attitudes are being discussed and B the relevant attitude). Since the presence of propositional attitudes means (if I am right) that these other possible worlds have to be discussed as well, in their presence the truth of the identity '$a = b$' does not guarantee that the same things can be said of the references of a and b without qualification, i.e., does not guarantee the intersubstitutivity of the terms a and b.

Our observations also enable us to deal with quantification in contexts governed by words for propositional attitudes as long as we do not quantify *into* them. However, as soon as we try to do so, all the familiar difficulties which have been so carefully and persuasively presented by Quine and others will apply with full force.[16] An individual constant occurring within the scope of an operator like B which expresses a propositional attitude does not specify a unique individual. Rather, what it does is to specify an individual in each of the possible worlds we have to consider. Replace it by an individual variable, and you do not get anything that you could describe by speaking of the individuals over which this variable ranges. There are (it seems) simply no uniquely defined individuals here at all.

It is perhaps thought that the way out is simply to deny that one can ever quantify into a non-extensional context. However, this way out does

[15] For a discussion of the problems connected with the substitutivity principle, see my exchange with Føllesdal: D. Føllesdal, 'Knowledge, Identity, and Existence', *Theoria*, 33 (1967), 1–27; J. Hintikka, 'Existence and Identity in Epistemic Contexts', ibid. pp. 138–47.
[16] See Quine, *From a Logical Point of View*, Ch. 8 [Essay I above]; *Word and Object*, Ch. 6; *The Ways of Paradox and Other Essays* (New York: Random House, 1966), Chs. 13–15.

not work.[17] As a matter of fact, in our ordinary language we often
quantify into a grammatical construction governed by an expression for
a propositional attitude. Locutions like 'knows who', 'sees what', 'has an
opinion concerning the identity of' are cases in point, and so is almost
any (other) construction in which pronouns are allowed to mix with
words for propositional attitudes. Beliefs about 'oneself' and 'himself'
yield further examples, and an account of their peculiarities leads to an
interesting reconstruction of the traditional distinction between so-called
modalities *de dicto* and *de re*.[18]

Another general fact is that we obviously have beliefs about definite
individuals and not just about whoever happens to meet a certain description. I want to suggest that such beliefs (and the corresponding
attitudes in the case of other propositional attitudes) are precisely what
one half of the *de dicto*—*de re* distinction amounts to.[19]

Furthermore, it does not do to try to maintain that in these constructions the propositional attitude itself has to be taken in an unusual
extensional or 'referentially transparent' sense. Such senses can in fact be
defined in terms of the normal senses of propositional attitudes. However,
these definitions already involve the objectionable quantification into
opaque contexts, and if one tries to postulate the defined senses as irreducible primitive senses, they do not have the properties which they ought
to have in order to provide the resulting quantified statements with the
logical powers they in fact have in ordinary language. For instance,
Quine's attempt to postulate a sense of (say) knowledge in which one is
allowed to quantify into a context governed by a transparently construed
construction 'knows that' has the paradoxical result that

$(\exists x)$ Jones knows that $(x = a)$

is implied by any (transparently interpreted) statement of the form

Jones knows that $(b = a)$

---

[17] Some arguments to this effect were given in *Knowledge and Belief* (ref. n. 11
above), pp. 142–6. The only informed criticism of this criticism that I have seen has
been presented by R. L. Sleigh, in a paper entitled 'A Note on an Argument of
Hintikka's', *Philosophical Studies*, 18 (1967), 12–14. As I point out in my reply,
'Partially Transparent Senses of Knowing' (forthcoming), Sleigh's argument turns on
an ambiguity in my original formulation which is easily repaired. Neither the ambiguity
nor its elimination provides any solace to the adherents of the view I have criticized,
however.

[18] One thing at which this old distinction aims is obviously the distinction (which I
am about to explain) between statements about whoever or whatever meets a description and statements about the individual who in fact does so. For the distinction, cf.
J. Hintikka, 'Individuals, Possible Worlds, and Epistemic Logic', *Nous*, I (1967),
32–62, especially 46–9, as well as ' "Knowing Oneself" and Other Problems in Epistemic
Logic', *Theoria*, 32 (1966), 1–13.

[19] Cf. below (Section XII).

and even by a similarly interpreted sentence

Jones knows that $(a = a)$.

This I take to show that the first of these three sentences can scarcely serve as a formulation of 'Jones knows who (or what) a is' in our canonical idiom. Yet no other paraphrase of this ubiquitous locution has been proposed, and none is likely to be forthcoming. (For what else can there be to Jones' knowing who a is than his knowing of some well-defined individual that Jones is that very individual?) And it is Quine who always insists as strongly as anyone else that the values of bound variables have to be well-defined individuals. It is not much more helpful to try to maintain that no true sentences of the form

Jones knows that $(b = a)$

(with the transparent sense of 'knows') are forthcoming whenever Jones fails to know who a is. The transparent sense in which this would be the case has never been explained in a satisfactory way, and I do not see how it can be done in a reasonable way without falling back to my own analysis. (What can it conceivably mean e.g. for Jones not to know in the transparent sense that an a, whom he knows to exist, is not self-identical? Can this self-identity fail to be true in a possible world compatible with everything Jones knows?)

Hence we have to countenance quantification into a context governed by an expression for an (opaquely construed) propositional attitude. Our semantical theory at once suggests a way of handling these problems. For instance, in order for existential generalization to be applicable to a singular term b occurring, say, in a context where a's belief are being discussed, it has to be required that b refers to the *same* individual in the different possible worlds compatible with what a believes (plus, possibly, in the actual world). This, naturally, will be expressed by a statement of the form

(*) $(\exists x)[B_a(x = b)$ & $(x = b)]$

or, if we do not have to consider the actual world, of the form

$(\exists x)B_a(x = b)$.

X. METHODS OF CROSS-IDENTIFICATION

This solution is simple, straightforward, and workable. It generalizes easily to other propositional attitudes. However, it hides certain interesting conceptual presuppositions. With what right do we speak of individuals in the different possible worlds as being *identical*? This is the problem to which we have to address ourselves.

It is not difficult to see what more there is given to us with our ordinary understanding of propositional attitudes that we have not yet dealt with. For instance, consider a man who has a number of beliefs as to what will happen tomorrow to himself and to his friends. Consider, on his behalf, a number of possible courses of events tomorrow. If I know what our man believes, I can sort these into those which are compatible with his beliefs as distinguished from those which are incompatible with them. But this is not all that is involved. Surely the same or largely the same individuals must figure in these different sequences of events. Under different courses of events a given individual may undergo different experiences, entertain different beliefs and hopes and fears; he may behave rather differently and perhaps even look somewhat different. Nevertheless our man can be (although he need not be) and usually is completely confident that, whatever may happen, he is going to be able to recognize (re-identify) his friends under these various courses of events, at least in principle. He may admit that courses of events are perhaps logically possible under which he would fail to do so; but these would not be compatible with his beliefs as to what will happen. Given full descriptions of two different courses of events tomorrow, both compatible with what our man believes ('believes possible', we sometimes say with more logical than grammatical justification), he will be able to recognize which individuals figuring in one of these descriptions are identical with which individual in the other, even if their names are being withheld. (Of course our man need not believe all this but my point is merely that he *can* and very often *does* believe it.)

The logical moral of this story is that together with the rest of our beliefs we are often given something more than we have so far incorporated into our semantical theory. We are given ways of *cross-identifying* individuals, that is to say, ways of understanding questions as to whether an individual figuring in one possible world is or is not identical with an individual figuring in another world.[20]

This is one point at which the obviousness of my claim may be partially obscured by my terminology. Let us recall what these 'possible worlds' are in the case of propositional attitude. They are normally possible states of affairs or courses of events compatible with the attitude in question in some specified person. Now normally these attitudes may be

[20] Cf. here my paper, 'On the Logic of Perception', forthcoming in *Perception and Personal Identity*, ed. by N. Care and R. Grimm (Cleveland: Case Western Reserve Univ. Press, 1969).

attitudes towards definite persons or definite physical objects. But how is it that we may be sure, sight unseen, that the attitudes are directed towards the right persons or objects? Only if in all the possible worlds compatible with the attitude in question we can pick out the recipient of this attitude, i.e. the individual at its receiving end. Although in many concrete situations the possibility of doing so is obvious, it has not been built into our semantical apparatus so far. There is so far nothing in our semantical theory which enables us to relate to each other the members of the different domains of individuals $I(\mu)$. In many, though not necessarily all, applications of such relations are given to us as a part of our understanding of the concepts involved. For such cases, we have to build a richer semantical theory.

The way to do so is to postulate a method of making cross-identifications. One possible way to do so is to postulate a set of functions F each member f of which picks out at most one individual $f(\mu)$ from the domain of individuals $I(\mu)$ of each given model μ. We must allow that there is no such value for some models μ. In other words, $f \in F$ may be a partial function. Furthermore, we must often require that, given f_1, $f_2 \in F$, if $f_1(\mu) = f_2(\mu)$ then $f_1(\lambda) = f_2(\lambda)$ for all alternatives λ to μ. In other words, an individual cannot 'split' when we move from a world to its alternatives. This question may seem to be a mere matter of detail, but it is easily seen that the question whether an individual can split in the sense just explained is tantamount to the question whether the substitutivity of identity can fail for bound (individual) variables, i.e. to the question whether a sentence

$$(x)(y)(x = y \supset B_a(x = y))$$

can fail to be logically true. This, again, is tantamount to the question whether a sentence of the form

$$(x)(y)(x = y \supset (Q(x) \supset Q(y)))$$

(with just one layer of operators for propositional attitudes in Q) can fail to be logically true.

In terms of the set F, the question whether $a \in I(\mu)$ is identical with $b \in I(\lambda)$ amounts to the question whether there is a function of $f \in F$ such that $f(\mu) = a, f(\lambda) = b$.

XI. THE ROLE OF INDIVIDUATING FUNCTIONS

Instead of speaking of a set of functions correlating to each other the individuals existing in the different possible worlds, it is often more appropriate to speak of these domains of individuals as being partly identical (overlapping). Then there would be no need to speak of correlations at all. This point of view is useful in that it illustrates the fact that the apparently different individuals which are correlated by one of the functions $f \in F$ is just what we ordinarily mean by one and the same individual. It is the concrete individual which we speak about, which we give a name to, etc. In fact, the members of F might in fact be thought of as names or individual constants of a certain special kind, namely those having a unique reference in all the different worlds we are speaking of and hence satisfying formulas of the form (*). Indeed, I shall assume in the sequel that a constant of this kind can be associated with each function $f \in F$.

However, emphasizing the role of the functions $f \in F$ is useful for several purposes. First and foremost, it highlights an extremely important non-trivial part of our native conceptual skills, namely, our capacity to recognize one and the same individual under different circumstances and under different courses of events. What the set F of functions embodies is just the totality of ways of doing this. The non-trivial character of the possibility of this recognition would be lost if we should simply speak of the members of the different possible worlds as being partly identical.

For another thing, the structure formed by the relations of cross-world identity (David Kaplan calls them 'trans-world heir lines') may be so complex as to be indescribable by speaking simply of partial identities between the domains of individuals of the different possible worlds. Above, it was said that in the case of many propositional attitudes an individual cannot 'split' when we move from a world to its alternatives. Although this seems to me to be the case with all the propositional attitudes I have studied in any detail, it is not quite clear to me precisely why this should always be the case. At any rate, there seem to be reasons for suspecting that the opposite 'irregularity' can occasionally take place with some modalities: individuals can 'merge together' when we move from a world to its alternatives. An analogy with temporal modalities may be instructive here.[21] If we presuppose some suitable system of cross-identifications between individuals existing at different times which turn on continuity, it seems possible in principle that a singular term should refer to the same physical system at all the different moments of

[21] For temporal modalities, see e.g. A. N. Prior, *Past, Present and Future* (Oxford: Clarendon Press, 1967). I am not saying that our actual methods of cross-identification in the case of temporal modalities (i.e. on ordinary methods of re-identification) turn on continuity quite as exclusively as I am about to suggest. It suffices for my purposes to present an example of methods of cross-identification that allows both 'branching' and 'merging', and it seems to me at least conceivably that temporal modalities might under suitable circumstances create such a situation.

time we are considering although this system 'merges' with others at times and occasionally 'splits up' into several. Some of these complications seem to be impossible to rule out completely in the case of some propositional attitudes, and because of them the idea of partly overlapping domains seems to me seriously oversimplified.

An extremely important further reason why we cannot reify the members of F into ordinary individuals is the possibility of having two different methods of cross-identification between the members of the same possible worlds, i.e. two different sets of 'individuating functions' although we are dealing with precisely the same sets of possible worlds. I have argued elsewhere that this kind of situation is not only possible to envisage but is actually present in our own ways with perceptual contexts.[22] It would take us too far to show precisely what is involved in such cases. Suffice it to point out that this claim, if true, would strikingly demonstrate the dependence of our methods of cross-indentification on our own conceptual schemes and hence on things of our own creation. The apparent simplicity of our idea of an 'ordinary' individual, safe as it may seem in its solid commonplace reality, is thus seen to be merely a reflection of the familiarity and relatively deep customary entrenchment of one particular method of cross-identification, which *sub specie aeternitatis* (i.e. *sub specie logicae*) nevertheless enjoys but a relative privilege as against a host of others.

The methods of cross-identification represented by the set F of 'individuating functions', as we might call them, also call for several further comments.

The main function of this part of our semantical apparatus is to make sense of quantification into contexts of propositional attitudes. The truth-conditions of statements in which this happens can be spelled out in terms of membership in F. As an approximation we can say the following: A sentence of the form $(\exists x)Q(x)$ is true in μ if an only if there is an individual constant (say b) associated with some $f \in F$ such that $Q(b)$ is true in μ. This approximation shows, incidentally, how close we can stick to the simple-minded idea that an existentially quantified sentence is true if and only if it has a true substitution instance. The only additional requirement we need is that the substitution-value of the bound variable has to be of the right sort, to wit, has to specify the same individual in all the possible worlds we are speaking of in the existential sentence in question. This is what is meant by the requirement that b has to be associated with one of the functions $f \in F$.

This approximation, although not unrepresentative of the general situation, requires certain modifications in order to work in all cases. The set **F** has to be relativized somewhat in the same way the unrestricted notion of a possible world was replaced by the notion of an alternative in the truth-criterion (S.B.) above. (Not everyone is in all situations 'familiar with' all the relevant methods of individuation, it might be said.) I shall not discuss the ensuing complications here, however, for they do not change the overall picture in those respects which are relevant in the rest of this paper.

XII. STATEMENTS ABOUT DEFINITE INDIVIDUALS VS. STATEMENTS ABOUT WHOEVER OR WHATEVER IS REFERRED TO BY A TERM

The possibility of quantifying across an operator which expresses a propositional attitude enables us to explicate the logic of the locutions in which we need this possibility in the first place. Perhaps the most important thing we can do here is to make a distinction between propositional attitudes directed to whoever (whatever) happens to be referred to by a term and attitudes directed towards a certain individual, independently of how he happens to be referred to. This distinction was hinted at above. Now it is time to explain it more fully. For instance, someone may have a belief concerning the next Governor of California, whoever he is or may be, say that he will be a Democrat. This is different from believing something about the individual who, so far unbeknownst to all of us, in fact is the next Governor of California.

In formal terms, the distinction is illustrated by the pair of statements

$B_a(g$ is a Democrat)

$(\exists x)((x = g) \\& B_a(x$ is a Democrat)).

Notice, incidentally, that my way of drawing this distinction implies that one can have (say) a belief concerning the individual who in fact is a only if such individual actually exists, whereas one can in principle have a belief concerning a, 'whoever he is', even though there is no such person. This, of course, is just as it ought to be.

The naturalness of our semantical conditions, and their close relation to the realities of actual usage, can be illustrated by applying them to what I have called a statement about a definite individual. As an example, we can use

'a believes of the man who in fact is Mr. Smith that he is a thief',

in brief,

$(\exists x)(x = $ Smith $\\& B_a(x$ is a thief)).

In order for this to be true, there has to be some $f \in F$ such that the value of f in the actual world (call it μ_0) exists and is Smith and that $f(\mu)$ has the property of being a thief whenever $\mu \in \phi_B(a, \mu_0)$, i.e. in all the alternatives to the actual world.

What the requirement of the existence of f amounts to is clear enough. If it is true to say that a has a belief about *the particular individual* who in fact is Smith, then a clearly must believe that he can characterize this individual uniquely. In other words, he must have some way of referring to or characterizing this individual in such a way that one and the same individual is in fact so characterized in all the worlds compatible with what he believes. This is precisely what the existence of f amounts to. If no such function existed, a would not be able to pick out the individual who in fact is Smith under all the courses of events he believes possible, and there would not be any sense in saying that a's belief is *about* the particular individual in question.

XIII. INDIVIDUATING FUNCTIONS VS. INDIVIDUAL CONCEPTS

One important consequence of my approach is that not every function which from each μ picks out an individual can be said to specify a unique individual. In fact, many perfectly good free singular terms fail to do so in the context of many propositional attitudes. Even proper names fail to do so in epistemic contexts, for one may fail to know who the bearer of a given proper name is.

Such arbitrary functions may be important for many purposes. They are excellent approximations in our theory to the 'individual concepts' which many philosophers have postulated.[23] (In Section VI above we already met a number of such 'individual concepts' in the form of the functions $\phi(a, \mu)$ with a fixed a.) Each such individual concept specifies or 'contains', as Frege would say, not just a reference (in the actual world) but also the way in which this reference is given to us. Each of them would thus qualify for a sense (*Sinn*) of a singular term à la Frege.[24] However, we do not need the totality of such arbitrary functions in the semantics which I am building up and which (I want to argue) is largely implicit in our native conceptual apparatus. Quine's criterion, however misleading it may be as a criterion of ontological commitment, still works as a criterion of commitment. If it is applied here, it shows that we are not committed (ontologically or 'ideologically') to these arbitrary functions,

[23] Cf. e.g. R. Carnap, *Meaning and Necessity* (Chicago: University of Chicago Press, 1947, 2nd edn.: 1956) pp. 41, 180–1, and Section VI, above.

[24] Cf. Gottlob Frege, 'Über Sinn und Bedeutung', *Zeitschrift für Philosophie und philosophische Kritik*, 100 (1892), 25–50, especially p. 26, last few lines.

since we do not have to quantify over them, only over the members of the much narrower class **F**.

The other side of the coin is that in our semantical apparatus we do have to quantify over the members of **F**. Does it follow that they 'exist' or 'are part of our ontology'? An answer to this question can be given along the same lines as to the corresponding question concerning 'possible worlds'. The members of **F** are not members of any possible world; they are not part of anybody's count of 'what there is'. They may 'subsist' or perhaps 'exist', and they are certainly 'objective', but they do not have any ontological role to play. The need to distinguish between ontology and 'ideology' is especially patent here.

The functions that belong to **F** may of course be considered special cases of the 'individual concepts' postulated by some philosophers of logic or as special cases of Frege's 'senses' (*Sinne*). No identification is possible between the two classes, however, for we saw earlier that not every arbitrary singular term (say b) which picks out an individual from each $I(\mu)$ we are considering goes together with an $f \in F$, although every such term is certainly meaningful and hence has a Fregean 'sense' and perhaps even gives us an 'individual concept'. As I have put it elsewhere, members of **F** do not only involve a 'way of being given' as Frege's senses do, but also *a way of being individuated*.[25] The primary care is in our approach devoted to ordinary concrete individuals. Singular terms merit a special honorary mention only if they succeed in picking out a unique individual of this sort.

Let us say that an $f \in F$ is (gives us) an individuating concept, and let us say that a term b does *individuate* (in the context of discussing a's beliefs) in so far as

$$(\exists x)B_a(x = b)$$

is true. Then we could have individuation without reference and reference without individuation: Both

$$(\exists x)B_a(x = b) \ \& \ \sim(\exists x)(x = b)$$

and

$$(\exists x)(x = b) \ \& \ \sim(\exists x)B_a(x = b)$$

can be true. We could even have both, but without matching:

$$(\exists x)(x = b) \ \& \ (\exists x)B_a(x = b) \ \& \ \sim(\exists x)((x = b) \ \& \ B_a(x = b))$$

---

[25] Cf. 'On the Logic of Perception' (ref. n. 20 above).

is satisfiable. Only if

$$(\exists x)((x = b) \ \& \ B_a(x = b))$$

is true does the successful individuation give us the individual which the term b actually refers to.

XIV. THEORY OF REFERENCE AS REPLACING THE THEORY OF MEANING

Here we are perhaps beginning to see what I meant when I said in the beginning of this paper that what is often called the theory of meaning is better thought of as the theory of reference for certain more complicated conceptual situations. Some of the most typical concepts used in the theory of meaning, such as Frege's *Sinne* and the 'individual concepts' of certain other philosophers of logic were in the first place introduced to account for such puzzles as the failure of the substitutivity of identity and the difficulty of quantifying into opaque contexts (e.g. into a context governed by a word for a propositional attitude). I have argued, however, that a satisfactory semantical theory which clears up these puzzles can be built up without using Frege's *Sinne* and without any commitment to individual concepts in any ordinary sense of the word. Instead, what we need are the individuating functions, i.e., the members of F. And what these functions do is not connected with the ideas of the traditional theory of meaning. What they do is precisely to give us the individuals which we naively think our singular statements to be about and which we think our singular terms as referring to. This naive point of view is essentially correct, it seems to me. The functions of $f \in F$ are the prime vehicles of our references to individuals when we discuss propositional attitudes. What is not always realized, however, is how much goes into our ordinary concepts of an individual and a reference. These are not specified in a way which works only under one particular course of events. They are in fact specified in a way which works under a wide variety of possible courses of events. But, in order to spell out this idea, we are led to consider several possible worlds, with all the problems with which we have dealt in this paper, including very prominently the problem of cross-identifying individuals.

The function of our 'individuating functions', i.e. the members of the set F, is to bring out these hidden—or perhaps merely overlooked—aspects of our concept of an individual (definite individual). This close connection between the set F and the concept of an individual appears in a variety of ways. One may for instance think of the role which the membership in F plays in the truth-conditions which we set up above for quantification into modal contexts. When it is asked in such a context whether there exists an individual of a certain kind, a singular term specifies such an individual only if its references match the values of a unique member of F in all the relevant possible worlds. Thus it is these functions that in effect give us the individuals which can serve as values of bound variables. As we saw above, it is mainly the possible subtlety and multiplicity of relations of cross-identity that prevent us from simply making the domains of the different possible worlds partly identical and thus hypostatizing my individuating functions into commonplace individuals.

This connection between individuating functions and the concept of an individual is part of what justifies us in thinking that in the traditional dichotomy their theory would belong primarily to the theory of reference, in spite of the fact that their main function in our semantical theory is to solve some of the very problems which the traditional theory of meaning was calculated to handle. This role is perhaps especially clear in connection with the substitutivity of identity. As we have seen, this principle does not hold for arbitrary singular terms a, b. However, if it is required in addition that both of these terms specify a well-defined individual, i.e. satisfy expressions like (*), depending on the context, then the substitutivity of identicals is easily seen to hold, presupposing of course here the prohibition against merging that was mentioned above. What this observation shows is clear enough. The failure of the substitutivity of identity poses one of the most typical problems for the treatment of which meanings, individual concepts and other paraphernalia of the theory of meaning were introduced in the first place. If the substitutivity of identity fails, clearly we cannot be dealing with ordinary commonplace individuals, it was alleged, for if two such individuals are in fact identical, surely precisely the same things can be said of them. This is what prompts the quest for individuals of some non-ordinary sort, capable of restoring the substitutivity principle when used as references of our terms. (This is almost precisely Frege's strategy.) We have seen, however, that the (apparent) failure of the substitutivity is due simply to the failure of some free singular terms to specify the same individual in the different 'possible worlds' we have to consider. Moreover, we have seen that this apparent failure is automatically corrected in precisely those cases in which it ought to be corrected, viz. in the cases where the two terms in question really do specify a *unique* individual. (That this depends on certain specific requirements concerning our methods of cross-identification, viz. on a prohibition against 'splitting', does not affect my point.) Substitutivity of identity is restored, in belief, not by requiring that our singular terms refer to the entities postulated by the so-called theory of meaning, but by requiring (in the form of an explicit premise) that they really succeed in specifying uniquely the kind of ordinary individual with which the theory of reference typically deals. One can scarcely hope to find a more striking example of the breakdown of the distinction between a theory of meaning and a theory of reference.[26]

XV. TOWARDS A SEMANTIC NEOKANTIANISM

The aspect of my observations most likely to upset many contemporary philosophers is the ensuing implicit dependence of our concept of an individual on our ways of cross-identifying members of different 'possible worlds'. These 'possible worlds' and the supply of individuating functions which serve to interrelate their respective members may enjoy, and in my view do enjoy, some sort of objective reality. However, their existence is not a 'natural' thing. They may be as solidly objective as houses or books, but they are as certainly as these created by men (however unwittingly) for the purpose of facilitating their transactions with the reality they have to face. Hence my reasoning ends on a distinctly Kantian note. Whatever we say of the world is permeated throughout with concepts of our own making. Even such *prima facie* transparently simple notions as that of an individual turn out to depend on conceptual assumptions dealing with different possible states of affairs. As far as our thinking is concerned, reality cannot be in principle wholly disentangled from our concepts. A *Ding an sich*, which could be described or even as much as individuated without relying on some particular conceptual framework, is bound to remain an illusion.

[26] Views closely resembling some of those which I am putting forward here (and in some cases anticipating them) have been expressed by David Kaplan, Richard Montague, Dagfinn Føllesdal, Stig Kanger, Saul Kripke, and others. Here I am not trying to relate my own ideas to theirs. It is only fair, however, to emphasize my direct and indirect debts to these writers.

XI

ON CARNAP'S ANALYSIS OF STATEMENTS OF ASSERTION AND BELIEF

ALONZO CHURCH

I

FOR statements such as (1) *Seneca said that man is a rational animal* and (A) *Columbus believed the world to be round*, the most obvious analysis makes them statements about certain abstract entities which we shall call 'propositions' (though this is not the same as Carnap's use of the term), namely the proposition that man is a rational animal and the proposition that the world is round; and these propositions are taken as having been respectively the object of an assertion by Seneca and the object of a belief by Columbus. We shall not discuss this obvious analysis here except to admit that it threatens difficulties and complications of its own, which appear as soon as the attempt is made to formulate systematically the syntax of a language in which statements like (1) and (A) are possible. But our purpose is to point out what we believe may be an insuperable objection against alternative analyses that undertake to do away with propositions in favour of such more concrete things as sentences.

As attempts which have been or might be made to analyse (1) in terms of sentences we cite: (2) *Seneca wrote the words 'Man is a rational animal'*; (3) *Seneca wrote the words 'Rationale enim animal est homo'*; (4) *Seneca wrote words whose translation from Latin into English is 'Man is a rational animal'*; (5) *Seneca wrote words whose translation from some Language S' into English is 'Man is a rational animal'*; (6) *There is a language S' such that Seneca wrote as sentence of S' words whose translation from S' into English is 'Man is a rational animal'*. In each case, 'wrote' is to be understood in the sense, 'wrote with assertive intent'. And to simplify the discussion, we ignore the existence of spoken languages, and treat all languages as written.

Of these proposed analyses of (1), we must reject (2) on the ground that it is no doubt false although (1) is true. And each of (3)–(6), though having the same truth-value as (1), must be rejected on the ground that it

From *Analysis*, 10, 5 (1950), 97–9. Reprinted by permission of the author, *Analysis*, and Basil Blackwell.

does not convey the same information as (1). Thus (1) conveys the content of what Seneca said without revealing his actual words, while (3) reproduces Seneca's words without saying what meaning was attached to them. In (4) the crucial information is omitted (without which (1) is not even a consequence) that Seneca intended his words as a Latin sentence, rather than as a sentence of some other language in which conceivably the identical words 'Rationale enim animal est homo' might have some quite different meaning. To (5) the objection is the same as to (4), and indeed if we take 'language' in the abstract sense of Carnap's 'semantical system' (so that it is not part of the concept of a language that a language must have been used in historical fact by some human kindred or tribe), then (5) is L-equivalent merely to the statement that Seneca once wrote something.

(5) and (6) are closely similar to the analysis of belief statements which is offered by Carnap in 'Meaning and Necessity', and although he does not say so explicitly it seems clear that Carnap must have intended also such an analysis as this for statements of assertion. However, (6) is likewise unacceptable as an analysis of (1). For it is not even possible to infer (1) as a consequence of (6), on logical grounds alone—but only by making use of the item of factual information, not contained in (6), that 'Man is a rational animal' means in English that man is a rational animal.

Following a suggestion of Langford[1] we may bring out more sharply the inadequacy of (6) as an analysis of (1) by translating into another language, say German, and observing that the two translated statements would obviously convey different meanings to a German (whom we may suppose to have no knowledge of English). The German translation of (1) is (1') *Seneca hat gesagt, dass der Mensch ein vernünftiges Tier sei*. In translating (6), of course 'English' must be translated as 'Englisch' (not as 'Deutsch') and 'Man is a rational animal' must be translated as 'Man is a rational animal' (not as 'Der Mensch ist ein vernünftiges Tier').

Replacing the use of translation (as it appears in (6)) by the stronger requirement of intensional isomorphism, Carnap would analyse the belief statement (A) as follows: (B) *There is a sentence* $\mathfrak{S}_i$ *in a semantical system* S' *such that* (a) $\mathfrak{S}_i$ *is intensionally isomorphic to* '*The world is round*' *and* (b) *Columbus was disposed to an affirmative response to* $\mathfrak{S}_i$. However, intentional isomorphism, as appears from Carnap's definition of it, is a relation between ordered pairs consisting each of a sentence and a semantical system. Hence (B) must be rewritten as: (C) *There is a sentence* $\mathfrak{S}_i$ *in a semantical system* S' *such that* (a) $\mathfrak{S}_i$ *as sentence of* S' *is intensionally* *isomorphic to 'The world is round' as English sentence and (b) Columbus was disposed to an affirmative response to $\mathfrak{S}_i$ as sentence of S'.*

For the analysis of (1), the analogue of (C) would seem to be: (7) *There is a sentence $\mathfrak{S}_i$ in a semantical system S' such that (a) $\mathfrak{S}_i$ as sentence of S' is intensionally isomorphic to 'Man is a rational animal' as English sentence and (b) Seneca wrote $\mathfrak{S}_i$ as sentence of S'.*

Again Langford's device of translation makes evident the untenability of (C) as an analysis of (A), and of (7) as an analysis of (1).

II

The foregoing assumes that the word 'English' in English and the word 'Englisch' in German have a sense which includes a reference to matters of pragmatics (in the sense of Morris and Carnap)—something like, e.g., 'the language which was current in Great Britain and the United States in A.D 1949.'

As an alternative we might consider taking the sense of these words to be something like 'the language for which such and such semantical rules hold', a sufficient list of rules being given to ensure that there is only one language satisfying the description. The objection would then be less immediate that (1) is not a logical consequence of (6) or (7), and it is possible that it would disappear.

In order to meet this latter alternative without discussing in detail the list of semantical rules which would be required, we modify as follows the objection to (7) as an analysis of (1). Analogous to the proposal, for English, to analyse (1) as (7), we have, for German, the proposal to analyse (1') as (7") *Es gibt einen Satz $\mathfrak{S}_i$ auf einem semantischen System S', so dass (a) $\mathfrak{S}_i$ als Satz von S' intensional isomorph zu 'Der Mensch ist ein vernünftiges Tier' als deutscher Satz ist, und (b) Seneca $\mathfrak{S}_i$ als Satz von S' geschrieben hat.* Because of the exact parallelism between them, the two proposals stand or fall together. Yet (7") in German and (7) in English are not in any acceptable sense translations of each other. In particular, they are not intensionally isomorphic. And if we consider the English sentence (a) *John believes that Seneca said that man is a rational animal* and its German translation (a'), we see that the sentences to which we are led as supposed analyses of (a) and (a') may even have opposite truth-values in their respective languages; for John, though knowing the semantical rules of both English and German, may nevertheless fail to draw certain of their logical (or other) consequences.

NOTES ON THE CONTRIBUTORS

WILLARD V. O. QUINE is Professor of Philosophy at Harvard, and is widely regarded as America's leading philosopher. Among his many publications are *A System of Logistic*, *Mathematical Logic*, *Elementary Logic*, *Methods of Logic*, *From a Logical Point of View*, *Word and Object*, *Set Theory and its Logic*, *The Ways of Paradox*, *Selected Logic Papers*, and *Ontological Relativity*.

ARTHUR F. SMULLYAN is Professor at Rutgers University. He is the author of *Fundamentals of Logic*.

RUTH B. MARCUS is Professor at Northwestern University. She is one of the principal founders of quantified modal logic, and she has written extensively on the philosophical foundations of the subject

DAGFINN FØLLESDAL is Professor at the University of Oslo and has been a regular visitor at Stanford University. His main work has been on the foundations of epistemic and causal logic, though he has also written on Husserl.

SAUL KRIPKE is Professor at Rockefeller University, New York. He has published widely on modal logic and in other areas of logic as well.

TERENCE PARSONS is Associate Professor at the University of Illinois at Chicago Circle. He has written on the problem of essentialism, and on ontological commitment.

LEONARD LINSKY, the editor of this volume, is Professor and Chairman of the Department of Philosophy at the University of Chicago. He is editor of *Semantics and the Philosophy of Language* and the author of *Referring*.

DAVID KAPLAN is Professor at the University of California at Los Angeles. His main work has been on intensional languages, referential opacity, and belief contexts. He has been influential through his participation in colloquia on these topics at philosophical meetings.

JAAKKO HINTIKKA is Professor at Helsinki and at Stanford University. He is the principal founder of epistemic logic, though he has published widely in other areas such as inductive logic, perception, and the philosophy of mathematics. He is the author of *Knowledge and Belief*, and edited *The Philosophy of Mathematics* in the present series.

ALONZO CHURCH is Professor of Philosophy at the University of California at Los Angeles. He has been an editor of the *Journal of Symbolic Logic* since its inception in 1936. He is the author of *Introduction to Logic*. Church's main work has been in logic, although he has also written much on philosophy, a good deal of it in the form of reviews in the journal which he edits. He has written on Frege's semantics.

Addendum to S. A. Kripke's
'Semantical Considerations on Modal Logic'

I could no longer write, 'Holmes does not exist, but in other states of affairs, *he* would have existed'. Such a fictional name as 'Sherlock Holmes' no longer seems to me to name some particular possible-though-nonexistent entity which would have existed under certain circumstances. Of course, there might have been *a person* in the nineteenth-century who performed exploits such as are described in the Holmes stories. Any actual person of the period (e.g., Darwin) might have done so, though I gather that none did; or, alternatively, some extra person (or persons), in $\psi(H)$ but not in $\psi(G)$, might have been born and had Holmes-like careers. But we would have no right to call any *particular* such entity, 'Sherlock Holmes'. The statement, 'Sherlock Holmes might have existed,' now seems to me to be inappropriate.

This change affects my view of the linguistic status of fictional names in ordinary language but does not affect the model-theoretic issue involved in the text, namely: (1) Some of the entities which actually exist might not have existed, and there might have been entities other than those which actually exist, so that $\psi(H)$ need not be constant for all $H \in K$. (2) In view of (1), if the variable 'x' is assigned an entity a, such that $a \in \psi(H_1)$, $a \notin \psi(H_2)$, should we give a value to $\varnothing\ (P(x), H_2)$, relative to this assignment to x? The use of fictional proper names to illustrate these points was incidental. Obviously I cannot elaborate on the linguistic question, though it is relevant to some philosophical problems about the status of 'un-actualized possible entities'.

Saul Kripke
11 January 1971

BIBLIOGRAPHY

(Not including material in this volume)

I. Books

R. CARNAP, *Meaning and Necessity* (Chicago, Ill.: Chicago Univ. Press, 1947 and 1956).

H. FEIGL and W. SELLARS, *Readings in Philosophical Analysis* (New York: Appleton-Century-Crofts, 1949).

P. T. GEACH and M. BLACK, eds., *Translations from the Philosophical Writings of Gottlob Frege* (Oxford: Blackwell, 1952).

J. HINTIKKA, *Knowledge and Belief* (Ithaca: Cornell University Press, 1962).

G. E. HUGHES and M. J. CRESSWELL, *An Introduction to Modal Logic* (London: Methuen, 1968).

S. KANGER, *Provability in Logic* (Stockholm: Almquist and Wiksill, 1957).

C. I. LEWIS and C. LANGFORD, *Symbolic Logic* (New York, 1932; 2nd printing, New York: Dover, 1951).

L. LINSKY, ed., *Semantics and the Philosophy of Language* (Urbana: University of Illinois Press, 1952).

L. LINSKY, *Referring* (London: Routledge and Kegan Paul, 1967).

A. PRIOR, *Time and Modality* (Oxford: Clarendon Press, 1957).

A. PRIOR, *Formal Logic* 2nd edn. (Oxford: Clarendon Press, 1962).

W. QUINE, *From a Logical Point of View* (Cambridge, Mass.: Harvard University Press, 1953; New York: Harper and Row, 1961 and 1963).

W. QUINE, *Word and Object* (Cambridge, Mass.: Technology Press, M.I.T.; New York and London: John Wiley and Sons, 1960).

W. QUINE, *The Ways of Paradox* (New York: Random House, 1966).

SOCIETAS PHILOSOPHICA FENNICA, *Proceedings of a Colloquium on Modal and Many-valued Logics.* Helsinki, 1963. (*Acta Philosophica Fennica*, Fasc. 16.)

P. F. STRAWSON, *Introduction to Logical Theory* (London: Methuen, 1952).

G. VON WRIGHT, *An Essay on Modal Logic* (Amsterdam: North Holland Publishing Co., 1951).

II. Topics

THEORY OF REFERENCE

K. DONNELLAN, 'Reference and Descriptions', *Philosophical Review* 75 (1966), 281–304.

G. FREGE, 'On Sense and Reference' in Geach and Black, 56–78; and in Feigl and Sellars, 82–102.

J. HINTIKKA, 'Modality as Referential Multiplicity', *Ajatus* 20 (1957), 49–63.

B. RUSSELL, 'On Denoting', *Mind*, n.s. 14 (1905), 479–93; reprinted in Feigl and Sellars, 103–15.

P. F. STRAWSON, 'On Referring', *Mind* (1950), 320–44.

SEMANTICS OF MODAL LOGIC

R. CARNAP, 'Modalities and Quantification', *Journal of Symbolic Logic* 11 (1946), 33–64.

174   BIBLIOGRAPHY

D. DAVIDSON, 'The Method of Extension and Intension', in *The Philosophy o*
Rudolf Carnap, ed. P. Schilpp (LaSalle, Ill.: Open Court, 1964), 311–50.

R. FEYS, 'Carnap on Modalities', in *The Philosophy of Rudolf Carnap*, ed. P
Schilpp (LaSalle, Ill.: Open Court, 1964), 285–98.

J. HINTIKKA, 'The Modes of Modality', *Acta Philosophica Fennica*, Fasc. 16 (1963)
65–82.

S. KANGER, 'On the Characterization of Modalities', *Theoria* 23 (1957), 152–5.

S. KRIPKE, 'A Completeness Theorem in Modal Logic', *Journal of Symboli*
Logic 24 (1959), 1–14.

S. KRIPKE, 'Semantical Analysis of Modal Logic I', *Zeitschrift für Mathematisch*
Logik und Grundlagen der Mathematik 9 (1963), 67–96.

S. KRIPKE, 'Semantical Analysis of Modal Logic II', in *The Theory of Models*
ed., J. Addison, L. Henkin, and A. Tarski (Amsterdam: North Hollan
Publishing Co., 1965), 206–20.

R. MONTAGUE, 'Logical Necessity, Physical Necessity, Ethics, and Quantifiers'
Inquiry III 4 (1960), 259–69.

R. MONTAGUE, 'Syntactical Treatments of Modality, with Corollaries on Re
flexion Principles and Finite Axiomatizability', *Acta Philosophica Fennica*
Fasc. 16 (1963), 153–68.

J. MYHILL, 'An Alternative to the Method of Extension and Intension', in *Th*
Philosophy of Rudolf Carnap, ed. P. Schilpp (LaSalle, Ill.: Open Court, 1964)
299–310.

R. STALNAKER, 'A Theory of Conditionals', *American Philosophical Quarterly*
monograph series No. 2, 98–112.

B. VAN FRAASSEN, 'Meaning Relations among Predicates', *Nous* I (1967), 161–179

LOGIC OF KNOWLEDGE AND BELIEF

H-N. CASTAÑEDA, 'On the Logic of Self-Knowledge', *Nous* I (1967), 9–22.

R. CHISHOLM, 'The Logic of Knowing', *Journal of Philosophy* LX (1963), 773–95

D. FØLLESDAL, 'Knowledge, Identity, and Existence', *Theoria* 33 (1967), 31–7.

J. HINTIKKA, ' "Knowing Oneself" and Other Problems in Epistemic Logic'
Theoria 32 (1966), 1–13.

J. HINTIKKA, 'Studies in the Logic of Existence and Necessity: I. Existence'
The Monist 50 (1966) 57–76.

J. HINTIKKA, 'Individuals, Possible Worlds, and Epistemic Logic', *Nous* I
(1967), 33–62.

L. LINSKY, 'On Interpreting Doxastic Logic', *Journal of Philosophy* LXV (1968)
500–2.

R. SLEIGH, 'On Quantifying into Epistemic Contexts', *Nous* I (1967), 1–31.

ESSENTIALISM AND PROBLEMS OF INTERPRETATION

B. BRODY, 'Natural Kinds and Real Essences', *Journal of Philosophy* LXXIV
(1967), 431–46.

R. CHISHOLM, 'Identity through Possible Worlds', *Nous* I (1967), 1–8.

A. CHURCH, Review of Quine's 'Notes on Existence and Necessity', *Journal o*
Symbolic Logic 8 (1943), 45–7.

A. CHURCH, Introduction to *Introduction to Mathematical Logic* (Princeton
N.J.: Princeton University Press, 1956).

R. CARTWRIGHT, 'Some Remarks on Essentialism', *Journal of Philosophy* LXV (1968), 615–26.

D. DAVIDSON, 'The Logical Form of Action Statements', in *The Logic of Decision and Action*, ed. N. Rescher (Pittsburgh: University of Pittsburgh Press, 1966), 81–95.

F. FITCH, 'The Problem of the Morning Star and the Evening Star', *Philosophy of Science* 17 (1949), 137–40.

J. HINTIKKA, 'Quantifiers in Deontic Logic', *Societas Scientiarum Fennica, Commentationes Humanarum Litterarum* 23 (1957), No. 4.

J. HINTIKKA, 'A Program and a Set of Concepts for Philosophical Logic', *The Monist* 51 (1967), 69–92.

S. KANGER, 'The Morning Star Paradox', *Theoria* 23 (1957), 7–11.

S. KANGER, 'A Note on Quantification and Modalities', *Theoria* 23 (1957), 133–4.

L. LINSKY, 'Substitutivity and Descriptions', *Journal of Philosophy* LXIII (1966) 673–83.

R. B. MARCUS, 'Modal Logics I: Modalities and Intensional Languages', *Synthese* 27 (1962), 303–22.

R B. MARCUS, 'Essentialism in Modal Logic', *Nous* I (1967), 91–6.

R. B. MARCUS, 'Modal Logic' in *Contemporary Philosophy*, ed. R. Klibansky (Florence: La Nuova Italia Editrice, 1968), 87–101.

R. MONTAGUE and D. KALISH, 'That', *Philosophical Studies* 10 (1959), 54–61.

R. MONTAGUE, 'Pragmatics' in *Contemporary Philosophy*, ed. R. Klibansky (Florence: La Nuova Italia Editrice, 1968), 102–22.

J. MYHILL, 'Problems Arising in the Formalization of Intensional Logic', *Logique et Analyse* 1 (1958), 74–83.

T. PARSONS, 'Grades of Essentialism in Quantified Modal Logic', *Nous* I (1967), 181–200.

A. PLANTINGA, '*De Re et De Dicto*', *Nous* III, No. 3 (1969), 235–58.

A. PRIOR, 'Possible Worlds', *The Philosophical Quarterly* 12 (1962), 36–46.

A. PRIOR, 'Is the Concept of Referential Opacity Really Necessary?', *Acta Philosophica Fennica*, Fasc. 16 (1963), 189–200.

W. QUINE, 'Notes on Existence and Necessity', in *Semantics and the Philosophy of Language*, ed. L. Linsky (Urbana: University of Illinois Press, 1952), 77–91.

W. QUINE, 'The Problem of Interpreting Modal Logic', *Journal of Symbolic Logic* 12 (1947), 43–8.

W. QUINE, 'Three Grades of Modal Involvement', in *Ways of Paradox*, 156–74.

B. RUNDLE, 'Modality and Quantification', in *Analytical Philosophy*, Second Series, ed. R. Butler (Oxford: Blackwell, 1965), 27–39.

R. THOMASON, 'Modal Logic and Metaphysics', in *The Logical Way of Doing Things*, ed. K. Lambert (New Haven and London: Yale University Press, 1969), 119–46.

INDEX OF NAMES

(not including authors mentioned only in the Bibliography)